CELTIC'S
GOALKEEPERS

CELTIC'S
GOALKEEPERS

DAVID POTTER AND MARIE ROWAN

DB
PUBLISHING

First published 2016 by DB Publishing, an imprint of JMD Media Ltd,
Nottingham, United Kingdom.

ISBN 978-1-78091-535-7

Printed and bound in the UK by Copytech (UK) Ltd Peterborough

CONTENTS

DEDICATION

To David Conner who we were fortunate to have as a friend

ACKNOWLEDGEMENTS

The authors would like to record their thanks to many people, notably men like Pat Woods, Tom Campbell, Jamie Fox and John MacLauchlan, fine Celtic historians who are always willing to share their extensive knowledge of the club.

Ricky Haggerty of the Celtic Visitor Centre, Jim Ryan and the Joe Kennaway Celtic Supporters Club, Montreal and various members of the Kennaway family have also shown a great deal of interest in this project and there was a real Donegal input from Pat Bonner's lifelong friends Mary Boyle and her daughter Pauline McGee. Also we are indebted to Fay Coutts of Oban for allowing us to use photos of Davy Adams' 1907 Scottish Cup winners medal and Alison Sinclair for alerting us to its existence. The Cardenden Celtic supporters including men like Alex Burns and Mark Cameron are similarly always interested to share their knowledge of John Thomson.

INTRODUCTION

The job of goalkeeper has never been an easy one. There is no hiding place for a goalkeeper – one mistake usually leads to the loss of a goal, and possibly the loss of a game as well. A team with the attacking instincts and traditions of Celtic must necessarily be resigned to the loss of some goals. Only very seldom does a Celtic team take the field with the declared intention to "keep it tight at the back". Can you imagine the uproar and outcry in the North Stand if this became a regular event?

It follows then that the goalkeeper must be very good. For most of Celtic's 130 years or so of history, the Parkhead side have been blessed with excellent custodians. This book is a tribute to eight of them in particular who have served the club with distinction, and others are mentioned in the Miscellany. The Miscellany does not claim to be comprehensive, and readers may well ask the question of why so-and-so has not been included. We apologise for omissions, but the ones we included usually have something interesting about them which deserves to be included.

The eight chosen for special treatment include a man of unbelievable courage in the rough days of the late Victorian era, the custodian of the greatest show on earth, the man who is best known for a song sung about him by opposition supporters, a dreadful tragedy, a Canadian, a man who never won a major honour with the club, a man whose career is astounding for its longevity and achievements, and a man who saved a famous penalty in the World Cup. But they all performed outstandingly for Celtic.

David Potter
Marie Rowan

July 2016

DAN MCARTHUR
(1892–1902)

by Marie Rowan

Dan McArthur was without any doubt a brilliant goalkeeper whose courage, it was reckoned, would have put a lion tamer to shame.Commenting on the game versus Hibernian on 1 January 1895, Willie Maley remarked that; 'the match will long be remembered as McArthur's game, our popular custodian giving an exhibition between the sticks never equalled in our history'. Dan had joined Celtic in 1892 and was with the club until 1903. He was quite possibly Celtic's greatest ever goalkeeper. A Scotland internationalist, he was skilful in judgment and fearless in action in an era where goalkeepers were given no protection and expected none. 'McArthur was not yet feeling any

ill-effects from his two head injuries,' wrote one newspaper scribe before adding, 'the third proved unlucky.' But this constant punishment eventually and inevitably took its toll and Dan McArthur retired in 1903. Dan had already received a benefit game versus Rangers in 1901 where a 1–1 draw prevailed in what was described as a 'magnificently contested game.' Despite his outstanding ability, Willie Maley declared that McArthur did not have the 'International temperament'. Dan played in goal versus England in 1895 at Goodison Park and he had his Celtic teammate Dan Doyle in front of him at left-back. Scotland were beaten 0–3. The second goal was initially saved by McArthur, but unfortunately the ball rebounded off the Scotland left-half Gibson of Rangers. The third goal was such an angled shot, it was generally conceded that it gave Dan no chance.

A description of the careers of goalkeepers in the last decades of the 19th century simply had to include the words nasty, brutish and short. That Dan McArthur's lasted from 1892 until 1902 was something of a minor miracle as was his predecessor Joe

Cullen's ability to come back from the near dead. But by the Final of the Glasgow Charity Cup on 12 May, 1894, Dan had assumed the mantle of the near-suicidal and opted to continue Celtic's reputation of having very good goalkeepers with a penchant for self-destruction. Along the way, McArthur changed that description of 'very good' into 'truly great' – perhaps even the greatest in Celtic's history. But, alas, memories are short and present-day Celtic supporters have virtually no knowledge of and perhaps even no desire to recognise and pay homage to a man who was a true Celt and gave his all for their club.

McArthur had kept goal for the Bhoys in both semi-finals of the 1893–94 Glasgow Charity Cup against Third Lanark, a draw in the first having necessitated a replay. The final was watched by some 18,000 spectators at Ibrox Park as Celtic took on the amateurs of Queen's Park.

Celtic's committeemen had been great admirers of the English team, Preston North End's close-passing, skilful, attacking style, but this kind of play was liable to be upset by the strength of the wind. As Celtic had kicked off with the wind against them, they were finding it difficult to get into a rhythm that would showcase their talents. The Rangers officials had, naturally, expected, as it was the Glasgow Charity Cup Final, that the magistrates of the city would grace the game with their presence and duly decked out the reserved seats for this august group in red and gold. A thoughtful touch, acknowledging the importance to the city of the tournament's charitable purpose. The expected guests failed to turn up. The newspapers were subsequently unanimous in their disapproval of them and all agreed that such a flagrant snub of what was a prolific source of revenue to the city's charities was nothing less than disrespectful. Lord Provost Bell was on the Continent, so it would appear that when their esteemed leader's eye was somewhat 'off the ball', the other civic dignitaries did what the old saying failed to predict, namely, 'When the cat's away, the mice – turn into rats.'

The game was still goalless at half-time despite a great effort on both sides, hard uncompromising tackling being the order of the day. Celtic were going for 'three-in-a-row' and Queen's Park desperately trying to stem a downhill spiral of bad defeats. In the second-half, the Spiders went ahead. A wake-up call to the Celts if one were needed. Madden slammed home the answering goal and six minutes from time-up, a Doyle free kick allowed Blessington to finish the tie off. Unfortunately for McMahon, he repeated his unfortunate fate of the previous season's Final and had to be carried off. Divers also suffered from having to play with a bandaged knee, having cut it badly at Hampden during the Wednesday replay by falling on a piece of glass. Celtic's defence had played well, their forwards' speed at Ibrox that day and

9

superior strength finally telling against their opponents. The Ibrox pitch was hard and sandy and this caused a great deal of complaints at the finish from the players as most of them ended the game with blistered feet. It was noted that Joe Cullen, McArthur's predecessor, who was a spectator at Ibrox that day, proclaimed himself delighted with Dan McArthur's performance.

The Glasgow Cup Final of 1894–95 versus Rangers at Cathkin was one during which Dan McArthur was at his brilliant best. For a Rangers man to have said after the game that he had not seen such goalkeeping in five years was, without doubt, praise indeed.

Having seen off Battlefield, Clyde and Cowlairs in the previous rounds, Celtic's opponents in the Final of the competition on 17 November 1894, were Rangers. In the words of John Glass who accepted the trophy after the game, Celtic had been forced to field a side in the second half sadly disorganised and greatly weakened. Sandy McMahon, their talisman goal-scorer, had been injured and failed to reappear in the second half.

Celtic had started the game as favourites and finished as winners. But it was a game of controversy if the after-match moans, complaints and general exhibitions of bad sportsmanship from the Rangers camp were anything to go by. Dan Doyle, that bête noir of all supporters bar Celtic ones, could do no wrong for the Parkhead team and absolutely no right for anyone else. His well-taken free-kick in the thirty-second minute managed to arouse Rangers' ire on four different points. Firstly, they damned it as no free-kick at all. Secondly, it was awarded to the wrong team

The Celtic squad 1892 – 1894. McArthur is second from the left in the back row.

and thirdly, the ball was already through before being touched and to add insult to injury, it was handled. One would think that would have been enough gripes for the first half, but no. Rangers should have had a penalty. Where had the referee been all this time? It seems that supporting Rangers even in those days was like taking a stroll through Heart Attack Alley. The first half injury to Smith simply put the tin lid on the whole proceedings. The fact that Dan McArthur's display in the Celtic goal, while thwarting the Rangers forwards, was reckoned to be good enough to earn him an International cap must have rankled a great deal except in the case of the Rangers adherent who did not let partisanship blind him to an excellent display by McArthur.

A crowd 20,000 had turned up to see the game and a fairly played one it was, with very little roughness on show despite Celtic's Cassidy getting a bloody nose and Rangers' Smith an accidental kick on the head. Celtic had lost their captain, McMahon, after twenty-five minutes but he had already won the toss and on a wet and slippery pitch, he had opted to play with the blustery, southeasterly wind at his team's back. Rangers, who were the holders of the trophy, emerged onto the pitch determined to retain it. The large crowd was full of anticipation, so much so that the crush of spectators at the East End goal was so great that the officials had to make hurried arrangements to shore up the palings. Not to be denied though, the fans simply jumped over it and the track was packed all round the ground within five minutes.

The game began and it was quickly obvious that neither team had turned up just to be cannon-fodder. Despite the wind disadvantage, Rangers were quick to stamp their authority on the game and Celtic would have been two goals down within twenty minutes had McArthur not performed heroically in the Celtic goal. As one commentator wrote, 'McArthur had all the goalkeeping and did it – rather.' (*Scottish Sport*, 17 November 1894) Victorian understatement at its best! The game was very hard on the players and their stamina was tested to its utmost. Dan Doyle accepted the responsibility for taking that hotly-disputed free-kick awarded to Celtic by Mr Lamb, the referee, on that day. The poor or courageous man, had been quickly surrounded by players angry, by players disputing his decision, by players disputing absolutely everything. No doubt he felt justified in refusing to accept responsibility for the strength of the wind. As far as the awarding of the free-kick was concerned, he stood his ground. One–nil to Celtic. (At the dinner and social later, Mr Lamb provided some songs and heard it suggested by Mr Sliman of the SFA that referees should be, 'experienced men who had played within recent years and who should keep themselves in training quite as much as players'. (*Scottish Sport*, 17 November 1894) Another ex-president of the SFA, Mr Crerar, suggested referees should be

11

endowed with unlimited powers. Perhaps the national drink had been distributed rather too freely by then. A newspaper suggested that unlimited fees might be more acceptable to the men with the whistle.) Mr Lamb ignored all of the Rangers' protests and the Celtic supporters saw their free kick specialist put the ball in the net. Just before half-time, Divers scored a beauty of a goal from a cross and, once again, his way of slipping the ball into the net sent the Celtic fans wild with delight. Celtic, therefore, went into the pavilion two goals to nil up at half-time.

Despite being two up, Celtic were the more nervous team and the second half was all about Dan McArthur in the Celtic goal. He was ably assisted by Doyle and McEleny in front of him but the diminutive figure kept his head and soaked up everything that got by the two backs. The team eventually settled down albeit with Willie Maley now limping on the wing. Despite massive pressure from Rangers in the second-half, Celtic, through Dan McArthur's brilliant performance, held the line and the Glasgow Cup was theirs.

The injuries to McMahon and Maley were sufficiently serious for both of them to leave for Matlock for specialist treatment a few days after the game. Willie Maley might have been injured in body but not in spirit for he fulfilled his promise to put the Glasgow Cup on show in the window of his shop in Glasgow's Gallowgate. Maley never missed a business trick. The Rangers team came in for some very heavy criticism after the game and no doubt during it from the folk on the terracing. Pure 'funk' and 'faint-heartedness' were the favourite descriptions used by the sports reporters of the day towards the players. The Celtic players were very fit and had put in extra training on the lead up to the game. But the inexplicable faltering of the team in the second half had allowed the opposition to capitalise on this and only the fearless McArthur had stood between Celtic and oblivion until the old Celtic spirit, flowing from the indomitable Dan, had seeped into the souls of his teammates. It took their efforts to greater heights and that strength of character could not be matched by Rangers. They huffed and puffed but they failed to blow the Celtic house down. Eventually, it was obvious to all that as the end of the game approached, Rangers were a spent force in the qualities of determination and resolve. The Celtic players were promised a little souvenir by the club to commemorate the victory. A *Scottish Sport* reporter wrote, 'This is the first time the Rangers have taken home those memorials of defeat, the runners-up badges.' There had been none awarded the previous time in 1887–88 when Rangers had suffered the same fate. No consolation trinkets. Henrik Larsson would have approved.

It is hardly surprising that McArthur so inspired his teammates. Although a strong wind blew in Rangers' favour in the second half, Dan was simply impassable.

He could not have helped being inspired by his captain, Sandy McMahon, that day, for he had witnessed him having three bandages put on his knee at different points in the game to keep the cartilage in place before he finally gave in and retired from the field. All subsequent complaints about the refereeing came to nothing.

It was with mixed emotions that the Hibs supporters of 1894–95 learned of their opponents at home in the second round of the Scottish Cup – the most desired trophy of the day. Celtic had been their old rivals and bitterest opponents when the Edinburgh team had graced the elite ranks of Scottish football. Hibs had shown no interest in joining the newly formed Scottish Football League and had clung tenaciously to a very definitely and official sectarian policy which, even in those days, was totally unacceptable. Now, having weathered storms of a financial nature plus the religious ones, the club now competed in a lower division and it had become a club open to all. Victory over the great Glasgow side was merely a dream. But dreams occasionally come true and on 15 December, 1894, Hibs emerged from a disastrous encounter, from a Celtic point of view, worthy 2–0 winners. Our Bhoys are out the Cup! The post-match verdict was that Celtic had been beaten by, 'their own cast-offs and a few colts.' It had all gone wrong for Celtic from the moment the referee had blown his whistle, exacerbated by the fact that the lead up to the game had seen Celtic suffer the misfortune of having top players on the injured list. It was also alleged that Divers and Blessington, keen to play at the top of their form, had unfortunately over-trained.

The game was played at Easter Road and the crowd, all 12,000 of them, were extremely vocal in their support for the home team and equally so in their loud loathing of the Celts, especially of that ex-Hibs man, Dan Doyle, although what Doyle had done to attract such vitriol forever remained a mystery. The Celtic full-back came in for persistent booing throughout the game whenever he was involved in the play. There had been no doubt beforehand that Celtic would defeat the second division side and that belief in no way faltered despite the fact that the Celtic forwards had failed to score in their three previous games, a statistic unparalleled in the club's history. In the pubs in Glasgow that evening, the question was asked as to why Celtic had failed to win.

Celtic had dominated the first-half, had had several great chances to open the scoring but had singularly failed to do so. A missed penalty and a resounding Madden effort, which cracked off the crossbar did not help morale from plummeting. But they rallied still. Hibs first goal came as the Celtic defence stood watching while Murray dribbled the ball past them unhindered and shot straight into the net. Doyle, Dunbar and McArthur, convinced Murray was offside, stood patiently waiting for Mr Donald, the referee, to blow for this infringement of the rules. Hibs were now one goal up as silence emanated from the man in charge. Doyle was still protesting loudly hours later. Doyle was in fact playing his first game in three weeks and Willie Maley his first in a month. Hibs second goal came from a foul by Doyle near the Celtic goal. Murphy's fierce shot hit the back of the net after a touch off a Celtic player and Celtic were out of the Scottish Cup. It was agreed that the Hibs half-back line had won the game, helped in no mean way by the Celtic forwards over-doing the fancy football with the ball frequently being gifted in the end to the opposition.

Seventy policemen were on duty that day and when it was decided that the stadium was full, thousands were turned away. The Hibs board had been prepared for the possibility of a break-in and had taken steps to prevent it by having men with, 'hatchets, hammers and paling-stobs' standing by to deal with that eventuality. The main reason given for the good behaviour of the crowd – the constant barracking of the Celts notwithstanding – was that most of the twelve thousand crowd were just interested spectators with it being thought that only one in six actually supported Hibs. Since most Celtic supporters had stayed at home, what a surprising number of 'neutrals' even in an era when some people actually were mainly interested in watching the game in a more detached way. Wonder who the rest supported as a rule! So our Bhoys were out of the Cup, but were they? Celtic duly protested that their opponents had played an ineligible player and were cheered to find their protest upheld. So once more to Edinburgh and lessons learned put into practice.

'This match will long be remembered as McArthur's game.' So wrote the *Scottish Sport*'s reporter of the replay held a fortnight later on 29 December 1894. With Reynolds and Doyle alongside him, it was deemed to be the finest defence seen in a Celtic team that season. It was a different Celtic that day. It was courage and determination that was the hallmark of the team at Easter Road as they took the field with nothing in mind but to erase the memory of the humiliating defeat of their previous match. As in most cup-ties, it proved to be a very physical encounter. But Hibs' strong-arm tactics were more than matched by a team of old campaigners who knew how to dole it out and still come up smelling of roses in the eyes of the match official. Celtic had long been noted for being 'cute and crafty'. Having learned the painful lessons of the previous defeat, Celtic neutralised the Hibs half-back line by simply playing through them and thus spoiled their tactics. The re-arranged forward-line performed admirably with Blessington and Madden superb and the Hibs wingers found themselves no threat at all to this much more focused Celtic team.

When Campbell scored in the first-half, the goal was ruled offside but at least a Celtic player had found his way to the net. Celtic's first goal came through a Doyle free-kick in the second half. It went in off Campbell's head according to the referee and Campbell and Celtic got their names on the score sheet. That so incensed the Hibs captain Murphy that he led his team off for some minutes as a protest. Rather childish behaviour was the only comment from the Press. Celtic continued to demonstrate how well they had learned their lesson from the previous game and McArthur continued to demonstrate that he was, at that time, the finest goalkeeper in Scotland. The game ended with a 2–0 victory to Celtic and the team plus officials left the capital to threats by Hibs ringing in their ears of their intended protest at Celtic having played an ineligible man, McEleny – in their eyes. McEleny himself thought it absurd and declared that there was no way he would have played and jeopardised Celtic's chances had he thought that. He declared that he had definitely not committed himself to play for another club.

Celtic's victory was not well received by the supporters of their opponents and the players had to have a police escort. An ex-Hibs player entered the fray in the stand and had a 'go' at an ex-Hearts player resurrecting some dispute of many years standing. It was also deemed in the Press as bad form for Celtic supporters in the hallowed reserved seats to wave their hats when Celtic scored.

Dan McArthur was applauded as the main player, man of the match, in the team and it was judged that his performance that day in goal had never been equalled in Celtic's history. Once back in Glasgow, the team and officials celebrated their hard-won victory in their favourite restaurant, The Mikado. Hibs protest was thrown out.

By 1895 it was quite obvious to all followers of football in Scotland that Celtic's Dan McArthur was a gifted member of the team and to all but the most partisan, an obvious choice to play for Scotland. Scotland's International team to face the other three home countries was chosen as a result of a series of trial matches, four teams being selected beforehand, from whom the final line-ups would emerge. These games were condemned as farcical by all and sundry except members of the SFA finance committee who greatly appreciated the funds and publicity these public trials generated. The teams playing for a berth included the entire Celtic team bar Kelly, Campbell and Dunbar. In fact, a player's form on the day mattered not a whit and in March 1895, despite a truly abysmal showing, Dan Doyle joined his Celtic team-mate Dan McArthur in the team to play England, the plum international fixture. The Scottish selectors still allowed no players playing in England to be considered for international matches. Thus Dan McArthur travelled with the Scotland team to Liverpool as the game was scheduled to take place at Goodison Park, Everton's comparatively new ground.

It was a game destined to be remembered for all the wrong reasons. Five foot ten and eleven and a half stones, Doyle could not have been more dissimilar to his five foot six and slender club-mate. In temperament they were poles apart and McArthur was no doubt embarrassed, but not surprised, at his Celtic teammates pre-match behaviour. Doyle simply disappeared from the moment they reached Liverpool on the Friday until one hour before kick-off.

This game was played before a crowd of 30,000 and they saw a player who was to become an English legend, Steve Bloomer, represent his country for the first time. This game also precipitated the abolition of the custom of not selecting players playing with non-Scottish teams. That the English team was superior to the Scots was generally acknowledged after the game but the two Celts were included in the three outstanding players for Scotland. Scotland had had the great misfortune to have an early goal chalked off due to the referee Mr Reid's very severe interpretation of the offside rule and the refereeing was generally regarded as having gone from bad to worse. It was said that the referee's 'microscopic' order of refereeing when he abandoned it in favour of a more 'telescopic' one was no more successful. On several occasions in the second-half he pulled up England players when they were obviously onside. As the saying goes in Glasgow, he 'started bad and fell away' and the crowd were not slow in letting him know their feelings. Immediately after the Scotland goal was struck off, he awarded England a free-kick for an infringement that mystified everyone on all sides of the great divide and England duly scored, as Bloomer blasted past McArthur from a Holt pass. Four minutes later and Dan pushed out a shot from Goodall only to see it rebound into the net off Gibson, the Scotland and Rangers right-half. Thirty minutes gone, two goals down and yet if that statistic had a disheartening effect on that Scotland team – as it surely must have had – there were no visible signs of quitting. The third and Final goal for England came just before half-time when an angled shot gave the little Celt no chance whatsoever of saving it.

Scotland's defeat was put down to the inadequacies of the half-backs who were slow at getting to the ball and reckless in parting with it. This lack of support had a devastating effect on the forward line. It was accepted by the sports journalists of both countries that a different half-back line would have rendered the Scotland team that day formidable. The back three had held up magnificently and despite the handicaps the forward line had endured from their team-mates behind them, Sutcliffe in the England goal had had three times as much work to do as Dan McArthur. The backs were brilliant with Doyle displaying such nerve and accuracy that was a delight to see. His partner, Drummond, was steadiness personified and eventually his stopping and tackling rendered him impassable. McArthur, despite the goal losses had a good game but not miraculous. As the *Scottish Sport* reporter wrote, 'That is the danger of being miraculous'.

A monumental battle was expected at Celtic Park on 28 November 1896, as Celtic was scheduled to face Hibernian in a vital League Championship match. A close contest was expected and great was the anticipation of both sets of supporters. Celtic had failed that season to secure even one point at Easter Road and likewise Hibs at Parkhead. The drama that was widely believed to be waiting in the wings as the two Irish teams went head to head, did not fail to manifest itself and its arrival would resound down through the generations. The Celtic team that had already been picked, had gathered in the dressing-room to get ready for this needle match. Even the wayward Dan Doyle had turned up. No doubt the racket coming from the throats of the 15,000 strong crowd would have been heard in the rather chilly dressing-room on that very cold November day. And Dan McArthur, like all 'keepers, would be anticipating a lot of action round the goalmouth where he could do two things, show off his brilliance and keep warm. There was no love lost between the two sets of fans by this time, as the Hibs supporters were still very bitter about the luring away of their seven best players in 1888 by the committeemen of Celtic for the new Irish club. But loyalty is a much abused word and expectations of it most unrealistic.

Today's custom of teams quietly walking out together might be geared to preparing fans for a sporting, gentlemanly contest but as hype, it's a non-event. Anticipation of a dual between two teams for supremacy that has fired the fans imagination for days suffers a severe case of deflation as measured steps, mini-mascots and 'all-pals-thegethir' acts are the official pre-match order of the day. Not so in 1896 where the Celtic order which lasted for several generations was, 'Run out on your own and show the fans that you're as keen to get the game started and won as they are'. No wonder then on that day the supporters were bemused by a team that took the field late and in Willie Maley's words, 'broken detachments'. As a journalist writing in the *Scottish Sport* later put it, 'The Celtic committee were on Saturday last presented with a position, which, for heartless acuteness, has seldom if ever fallen to the lot of management to face'. Although the team had begun to strip for the game, three players, Meehan, Battles and Divers, intimated their refusal to play and proceeded to carry out the threat. A reporter from the *Scottish Referee* had been giving the Celtic players, especially Battles, a hard time of it specifically because of the team's rough play in previous games. The players gave the club the ultimatum that they would only participate in the match if they removed the

THE SCOTTISH TEAMS SERIES.

CELTIC

GROUND–CELTIC PARK,
PARKHEAD, GLASGOW.

The Bould Bhoys!

offending reporter forthwith from the Press box. Freedom of speech was cited by the committee for doing nothing right then, but they gave the promise that the matter would be discussed later. The three men considered that promise inadequate and refused to play. The game was against the club's closest rivals in the League and there was now no time to have a full team ready and on the pitch in time for the kick-off. It is interesting to speculate how much sympathy the fans would have had for the three men who were very well paid compared to them. The committee refused to be held to ransom as they saw it and Celtic began the game with eight of the players selected, plus Willie Maley who had in fact all but retired, dragooned into donning his boots again and Barney Crossan making up a tenth man.

The crowd had by this time begun to get impatient and foot stamping was the order of the day. The Celtic team, and a makeshift one at that as could be seen by Hibs and Celtic supporters alike, lined up and the whistle was duly blown. The referee was probably the only person in the ground that day who missed the fact that Celtic numbered only ten. The Celtic reserve team was in action versus Queen's Park that day and a hurried request was sent to Hampden Park asking for Tom Dunbar to be allowed to play for the first team. Understandably, that plea was immediately granted but Dunbar did not manage to take his place until fifteen minutes into the second-half. Dan Doyle had given the wrong call when the coin was tossed that day and all were agreed that things did not bode well for Celtic.

Labelled variously erratic, unorthodox and unflinching, those Celtic players that day fought for a club the three men in the dressing-room had deliberately placed in peril. It was a story of undiminished courage and a demonstration that the legendary fighting qualities of Celtic were alive and flourishing in the form of those players on the pitch that day. In captaining the side through this unprecedented setback, Dan Doyle was at his inspirational best. A team that should have been obliterated from the trauma in the dressing-room and the prospect of a hopeless struggle against the prospective League Champions was in fact winning with three minutes to go. A Jimmy Blessington goal had put Celtic in front and the Celtic players were inspired by the superb goalkeeping of Dan McArthur who was under heavy and persistent pressure from a Hibs team which could have been forgiven for thinking they were onto a good thing when ten men were all Celtic could muster for most of the game. Celtic were in the lead and deservedly so until an overcrowded goalmouth allowed a Martin of Hibs' shot from twenty-five yards out to be unsighted by McArthur. Dan's play in the Celtic goal that fateful day was judged by all to have been superb. With Hibs and Celtic placed first and second at the top of the league table and the players promised by the Celtic committee a bonus of £10 each for winning the game, a small fortune in those days for a working person, this had been a peculiar time for the three players to register their grievance against the Press and club officials who had been slow to take their previous complaints seriously. The team that day, by their wonderful play, had very effectively put to shame all the carping criticism from the sports reporters of unjustifiably rough tackling in the most erudite way – on the pitch. That team was, after sixty minutes, McArthur; Dunbar, Doyle; Russell, Kelly, A. King; Blessington, Gilhooly; Crossan; W. Maley, Ferguson.

'This scratch lot saved the club's colours and credit in circumstances of most wanton peril, and deserve to be gratefully remembered by all true Celts for so bravely filling the breach.' (*Scottish Sport* 1 December 1896).

There is a glamour, an excitement and an instant gratification in a Cup tie that can never be emulated by a League match. It is a gladiatorial contest versus the Punic Wars, a war of attrition. Even a century after it is was first inaugurated, the Scottish Cup competition was the more prized possession of the two in the hearts of those Celtic supporters nurtured on stories of the feats of players long dead whose great run in the Scottish Cup that first season put the new Irish club firmly in the ascendancy. No League then, no watching teams slogging it out week in, week out, piling up the points. Maybe just settle for a draw. Cup-ties did not breed that mentality. Cup-ties were made for the skilful attacking play of Celtic, where the fate of a club was decided instantly or, at worst, in a replay. Looking back at Celtic's very earliest days, it is difficult to believe that the initial success, which was beyond all reasonable and probably unreasonable, expectations, too, that that fulfilment of dreams could continue indefinitely. That flirtation with the Scottish Cup in the club's first season – that so near and yet so far hope – had made Celtic feel that by any moral standards, the Scottish Cup belonged to them – indefinitely. Being knocked out of that competition at any stage was looked upon as a disaster second to none. Glittering prizes were there for the taking in football but the one that glittered more brightly than all the rest put together was the Scottish Cup. No chances were ever taken, even when meeting a team less fancied and in the competition of season 1898–99, the result when Celtic met the Sixth Galloway Rifle Volunteers (Dalbeattie) away from home reflected that. An 8–1 victory – no prisoners taken! If Celtic ever needed a reminder that everything is possible in football, that very salutary lesson was learned in the defeat of Glasgow's East End team by lowly Arthurlie only two season's previously, was sure to be still fresh in the memories of the players.

In the next round, a home game against St Bernard's, produced a decent result of 3–0 and Celtic were into the quarter-finals. Dan McArthur was going all out for his first Scottish Cup medal, as there had been a severe drought of victories since the great team of the early days had last lifted the Cup in 1892. From winning the League in the previous season without suffering a single defeat, this present season had seen Celtic slip into third position, so a Scottish Cup was desperately and definitely needed to appease their very vocal support. The next team they were drawn to meet was Queen's Park at Hampden Park on 18 February, 1899. The Parkhead club was most unfortunate to have a 4–2 lead wiped out as the game was abandoned when the light became too poor to allow the game to continue. The game had kicked-off at the somewhat late hour of 3.30pm and on a misty Glasgow day in February, it was hardly surprising that as the afternoon wore on, a combination of winter darkness and the mist, probably fog in that heavily industrialised city, made seeing the action for the spectators a near-impossible task. As each spectator had paid double for the privilege of entering the ground, it was hardly surprising that they revolted when the game was abandoned halfway through the second period. The police were called to ensure anger did not spill over into something more serious than verbal abuse. The game had to be played all over again and, for some inexplicable reason, as it was an abandoned game not a replay, the venue was now moved from Hampden Park to Celtic Park and the 35,000 who turned up saw Celtic win 2–1 and had the satisfaction of knowing that they had only paid half the entrance money charged for the original game. All on course for Dan's first Scottish Cup medal in the competition.

Celtic seemed to have managed to avoid a lot of serious contenders that season for the semi-final saw them matched with Port Glasgow Athletic at home. Port Glasgow Athletic were not reckoned to be capable of delivering any shock result and that suited every Celtic fan on the planet. It had not been the best of seasons with the team's performance, especially in the beginning, having been on numerous occasions nothing short of dire. No surprises this time as Celtic ran out the winners by four goals to two although the visitors from 'The Port' had given Celtic a good run for their money and had held them to a 2–2 draw at half-time.

But it was with some trepidation that the Celts now learned that their opponents in the Final were to be Rangers. The teams had met twice in the League that season and both times Celtic had endured severe drubbings of 0–4 and 1–4. Rangers had won the League and now they were going for the 'double'.

As Rangers prepared for the game at a resort on the Clyde Coast, Celtic abandoned their usual visit to Seamill and opted for the polluted air of Glasgow's East End for their players. Bet they were pleased! Was the biscuit tin mentality beginning to rear its ugly head? The Final was scheduled to be played on 22 April 1899, and 25,000 people turned up to see the two Glasgow teams battle it out despite the entrance fee being doubled yet again. It was irritating then, as it still is today,

Dan is sitting on the ground on the left in the front of this picture of Celtic in their green and white vertical stripes with the Scottish Cup of 1899.

that the decision regarding the ticket price is made by the very people who get in for nothing. The crowds basked in the sunshine of a late Spring afternoon and it proved to be the weather that truly did outshine the football.

It was a canny sort of game with McArthur keeping his goal with his usual daring and panache, with his old mate Barney Battles encouraging Marshall and King to follow Dan's example. The League Champions were not having the stroll in the park they expected for the Celtic defence grew in confidence as the first-half progressed. A shock, though, came when Sandy McMahon headed off his own line as McArthur was beaten in a Rangers attack. Half-time came and still no goals scored by either one of two very equal teams. Mr Robertson, the referee was having an excellent game. All changed in the 67th minute when the excellent Sandy McMahon, 'The Duke' to his adoring Celtic fans, headed home the opening goal while the Rangers players were arguing with the referee about a corner he had awarded to Celtic. The Parkhead Bhoys had quickly taken it in the form of a Johnny Hodge cross and Sandy had done the rest. Sheer ecstasy! The roar of the crowd had no doubt conveyed the fact that Celtic had scored to the thousand or so who had been locked out half-an-hour before the kick-off, for the noise at one end and the silence at the other would tell whose goal had been breached.

Dan McArthur came into his own as Rangers heeded the wake-up call but McArthur and his defence held firm regardless of the severe pressure they were put under. Celtic, though, were equally awake and buoyed-up by this McMahon gift.

Celtic scored the second and final goal of the game when Rangers were once more arguing with the referee. With their usual conviction that they were right and the referee was wrong in not blowing for offside, they merely succeeded in distracting themselves from the task in hand and Hodge simply ran through the unresponsive Rangers defence and put the ball into the net. Celtic's second Scottish Cup and Dan's first Scottish Cup-winner's medal.

It is no exaggeration to say that the interest in the first-round game of the Scottish Cup of season 1900–01 involving Celtic FC generated as much interest as a Scotland international game. Perhaps it was because of the opposition – Rangers FC! It was fair to say that the exit of one or other of these teams would inevitably diminish the excitement of further rounds, certainly in the West of Scotland.

Celtic had been training assiduously at one of their favourite haunts, Rothesay. Willie Maley had always harboured a penchant for 'doon the watter'. Speculation as to team selection had been mounting as Celtic had been having difficulty finding a permanent outside-right and it was rumoured that one of Queen's Park's amateurs was being considered to fill that berth in this most important fixture. It was also thought that the very promising young player, Jimmy Quinn, was too inexperienced to be considered at all although he had been training with the team in Rothesay. A spate of injuries and influenza had pitched the youthful Willie Loney into the side, but he was considered at this time to be merely a stop-gap and too young for a match of this importance despite what was considered a rosy future being predicted to lie ahead of him. Problems in the forward line, problems in defence. Maley did not have his sorrows to seek for even that stalwart and ever-present Dan McArthur was still recovering from an injured wrist and not expected to be fit enough to start against Celtic's main rivals. But that was really one position where Maley, in his heart of hearts knew he need not worry when push came to shove. McArthur was an uncomplaining sort and Celtic had always taken full advantage of his determination to shrug off the most serious of injuries and simply get on with the job. How did he manage to play for more than a decade without the aid of a sports scientist?

The game described as 'lusty and vigorous' by some took place on 12 January 1901, in ideal weather conditions in front of some 30,000 spectators. It was soon obvious that a classic game of skilful passing and dribbling would not be on show as the Parkhead pitch was in an abominable state and cut up right from the kick-off. Celtic were considered the fittest side and lasted the game better than their opponents. This was put down to their special training at Rothesay as it seemed a bit of bonding and fresh air went a long way. Celtic had by this time developed a reputation for consistently bringing their Ibrox rivals' high expectations of winning the celebrated trophy to a grinding halt and tradition was what the Celtic psyche was all about.

Despite the Celtic forwards consistently forcing the play and at one point Sandy McMahon had a shot, backed with terrific force, saved by an enormous effort from Dickie in the Rangers goal, these efforts came to nothing in the way of goals. The single goal on the sheet that sent the Bhoys through to the next round came as a result of a corner kick. Drummond, the Rangers right-back, whilst attempting to clear a shot from Findlay, Celtic's outside-left, somehow contrived to put the ball into his own net. Shades of Sandy Jackson! Twenty-two minutes gone and the Celts were 1–0 up. The younger players Celtic had been forced to play and their fearlessness at close quarters was a feature of the game. Celtic's forwards had an excellent game considering the pitch was in a deplorable state and made the ability to dribble the ball almost impossible. A terrific shot from Campbell had hit the bar so hard that it quivered for a considerable time afterwards. Eight minutes from time, McMahon raced through the Rangers' defence and fired a ferocious shot at goal. Rangers were saved yet again by their goalkeeper and the final score of 1–0 to Celtic saw Rangers exit the Scottish Cup in the first round.

All plaudits for keeping the score down went to Rangers' keeper, Dickie. He had been lamentably – from a Rangers fan's point of view – let down by the disastrous performance of his full-backs. Their play alone was reckoned to have been enough to take the heart out of the entire team. Dan McArthur gave a fine display of goalkeeping, too, as he had done consistently for all the years he had occupied that unenviable berth. The price he paid, though, and the cumulative toll it took on the wee fellow's health was great indeed. In this particular game, Dan had had to retire fifteen minutes from the final whistle. Yet again, he had suffered a bad head injury. Whereas in other games, the Celtic 'keeper had allowed his head to be bandaged as he eagerly awaited his return between the sticks, in this instance he had no say in the matter as he had been kicked semi-conscious. He had gone down to save the ball and his team's slender lead from Hamilton, the Rangers centre-forward. Unfortunately, with near-fatal results, the forward tried to kick the ball out of the prostrate McArthur's hands and the kick intended for the ball was taken full on by the Celtic goalkeeper's head. The two teams' doctors attended him for four minutes before he was helped from the pitch. The wound to the back of his skull required four stitches but, later that night, he was reported as being out of danger. Dan, the bravest of the brave, had only just returned after suffering another severe injury that had kept him absent for several weeks. Divers took his place for the remaining quarter of an hour so as not to weaken the defence. Despite the chance given to them as Celtic were now a man down, Rangers were unable to capitalise on this. Divers had only one real shot to deal with and he managed that whilst giving away a corner-kick, which came to nothing.

An English visitor in an interview after the game declared that he was left unimpressed by the play on show that day. It was too vigorous, too exciting for his taste and he noted that tackling in the Scottish game was very severe.

The trophy which aroused the greatest emotional response within football-supporting circles was still, in 1901 the Scottish Cup, and to the delight of their followers, Celtic had reached the Final yet again. This time their opponents were to be Hearts and the venue Ibrox Park. Celtic had defeated Queen's Park in the previous season's Final and thus came to this match as the holders of the Blue Riband of Scottish football. Dan McArthur had played a lion's part in that 4–3 victory and had many people wondering why he had not at that time been selected to play once more for his country the previous week when the international match against England had been played on Dan's home ground, Celtic Park. But the persistent toll on McArthur's health, the repeated injuries he suffered were threatening to make themselves felt and when it finally happened on that most public of Scottish stages, a Scottish Cup Final, with the entire country focused on it, the victim was not only McArthur but the club in whose name and for whose sake he had endured them for so long. It was a disaster waiting to happen.

This significant game was a defeat for Celtic, Hearts scoring four goals to Celtic's three. But the brilliant and courageous uphill battle which the Celtic team fought in the most discouraging of circumstances was the outstanding and the most talked about feature of the game. Although the Cup was safely stowed away in their trophy room, after reading newspaper accounts of the game, Hearts must have wondered who were the true victors.

The game started off very well for McArthur, as an excellent Thomson shot was beautifully dealt with by him. The game flowed from end to end with the Celts sticking to their traditional style of play. The first goal came as a result of a free movement between Hearts' Walker and Thomson who then passed the ball out to Porteous, their outside-right. That player ran no more than two metres before his fast shot had McArthur beaten. Dan had managed to get his hands to the ball but was unable to clear it and it went spinning off his hands and into the net for a goal with only fifteen minutes gone. Celtic stepped up the pace and the equaliser seemed almost inevitable. Barney Battles equalised in the twenty-seventh minute from a free kick much to the relief of the Celtic supporters. With the game being in full swing, a brief halt was called so that the ball's lace could be attended to. Hearts took the lead once more and this time McArthur was aided and abetted in the blunder department by Davidson, his right-back. Walker's shot had been smothered by the Celtic 'keeper and then he held it securely in his grasp. But Bell of Hearts was rushing in and McArthur had the option of either putting it round the post for a corner or throwing it out to a teammate. Cup Final nerves came into play right then and Dan simply dropped the ball at his right-back's feet. Davidson had less than a metre to turn with the ball but unfortunately failed to do so. The ball rebounded off his legs and into the goal with Bell making certain it crossed the line. Half-time and Celtic were 2–1 down and McArthur was taking all the stick from the crowd. But the commentators of the day were more generous towards McArthur than some present day Celtic historians. Being present and knowing the conditions at first-hand, they suspected that the greasy ball might have played its part although, on the general run of play, Hearts deserved, in their opinion, their slender lead.

Play resumed with Hearts getting into their stride immediately and McArthur having to be more alert to parry their frequent efforts to score. Celtic finally woke up and tested the Hearts 'keeper till disaster struck once more and Walker was once again the playmaker for the Edinburgh side. His pass to Thomson saw the centre-forward shoot into the Celtic goal. McArthur did manage to reach it but it went off his hands and into the net. The wee man was truly having a nightmare of a game. Thus with half-an-hour remaining, Hearts had gone 3–1 up. Celtic finally changed tactics and two goals followed, one from McOustra and the third Celtic goal coming from McMahon. A draw would have been a fair result considering the heroic effort the Celtic players had put it to achieve it but no, it was not to be. With only two minutes remaining, Walker had yet another shot at the Celtic goal. This time McArthur saved the shot but the ball unfortunately went out as far as Bell. The Hearts forward kept possession in the few minutes left then Thomson fired home the winner with the goal at his mercy. A 3–4 defeat and for Dan McArthur, that truly great Celtic 'keeper, it was the beginning of the end. Ill health and savage injuries had done the damage and the wonder is, it had not happened sooner.

The crowd had been a poor one at least by Celtic standards, only some 16,000 having paid an increased price and had seen the pre-match favourites defeated. At the reception in the Alexandra Hotel, Celtic's J.H. McLaughlin suggested that the crowd would have been larger had the price been a more popular one. That suggestion or hint to the exalted personages of the SFA went down, needless to say, like a lead balloon.

Celtic was a club whose whole ethos in the very early days was charity. A glance down the list of benefit/testimonial matches played in Dan McArthur days with the club reveals a great variety of worthy causes and McArthur took part in most of them. They ranged from helping players' widows and children to colliery disasters and lockouts. Players needs were, of course, the initial reason for such matches, but as the game of football developed in Scotland and professionalism came to the fore, it became, for players themselves, more of a 'golden handshake' at the end of a career or a financial inducement for ones still at their peak in skill and popularity to remain with the club. Dan McArthur was fully deserving of the very best testimonial the club could deliver as he had given his all for Celtic. It is doubtful if any player sustained and survived such brutal treatment on the pitch on a regular basis as Dan.

Dan McArthur had joined Celtic in the season 1892–93 and is almost certainly Celtic's greatest ever goalkeeper and that's saying something. A Scotland internationalist, Dan was skilful in judgement and fearless in action in an era where 'keepers were given no protection and expected none. McArthur had done his fair share in playing in the testimonial matches for both his own team-mates and other players in Scottish football and deserved the best opposition for his own that Celtic could provide.

The constant punishment Dan McArthur was subjected to eventually took its toll and the great Dan retired from football in 1903. Celtic met their rivals Rangers on 28 August 1901, to play a benefit for McArthur, Celtic's goalkeeper par excellence of the previous seven years.

Celtic: McArthur; Watson and Davidson; Moir, Loney and Orr; Hodge and Campbell; Mair, McOustra and Quinn.

Rangers: Dickie; Smith and Crawford; Stark, Neil and Munro; Graham and Sharp; Hamilton; Wilkie and Campbell.

The day of Dan's testimonial dawned with the weather being dry but rather windy and the strength of the wind looked like it might just cause trouble for players who liked to indulge in fine ball-play. Rangers lost the toss but this did not prevent them from being the first to threaten the opposition goal, Davidson heading the ball very close. But testimonial or no, Celtic had no intentions of being outplayed that day. Picking the ball up, Loney neatly passed to Campbell who tested the Rangers' 'keeper with a high ball but Dickie had it covered. Celtic were by now taking full advantage of the wind in their favour and constantly tested the Rangers' 'keeper. They repeatedly bore down on the Rangers' defence but it held firm, Smith in fine form clearing repeatedly. The Celtic players made the most of the wind advantage and laid siege to the Rangers goal, hemming in the opposition in their own penalty area and the crowd were treated to an exhibition of fine shooting. Rangers' only answer was an occasional badly rushed attempt to break out. The play was by now centred on the unfortunate Dickie and it was with some relief that he saw Hodge's goal chalked off for offside. The one-sidedness of the game is illustrated by the fact that it was a full thirty minutes before

Dan had his first touch of the ball! But the shell-shocked Rangers defence held on and half-time came with no score from either side.

The second half opened with more of the same, Celtic pummelling the Rangers goal. For all Celtic's efforts, they had nothing to show for it as Dickie in the Rangers goal was playing a blinder and while the rest of his team were struggling badly to get into the game, he alone was beating back the Celtic forwards. But, against the run of play Rangers scored first, Graham beating McArthur at close quarters. Celtic continued to bear down on the Rangers goal, a single-handed run by McOustra was stopped on the goalline and Muir, guilty of earlier squandering the perfect chance to draw level, was brought up on the post. Celtic had never at any time contemplated defeat at the hands or feet of the Ibrox men and they now tried desperately to get the draw they so richly deserved. Whatever they tried, however clever, none of it produced the desired result. But luck had not completely deserted the boys in the green and white and Johnny Campbell finally gave Celtic the goal they so richly deserved. With five minutes left and Dickie having pulled off yet another magnificent save, Johnny Campbell scored from a corner. This 1–1 draw ended a greatly contested game, the best Celts reputedly being Watson, Loney, Quinn and Campbell. Dan pocketed £80 at the turnstiles and a fair amount from a considerable number of tickets sold.

Dan McArthur's career with Celtic FC could be described in his later years with the club as the 'Twilight of the Gods' for Dan's brilliance only dimmed in the last few appearances in his long service as the constant physical injuries he had suffered finally took their toll. Words used to describe his performances were truly heroic; consistently brilliant, miraculous, marvellously agile. Horatius held the bridge magnificently in Lord MacAulay's epic poem and helped save Rome. Dan McArthur held his line with equal fortitude and bravery but with less acknowledgment from history.

In the roll of truly great Celts, Dan McArthur's name should be one of the most revered in the firmament of stars. We will almost certainly never see his like again and football is the poorer for it.

CAREER:

Appearances: 151
Scottish Cup Medals: 2
Scottish League Medals: 2
Glasgow Cup Medals: 2
Glasgow Charity Cup Medals: 4
Scotland Caps: 2
Shut Outs: 44

DAVY ADAMS
(1902–12)

by Marie Rowan

Born in Oathlaw in Angus, Davy Adams left Dunipace Juniors to sign for Celtic in 1903. He had already been a Junior International 'keeper in 1902–03 season when Willie Maley decided he was Celtic material and signed this tall, hefty lad. Being an internationalist and a great prospect, Maley had stiff competition especially from a determined Falkirk who had been quick to recognise real talent when they saw it and were not easily outwitted. But Maley was as fly as a jailer and issued an  invitation to Davy suggesting he might like to accompany the Celtic team on a trip to Ireland, which the young Adams accepted with alacrity. The return trip saw him agreeing to sign for Celtic and the way was now open for him to become a member of the legendary six-in-a-row team. Adams rarely missed a game and on the few occasions that he did, it was because he once tore his hand open on a nail in a goalpost at Ibrox Park and another time when he was suffering from pneumonia. When complimented on his natural goalkeeping abilities, Davy Adams' modesty only allowed him to say that it would be difficult to be anything other than good when operating behind such great backs as McNair, McLeod, Weir or Orr. His only complaint was that they were such great defenders with Young, Loney and Hay in front of them that he was frequently suffering from cold as he had virtually nothing to do most of the time.

Davy Adams had been in goal for Celtic during a weekend when several Scottish teams went south to play English clubs in friendly matches. On 1 September 1903, Celtic met Middlesbrough and both teams fielded makeshift teams. The 8,000 crowd saw a hotly-contested game with a number of Scottish players in the Middlesbrough side. Celtic went down 0–1 to a home side which was reported to have played 'a splendid game' and it was noted that it was only due to the 'brilliant goalkeeping' of Adams in the Celtic goal that had kept the score down. The only goal had come from a penalty.

A few weeks later, a *Daily Record* journalist commented on how strong was the Celtic defence in all positions. 'Adams, the tall Dunipace goalkeeper, has been exhibiting magnificent form at practice.' Davy was definitely on a roll! Celtic met Hibs on 26 September 1903, and it proved to be an easy victory for Celtic although Hibs did not give up entirely until fatigue got to them in the last 30 minutes of the game. The Celts had proved to be far too skilful and a class apart that day and Adams and the defence had held fast during what pressure there was from Hibs. That day also saw Davy Adams become Celtic's regular goalkeeper.

For Davy Adams, the Scottish Cup Final, due to take place on 16 April 1904, was his first opportunity to walk away with the much-sought-after winner's medal. The opponents could not have been better – Rangers. They were by now Celtic's greatest rivals and it was certain to be a match that would attract a great crowd. And it did, for 65,000 souls turned up to cheer on their own particular team. Celtic would be fielding a young team at Hampden Park, Rangers a poor one. The Ibrox club's fine team that had lifted the League Championship trophy four years in a row, were now looking distinctly jaded. Despite being the holders of the dreaded runners-up medals in 1902 and 1903, it had now been three years since the Scottish Cup had graced Parkhead as they had beaten Queen's Park in the 1900 Final. Both teams had their own reasons for being absolutely determined to lift the silverware in 1904.

The weather was fine, the crowd exceptional and good-humour the order of the day. In the previous four years, two more 'finals' for a trophy had seen the teams now standing at one victory each. The 1901 International Exhibition Trophy had headed south of the Clyde when Rangers had beaten Celtic in the Final. The first of the Ibrox disasters occurred the following year when part of the new terracing at Ibrox Park collapsed and twenty-six spectators were killed with over five hundred injured during a Scotland versus England match. The International Exhibition Trophy was put up by Rangers as the prize in a very special tournament to raise money for the Ibrox Disaster Fund. The League Champions of both Scotland and England plus the runners-up played for this trophy in a contest billed as the unofficial British Championship. The four teams were Celtic, Rangers, Everton and Sunderland. Celtic beat Sunderland and Rangers beat Everton. In the Celtic versus Rangers Final it was 2–2 until the last minute of extra-time when the very young Jimmy Quinn completed his hat-trick that day. The trophy still rests in Paradise. Davy Adams and his teammates were determined to place the Scottish Cup right alongside it for the first time.

When referee, Tom Robertson of Queen's Park, blew for the kick-off, the Celtic team, youthful and talented to the nth degree and ever optimistic, sprang into action full of promise and vitality. Ten minutes later, they were two goals down and wondering how it had happened. No-one more so than Davy Adams in the Celtic goal and his character references from the Celtic supporters told him in no uncertain terms what they thought of the prowess of Celtic's new, regular goalkeeper. Davy had indeed got off to a horrendous start. If there had been a Rangers player to be singled out for close watching, it was Finlay Speedie, the Rangers inside-right. Against the run of play, Speedie threatened the Celtic goal and a good header by him was well taken by Adams. The danger seemed to be past, but not so. Adams gifted his opponents their first goal as he collided with the post, dropped the ball and saw it dally its way into the net. Celtic were one goal to nil down but not for long. Worse was to come a few minutes later as Speedie made yet another raid on the Celtic goal. Shooting from the edge of the penalty area, he watched his shot snake past a ruck of players and Adams was once more picking the ball out of the net. Two nil down and Big Davy, the most likeable of men, was wondering what had happened – as were thousands of supporters of the green and white. No doubt there were many blaming not Adams nor his defence, but the kit now being hoops instead of their beloved stripes. A love of tradition was, and still is, an Irish trait and no doubt the fabled Deirdre of the Sorrows had a lot to 'greet' about right then. One great difference between the teams that day was the youthfulness of one and the solid professionalism of the other. Hope springs eternal in youth, though, and there was no way that that Celtic team was down in spirits. The incomparable Jimmy Quinn took the first-half by the scruff of the neck, taking on the entire Rangers defence by himself. He got the ball, took off towards the Rangers goal and powered his way past opponents, neatly avoided challenges, gave short-shrift to any foolish enough to attempt to tackle him and rested only after he had struck a ferocious shot from inside the penalty area past Watson in the Rangers goal. Now 1–2 down and all to play for and Mr Robertson had not yet blown for half-time. The Celtic faithful took heart for Quinn had demonstrated that whatever nightmare his goalkeeper was enduring, he himself was on song. Davy Adams was slowly recovering from the hammering his confidence had taken and was trying to assuage his guilt. Quinn then gave him the boost he needed as just before half-time, he accepted a terrific cross from Muir on the bye-line and slammed it where it belonged. Two goals each and Davy could pretend the match was just beginning when he came out for the second-half.

Despite a spirited revival of sorts from Rangers who had seen their inexplicable lead vanish in an equally inexplicable way, Celtic once again began to play the beautiful passing game for which the club was famous. The Rangers' efforts were to no avail as the soon to be legendary half-back line of Young, Loney and Hay took control and stifled any Rangers attack before it got into its stride. Confidence was rapidly filtering through the team. The dreaded replay loomed with its attendant big bucks for the clubs and lighter pockets for the fans. These happened so often in those days that they were viewed with great suspicion and very definite resentment. No doubt the usual mutterings of stitch-ups were wending their way round the new showpiece ground that was Hampden Park. But such thoughts were finally dispelled by Celtic's magician, Jimmy Quinn, the man who could make something out of nothing. This time, though, he had a glorious pass from his captain, James Hay, to work with and Quinn needed no prompting. As he tore through the Rangers defence yet again, he was needlessly felled by Nick Smith. But stumbling and regaining his balance, still holding onto the ball, he answered the somewhat brutal tactics employed by the Rangers players to stop him in the most eloquent way he knew. Quinn scored the goal that put the Celts ahead and the Scottish Cup back where it belonged.

Both the team, Adams (and the huge Celtic support) were pleased with the victory and the medals but Davy himself had had a nightmare of a game and had also learned a very hard lesson. He went on to save Celtic's 'bacon' on numerous occasions as an important member of a team that has never quite been equalled in Celtic's history. He was also privileged to see Quinn score the first ever hat-trick in a Scottish Cup Final.

The Glasgow Cup Final against the same opposition five months later could now provide Adams with an opportunity to make amends. Celtic were the less fancied team, Rangers, class and skill personified if some elements of the Press were to be believed. The great six-in-a-row team had only just taken its first positive steps on its epic journey and none could see how this record-breaking run would enter the annals of football history.

It was a hard game as these encounters tend to be and doubts about the Rangers defence that had surfaced tentatively over the previous weeks were proved to have some substance to them. Some 55,000 supporters turned up on a glorious 8 October 1904, to see the Old Firm do battle yet again for silverware. The Glasgow Cup was much coveted by Celtic but had proved somewhat elusive since the team containing such iconic names as McArthur, Doyle, and Madden had lifted it in season 1895–96. The 1901–02 Glasgow Cup Final versus Rangers at Ibrox had necessitated a replay after a 2–2 draw before 40,000 fans on 26 October 1901. The Glasgow Association held a ballot for the venue for the replay and Ibrox Park was selected yet again. Celtic complained about the fairness of this decision, Rangers did not support them. Celtic scratched so any chance of regaining the trophy after a long time had now gone. But Celtic's chance had come once more against Rangers and the team was determined to grasp it with all their collective hands. Big Davy, the well-liked 'keeper from the East Coast, had no intention of giving a repeat performance of that fierce Scottish Cup battle.

The Rangers defence wavered alarmingly from the whistle and never looked like they could withstand any pressure the Celtic forwards cared to apply. With the firm conviction that there is no such thing as bad publicity, the famed half-back line, which had almost guaranteed Rangers success in recent years, decided to emulate their quivering comrades behind them. From his position between the posts at the other end of the pitch, Adams must have wondered why he had got the wind up so badly in May. But Dame Fortune smiled upon that Rangers defence and they somehow managed to extricate themselves from their self-imposed fankles time and time again. Celtic had the disadvantage of a crosswind and playing into the sun in the first-half. But despite all the Celtic pressure and their own panic, Rangers found themselves a goal up scored by Hamilton, the Rangers forward, with barely five minutes gone. It made no difference to their shaky defence and the Celtic pressure was heaped upon them in even greater measure as Celtic looked for a goal to reward their efforts and twenty minutes later, it came. Celtic's Hamilton parted with a telling pass right to the feet of Jimmy Quinn. A low, ground cross-shot beat Allan in the opposition's goal all ends up. Bennett came rushing in to make certain it was a goal but the ball had already crossed the line and the credit for the equalising goal was given to Quinn. The defensive play from both sides had the effect of almost stifling the attacking efforts of both sides much to the annoyance of many spectators despite furious attempts by the forwards to break loose. There had been no individual performances of brilliance, no displays of wonderful, sustained passing. It was just a dour, hard struggle.

Celtic came out for the second-half in a determined frame of mind. That was in complete contrast to the Rangers team that seemed to have lost heart completely. But it was still one goal each and the Celts were set on getting their hands on that trophy. Egged on by their massive vocal support, it was not very long before their more free-flowing and inventive moves paid off and put them into the lead in the fifty-second minute of the game. One of their most dangerous moves in the first-half from Celtic had been a tremendous shot on goal from deep in the midfield by Willie Loney. The magnificent half-back trio of Young, Loney and Hay – three names that together have resounded down through the generations like a mantra in Celtic's history – this almost impregnable wall had allowed Loney to indulge in the occasional foray into Rangers territory and an incredible, long-range shot had almost paid off before Quinn had equalised. Sweet revenge and a much happier Davy Adams.

Back in the 'Good Old Days' of Scottish football, it was considered tough enough on the paying-public's fraught nerves only to have points to worry about in the League Championship competition. In addition to this, of course, was added the uncertainties such as injuries to favourite players, the charabanc turning up late, dodgy fish suppers eaten by recalcitrant players coming out of the dancing the previous evening and such matters. But these were beyond the legislative responsibilities of those in authority. If it had ever occurred to that august body, the Scottish Football League, that goal difference might also be included in the equation, it had made no lasting effect on their brains. So many games were played over the course of a season that a tie for first place seemed a remote possibility. But even so, the men in charge prided themselves on covering all eventualities and had decreed from the first League Championship season that in the event of two teams having an equal number of points, a play-off at a neutral ground would be sufficient to settle it all. Strangely enough, this did happen immediately. Dumbarton and Rangers, at the end of season 1890–91 had tied on points and the deciding 'rubber' was played at Cathkin Park. A draw was the result and as both teams were content to share the Championship, the League committee agreed to buy another flag.

The second time two teams tied for first place was in season 1904–05 and Rangers were, once again, one of the concerned parties. Equal on forty-one points was Celtic and a game to settle the flag's destination set alight the final weeks of a dying season that seemed to be finishing with a whimper, not with a bang. Great expectations, renewed enthusiasm, massive excitement and anticipation wiped away the lethargy. Over the course of the season, the teams had met each other eleven times in various competitions, each having won five and drawn one. The neutral ground chosen was the home of Queen's Park, Hampden Park. The date was set for 6 May 1905, with a 3.30pm kick-off, extra-time to be played in the event of a draw. A huge crowd was anticipated for this unexpected, high-profile match and it had set alight the imagination of the fans as much as the Scottish Cup Final itself. One game to decide the destination of the League Championship flag.

The build-up was intense and Celtic were reckoned to be the favourites to win the title but only marginally so. As one reporter noted, when these two teams met, form had a habit of flying out the window. When an eye is cast over the Celtic team that day, who would have bet against them? Davy Adams' name was first on the team-sheet followed by Watson and Orr; McNair, Loney and Hay; Bennett,

McMenemy, Quinn, Somers and Hamilton. After one of the best and most hard-fought games of the season, Celtic emerged the winners in front of a crowd of some 30,000 spectators and the Scottish Football League did not have to consider purchasing a second flag. £652.10.6 was taken at the gates and divided between both clubs with the £97.10.9 from the stand and reserved enclosures going to Queen's Park for the use of the ground.

McNair replaced the suspended Sunny Jim Young in the half-back line but it was still a mighty team. Rangers won the toss and for some inexplicable reason, opted to play against the breeze. Despite this self-inflicted disadvantage, it was the Ibrox team who were quickly settled and into their stride and firing hard at Davy Adams in the Celtic goal. The big 'keeper had to be on his mettle as the Rangers forwards continually broke through what was a very strong Celtic half-back line and a brilliant shot from McColl, the Rangers centre-forward, after he had taken a pass from his left and driven it goalwards as it came to him, was equally brilliantly saved by Adams. Celtic's half-back line settled down after that scare. Although the Celtic forward line did their fair share of threatening to score, no attempts by them came anywhere near to looking as dangerous as McColl's. Half-time came as Mr Kirkham of Preston blew the whistle without that official having entered a single goal in his wee notebook. Two Celts had suffered injuries, Adams and Willie Loney. Despite the lack of scoring in the first half, the crowd had been treated to a first-class demonstration of excellent defending by both teams and the constant threats of the forwards to score kept the anticipation and tension at peak levels. Celtic's forwards were now moving together like the legendary team they were about to become, this unison of movement a hallmark of their play.

Twenty minutes into the second half and still the play raged from end to end with the half-backs of both teams tackling superbly and excelling in passing. But winning was the name of the game and the magnificent McMenemy put Celtic one goal up and his team's
supporters into raptures. They were still rejoicing on the terracing when the Bhoys went two up as Hamilton emulated his colleague. 2–0 to Celtic and that Championship flag was almost in their stadium. But Rangers hit back through a shot from Robertson five minutes later and the game now seemed to hang in the balance. Nerves throughout Hampden were shredded by this time as Adams' goal came under determined attack upon attack from the Rangers forwards, as they tried desperately to find the equaliser. But Celtic finished the stronger team and one goal better off. They had been beaten by Rangers 0–2 in the semi-final of the Scottish Cup in April at Ibrox and so this 2–1 victory, which gave them the League

Championship was looked on as revenge for that game. The semi-final had been abandoned because of crowd trouble. The score had been 2–0 to Rangers at the time and, despite Celtic protests, the result had been allowed to stand and Celtic were out of their favourite competition. This 2–1 defeat of Rangers had given Celtic their first League Championship in seven years and Davy Adams his first medal in the competition. He did not realise it at the time but they were about to pile up.

The ultimate success, the laurel wreath, for every Scottish team was the winning of both the Scottish Cup and League Championship in the same season. In fact 'The Double'. By the time Celtic took to the field on 20 April 1907 in the Final of the famous cup, such a feat as winning the 'double' had never been achieved. The Lisbon Lions were famous, and rightly so, for having won every competition they had entered in season 1966–67. A magnificent achievement indeed. The BBC *Quizball* is invariably added to this by the Celtic supporters of that period. Wha's like us? But in the days of the truly brilliant six-in-a-row side, only four trophies were available for them to win. That season, Celtic did win a treble of sorts for they won the League Championship, the Scottish Cup and the Glasgow Cup. Why do we not boast about Willie Maley bringing home 'The Treble' that season? Naturally, Maley was furious at losing out on the Glasgow Charity Cup, but the money earned for the city's charities might have compensated a little – a very little, for Maley was a winner first and foremost. The charities had won but Celtic had not in any material sense.

Season 1906–07 was truly magnificent with Celtic's Davy Adams in goal managing 15 shut-outs when 34 games were played, there being 18 teams in the League. Celtic got off to a flying start that season and before October had hardly begun, they had won the Glasgow Cup and their goalkeeper had notched up six consecutive shut-outs. The 'keeper, though, was not Davy Adams but Tommy Sinclair, Rangers' reserve goalkeeper, whom Rangers had offered Celtic as a temporary replacement for the injured Adams. Guilt had played a large part in this generous offer as Adams had cut his hand on a nail on an upright of the goal at Ibrox while playing in a testimonial match for the redoubtable Rangers' player, Finlay Speedie. Celtic did not believe in the need for reserve goalkeepers. They baulked at the idea of paying a player who would simply be standing about in the off chance he was needed. Outfield players could be drafted into various positions as required, not so goalkeepers. Besides, Sunny Jim Young had frequently taken over between the posts to the Board's satisfaction. It turned out very well for Sinclair but he was in fact playing behind a superb defence who were aware of the potential fragility of a reserve 'keeper and pulled out all the stops to shield him. Still, when Sinclair left

Parkhead to return to Ibrox, he took with him a Glasgow Cup medal. Davy Adams' hand had now healed and he was back between the posts. It would be interesting to know if Mr Sinclair had the courage to show off his medal in the Ibrox dressing-room.

That season, that Celtic team were undefeated until New Year's Day. With Adams in goal, Celtic marched on relentlessly and looked as if winning the League to make it the seventh time for Celtic since the competition began and three in a row for that particular team was inevitable. In that entire season, they were only to lose twice, going down 1–2 to both Rangers and Third Lanark away from home.

Thoughts of winning, in the minds of the fans, the League Championship and bringing the flag yet again to Parkhead were now being linked to the possibility of winning the Scottish Cup, too, and doing the 'double'. The quarter-final draw, though, was destined to bring about a reality check. In the cup, at any rate, Celtic seemed determined to make life difficult for themselves. A 2–1 victory over Clyde at home saw them face Morton in Greenock. Jimmy Quinn had been suspended for two months and as he disappeared, so did Celtic's ability to score, it seemed. Fortunately Davy Adams and that supreme half-back line compensated for the near-drought of goals from the forward line. It took a second replay before Celtic could shake off their opponents by two goals to one.

Their next opponents in a quarter-final tie were Rangers at Ibrox. If Celtic were destined to win the Scottish Cup that season, they were getting absolutely no help

J. Bennett, A. M'Nair, D. M'Leod, J. Young, D. Adams, W. Orr, R. Templeton, J. Hay, R. Davis, D. Hamilton, J. M'Menemy, P. Somers, R. Craig, J. Bauchop, W. Loney, J. Quinn, A.J.Wilson, E. Garry.
CELTIC F.C., 1906-07.

so far from Fate. The good news, though, and it had nothing to do with outside help, was that Jimmy Quinn's two months suspension was now served and he would be free to play in the tie. The great man resumed his career on St Patrick's Day 1907. A long lay-off by Quinn had not dimmed the memory of his immense ability in his opponents' minds and Celtic were determined to make the most of Rangers' very obvious tactics. Quinn proved he was a real team player, always willing to utilise Rangers' pre-match plan of choking off any initiative of his or his team-mates' attempts at playing him in to Celtic's advantage. Whilst three Rangers players had been put on to shadowing him very closely indeed, Quinn made the most of it by pulling them out of the way of Celtic's other forwards and thus virtually rendered their presence on the field impotent. Celtic romped home by three goals to nil.

A sterner test faced the team in the semi-final as they met a determined Hibs side whose supporters showed no love for Celtic, still apportioning some of the blame on Celtic for their temporary demise from top-flight football in the early 1890s. Hibs pushed the Bhoys all the way but after two goalless draws and the consequent reappraisal by the Press of the possibility of the team failing to win the 'double', Celtic made the breakthrough in the third game and reached their 10th Scottish Cup Final by beating Hibernian 3–0. Davy Adams knew it not, but in this entire Scottish Cup campaign, he was to concede only three goals in nine games. Those dreams were becoming a reality.

Could Celtic complete the 'double' against the other very good Edinburgh side, Hearts? Celtic's eventual comprehensive victory over Hibs in the second replay said they were back on song and as the Final was only one week away, things were looking good for the Bhoys. Cold, blustery, heavy showers – a typical sodden day at Hampden Park for the Final on 20 April 1907. Both teams were going for a fifth victory in a Final in this competition. As usual, all form was reckoned to be as of no importance as cup competitions brought out the best in a team.

The kick-off was delayed for fifteen minutes because Hearts were a man short. Their goalkeeper had been held up by the large crowds attending the game. Some 50,000 souls had turned up ready for an East versus West battle. No delayed kick-off for Celtic in 1896 versus Hibs when the Celts had to play most of the game with ten men in a crucial League match. But this was death or glory in the Scottish Cup. When play finally got underway, the first-half was a very equal affair with neither Hearts' nor Celtic's big guns such as Walker or McMenemy making any show of their undoubted abilities. Of goals in the first forty-five minutes, there were none.

When the whistle sounded to begin the second-half, both sets of fans were anxious to see the opposition goalkeeper pick the ball out of the net. Hearts had tested Adams on a few occasions but he dealt with their best efforts with his usual aplomb. The teams were judged to be evenly matched until a penalty was awarded to Celtic. Hotly disputed and a surprise to all, Celtic accepted this result of a bit of a harmless ruck as mana from heaven and Willie Orr stepped up to open the scoring for his team. Celtic, always ready to take the moral high ground and great advocates of fair play, did nothing to support Hearts' justified complaint and went on to take full advantage of a distracted opposition. A sublime Alec Bennett cross to Peter Somers saw Celtic go two goals up as Somers, a superb passer of the ball himself, slipped the ball into the net. Celtic were now on a roll as Hearts seemed incapable of moving on from that very harsh penalty decision. Bennett and Somers repeated the movement minutes later and the Parkhead bhoys were now three up and coasting to their fifth Scottish Cup victory. Davy Adams had once said that being behind that great defence meant that he was frequently cold and lonely. That day he could add 'soaked' to the list and he would go down in Celtic history as a member of the first Scottish team ever to win the League and Cup double.

Possibly Celtic's greatest ever team. Adams is the tall man fifth from the left in the middle row. Goalkeepers did not wear different jerseys form the rest of the team in 1908.

As Celtic had been the first team to win the League and Cup double in Scotland, they felt that they really had to do it again the following season, 1907–08, just to show it had not been a fluke. Fortunately Celtic had a side that season that were more than capable on their day of sweeping the board of all the trophies going, the League Championship, the Scottish Cup, the Glasgow Cup and the Glasgow Charity Cup. In his career, Davy Adams had 137 shut-outs which shows just how valuable he was to that great team.

As the season began, it must have dawned on Celtic that they were now going to have to do it all over again. But they set out to accomplish it and that is exactly what they did and did it in style and with flair. They won the League four clear points ahead of their nearest rivals, Falkirk. As well as Adams' astonishing number of shut-outs, the defence only conceded 27 goals in those 34 games. Celtic also that season seemed to indulge in a bit of the Swap Shop mentality as Kivlichan came east from Rangers and Bennett went south some time later that season to the same team. A few weeks before leaving, Bennett had scored the only goal of the game in a vital 1–0 victory over the hand that was about to feed him. That game was a crucial step taken by Celtic on the road to lifting the Championship. Also in that season of 1907–08, both Edinburgh teams, Hearts and Hibernian, were soundly thrashed 6–0 and 4–0 respectively as Celtic powered their way to the title. It was to be their eighth Championship and fourth successive one.

In September of 1907, Celtic found themselves drawn against Queen's Park in the semi-final of the Glasgow Cup and it was no surprise to anyone that they were favourites to beat the amateurs. But, although it was so early in the season, injuries and accidents had reduced the potency of the team and Queen's Park reckoned they had a chance, if somewhat slim, against the League Champions. Celtic had a particular love of success, had become used to it, and the Glasgow Cup was a special favourite. Their worries had encouraged dreams to be dreamt by Queen's Park and the Spiders' attacking style gave them hope against a team that by this time had some acute problems in defence where Sunny Jim Young, a mainstay of the Celtic defence, was injured along with McLeod and was now battling to be fit for a place in the team. This casualty list had now left Davy Adams with two young players in McNair and Craig as the support immediately in front of him.

This game at Hampden, played in beautiful late summer weather, was deemed a pleasure to watch as it was played completely in a spirit of excellent sportsmanship; a model game, an exposition of cup football where every man was allowed to demonstrate his skills and to play the game. For Davy Adams, the first-half was uneventful due to the constant pressure of the Celtic forwards attacks on the opposition goal. Somers and Quinn scored one goal each, Somers in the first-half and Quinn in the second. All in all, the Celtic attack was simply formidable. Still, Paul and Entwhistle of Queen's Park allowed Adams to demonstrate his own brilliance as he pulled off two superb saves from great shots.

The Final saw Celtic pitted against a team that was bound to give them a much harder game – three in fact, as Ranger had every intention of removing the Glasgow Cup from Paradise. The encounters between Celtic and their opponents in the Final were described in this much-anticipated encounter as 'the delightful charm associated with past encounters'. Celtic's hopes of winning the Glasgow Cup four times in succession were blighted, it seemed, by their continuing list of injured first team stars. There were six of them out and some playing while not fully fit and the season not two months old. Yet again, Celtic decided that the half-backs available would be utilised as the entire defence save Davy Adams in goal. Celtic was now going into the Final to defend the trophy with five half-backs, Hay and McNair, filling the full-back positions. Although Celtic were entitled to utilise players from outwith the club, the directors decided to stick with the players they already had and whose abilities and fitness were well understood.

Hampden Park was the venue chosen to hold the Final and with its ability to accommodate 100,000 people, it would still be comfortable for even the largest crowd expected. The pitch was so well drained that the recent change in the weather with its attending moisture was reckoned to be of no import.

Celtic, with their necessary changes to the team, were considered the weaker side but the journalists of the day noted that the Glasgow Cup underdogs usually prevailed.

The first-half was for Celtic a period of complete supremacy, Bennett especially delighting the huge crowd with his perfect dribbling and accurate shooting and it was quite appropriate that he should have scored the first goal. It came after seven minutes to the intense delight of the Celtic supporters. But Rangers equalised and the teams headed into the second half a goal apiece. Despite Jimmy Quinn putting the Bhoys ahead again five minutes after play had restarted, Rangers took control of the game and with just over twenty minutes remaining, they equalised. Davy Adams had an excellent game, as did his opposite number, as both attacks tested them to the limit. Hamilton's contribution to the team was very badly missed. Of the two 'keepers, Adams was the busier and his most crucial save was when Sunny Jim Young scooped the ball over his head and almost scored for Rangers. The final whistle went and the Glasgow Cup was still up for grabs.

The replay was scheduled for the following Saturday, 18 October, 1907, and from Celtic's point of view, that week long respite was more than welcome. Sunny Jim had failed to last the whole of the previous game but now the Bhoys had all the injured players back in training. Most of the injuries had been ankle ones. The same team was expected to take on Rangers once more with the exception of Davy Hamilton who was not injured but suspended. Another large crowd was expected and it was hoped that the Queen's Park officials had taken to heart the lessons learned from the previous week's crushing at the pay-boxes. Celtic still had their sights firmly fixed on the 'four-in-a-row' record and Rangers were pulling out all the stops to stymie this record going Celtic's way. The Ibrox team were being given the benefit by their club of a week's stay at a Clyde Coast resort with the ozone breezes, brine baths and a rest cure to brace them up. Celtic, as usual, favoured Seamill.

The headlines after the game proclaimed 'PARKHEAD GOALKEEPER SAVES THE SITUATION'. 'DESPERATE FINISH' was also a favourite. Although it was an earlier kick-off and the crowd expected to be smaller, a large influx at half-time brought the crowd up to 55,000, the same as had witnessed the first replay the previous Saturday. Over the three games, £4,980 had been taken in – a club record. Celtic stuck by the team that had drawn with Rangers and McNair and Hay returned the board's confidence and faith in them in magnificent style, eclipsing with their boldness in the tackle and keeping the ball in play. In this, they completely outshone their opposite numbers. Celtic resorted to their first-game, forward line formula with Davie Mclean going centre and Jimmy Quinn at outside-left.

Once more the Celts dominated the first-half and led at half-time by two goals to nil. On the fifteen minute mark, Somers had taken advantage of a goalkeeping error to slip the ball past Newbigging in the Rangers goal and McLean earned the second eleven minutes later as he fired in a ferocious, well-judged shot. In the second-half, Rangers' determination and sudden domination reduced the difference between the teams by a goal with twenty-one minutes remaining. Their forward line play was now deadly but Davy Adams gave a tremendous display of 'courageous and clever saving' whilst under severe pressure and this exhibition of superlative goalkeeping was credited for Celtic being the holders of the Glasgow Cup for four years in succession. Adams defied every attempt to breach his goal and to level the score and the favourites were this time beaten. The underdogs had triumphed yet again. It had been a dogged Celtic display in the second-half with Adams' performance giving his defence great heart and encouragement. The referee had made some questionable decisions with some of them coming a bit late. It was suggested that, as this latter action had resulted in players wasting energy, perhaps he would have benefited from having a louder whistle. The stunning Glasgow Cup was presented later on the pavilion steps by President Wm. Reid of Partick Thistle and Mr Tom White accepted on behalf of Captain Hay.

With the League Championship safely sewn up, Celtic thoughts all turned to the other half of the 'double', the Scottish Cup. If the Celtic players were feeling the pressure of having made a rod for their own backs by doing it the previous season and raising all sorts of wild hopes of a repeat performance, it was nothing to the nervousness that had raced through their opponents in the Final, St Mirren, that day 18 April 1908, at Hampden Park. The Celts had seen off the comparatively new club, Aberdeen, in the semi-final, beating them by a slender one goal to nil away from home in front of a crowd of 20,000. This time the crowd on a windy – what else at Hampden? – day had soared to 58,000.

The final score line of 5–1 in Celtic's favour clearly reflects the superiority of Celtic against a workmanlike but very much overawed St Mirren team. But it was a great day out for their supporters who had expected nothing more and were rightly proud of their team for reaching the Final.

Celtic, once the whistle blew, went into their composed mode, showing their style and flair, knowing there was in all honesty nothing now to stop them completing the 'double' as for some inexplicable reason, St Mirren showed their acute nervousness by opting to play against the wind. The importance of the game and the daunting reality of playing in their first ever Scottish Cup Final before such a massive and very vocal crowd, had kicked in even before the kick-off, it seems.

The first-half saw St Mirren trying to match the greatest team in Celtic's history – a hopeless task – but fair play to them. Bennett scored and Celtic were out of the blocks. The second half saw Celtic step up a few gears and St Mirren buckled under the pressure. Another goal from Bennett was quickly emulated by Quinn, Somers and Hamilton and these were all duly appreciated by the vast crowd inside and probably outside the stadium. They were roaring Celtic on to the first ever successive League and Scottish Cup double in Scottish football history. The sheer size and noise of the crowd, nothing new to the Celtic players, plus some questionable refereeing decisions – Quinn was yards off-side when he scored – were simply too much for the St Mirren players to cope with and the team fell apart. St Mirren's Cunningham could at least be toasted that night in Paisley pubs as he had managed to make Davy Adams, the Shut-Out King, pick the ball out of the net once. It would, of course, be ignored that this had been a sure sign that the Celtic defence had eased up. It was also no consolation to the St Mirren supporters that Celtic's first opponents on the long road to Hampden and glory had been Peebles Rovers and the Bhoys had

Scottish Cup medal won by Adams in 1907

only beaten them 4–0 at Parkhead – four months and a hard-fought season before. In all, Celtic had scored 15 goals in the competition for the loss of two. It was a sixth Scottish Cup victory for Celtic.

By the time the Final of the Glasgow Charity Cup approached, due to be played on 30 May 1908, Celtic had won everything else and this trophy was the only glittering prize left. The Glasgow Charity Cup, first put up for competition in 1877 was the last big game of the season and had always attracted a lot of attention with the distinct possibility of a Celtic versus Rangers game in the contest. That season, 1907–08, Celtic had met and defeated Partick Thistle and now faced Clyde in the Final at Celtic Park.

The match attracted a crowd of 34,000 with all Celtic supporters there eager to see the team sweep the board. In all the Charity Cup matches that season, £2,780 was raised beating the previous best total of the 1888–89 season by £1,000. The end of May saw Glasgow sweltering in a mini-heat wave and the sports journalists afterwards could not decide whether the nastiness displayed by the players was a result of the tremendous heat or just the Celts being over-anxious to establish a new record. The Celts were obviously being made the fall guys, the naughty bhoys, in a none too subtle fashion. One of the Celtic half-backs, not Hay, was deemed responsible for a bit of rough handling of a Clyde player and these tactics apparently upset a knighted gentleman and his guests in the stand. Shame. The game was dubbed 'a distinctly unpleasant game', but in the end, the record was established as the Celts with their irritating ways beat Clyde 2–0.

The first-half began and Celtic's apparent strong-arm tactics did not appear to stop Clyde from giving Davy Adams in the Celtic goal more work than the Celtic forwards were giving his opposite number in the entire game. Clyde had won the toss and were playing with the wind behind them, but when the whistle blew for the end of the first-half, the score was still 0–0. The second-half saw a Celtic revival and frequent clashes of temper. But Celtic were out on that pitch to win and in the strength-sapping heat, two goals from McMenemy and one from Quinn saw them bring that epic season to a successful conclusion.

All the efforts of Davy Adams and his teammates over two hard and very good games in the Final of the Scottish Cup in 1909 have been consigned to the bin of footballing history by the riotous behaviour of some fans after the game and the condemnation for irresponsible actions being heaped on the heads of the Celtic team that day. All eyes, thoughts, words and hyperbole have rendered two excellent cup-ties irrelevant and have done a disgraceful injustice to the players of both Celtic and their opponents, Rangers. Little has been written in detail of both games in which the players, whose number of fixtures they had featured in would have modern-day players begging for a stint down a 19th century coal mine as an option, had given their all.

The replay on 17 April 1909 had been the result of a very hard-fought draw a week earlier. As usual in Old Firm games, tension was at its highest both on the pitch and on the terracing and so the scene was set for a gigantic tussle. A crowd of 70,000 had turned up on 10 April hoping for an entertaining game and they were not disappointed. The roar of the crowd when the first goal went in was prolonged and joyous in the Celtic half of Hampden Park as the incomparable Jimmy Quinn did what he did best, scored for the Bhoys. Celtic went in at half-time one goal up and determined not only to maintain that lead and lift the coveted Scottish Cup but also to add to it. Rangers, though, had other ideas. Two goals later for them and it looked like they were on track to lift the Cup when Jimmy Quinn's attempted shoulder charge resulted in the Ibrox 'keeper, the ball firmly grasped in his hands, stepping over the line to avoid Quinn. 2–2 and that was the Final score. The replay was scheduled for the following Saturday

The first half of the replay, which had attracted some 60,000 that Saturday was largely dominated by Rangers. Despite Adams most heroic performance in the Celtic goal, Rangers were one goal ahead when Celtic had to cope with the blow of losing Jim Young for a time. Young had suffered an injury, which required him to leave the pitch to have stitches put in a gash over his eye. The firsthalf finished with only that one Rangers goal on the score-sheet and it would be all to play for Celtic in the remaining forty-five minutes.

Celtic came storming out of the blocks after the interval and bombarded the Rangers goal and how they failed to score was amazing. Somers had two near misses and Quinn, Kivlichan and Hay followed suit and Rangers were really pushing their luck. Had the aforementioned luck been even marginally on Celtic's side, there would have been no mention of extra-time or of a replay that had been engineered by the clubs to earn them more money. Davy Adams in Celtic's goal was as sound as ever. Celtic's forwards were explosive and determined to equalise. Sunny Jim's heading ability had obviously been voided by that injury and Smith took full advantage of this. But Quinn was Celtic's saviour yet again and with the score now a level 1–1, Celtic laid siege to the Rangers goal but to no avail. The final whistle went and Fate stepped in.

The famous photograph of Celtic and a few Rangers players lingering on the pitch is a study in indecision. Bafflement, bewilderment, what happens next? It is all there in their body language. They were obviously under the impression extra-time would be played and were no doubt wondering why most of their opponents had left the pitch. Seasoned footballers, internationalists who knew the rules. The obvious inference is that they had been told otherwise. At the conclusion of this drawn, second match and the lack of communication to both players and crowd that there would have to be yet another replay must have greatly contributed to what followed. No doubt the players, tired as they were, would have preferred to play the game to a conclusion. The crowd definitely had no doubt that yet another replay simply meant more money for the clubs, Queen's Park and the SFA. Was the whole thing rigged? That was now the idea uppermost in their minds. Whatever the reason, once all the players had eventually left the pitch, two hours of wanton destruction and hooliganism followed and a small section of the 60,000 crowd subjected police and firemen to sustained stone throwing. They also set fire to pay-boxes, tore up goalposts and the pitch and assaulted ambulancemen who had come to the aid of the injured, very many severely so.

The game of football had grown substantially in Scotland and in Glasgow in particular and its popularity as a game was being marketed as a family pastime. Parents were now encouraging their children to take up the game and schools football was taking off. It was now thought that this image would be irreparably damaged because of the Cup Final riots. That this did not happen is something as inexplicable as the 'mobocracy' itself on that day. The Press came in for a high degree of criticism for having published on the Tuesday preceding the match, although it was in fact their right to do so, the information that the Celtic directors had held a meeting and the possibility of playing extra-time had been discussed. Willie Maley told one newspaper reporter that he had been instructed to ask Rangers FC and the Association if this could be arranged as the rules stated extra-time would only be played if the third replay was drawn. The Celtic players were also aware of this request by their club. As no further word was heard, it was obvious that both players and public alike assumed it was a 'done deal'. Certainly some of the Celtic players thought so. In fact it turned out that the Rangers director Maley had approached and who was to have consulted his board had simply forgotten all about it. Rangers FC knew nothing at all about it, they said. They obviously did not read the sports section of the newspapers or in fact the newspapers read by the players and paying public who traipsed through the turnstiles.

The SFA inquiry threw up an astonishing number of officials claiming, 'It wisnae me, sir.' With Celtic, it was a case of, 'Riot? What riot?' as both players and officials were comfortably ensconced in a city restaurant when they first heard of it. Some idea of a disturbance, though, must surely have registered as it took several policemen to shield the players and officials as they left Hampden. Willie Maley many years later claimed he had watched it all happen. Odd. The disturbance continued outside the ground with all street lamps and shop-windows broken in both Aitkenhead Road and Polmadie Road. Willie Maley told the official enquiry that he could give no explanation as to why the Celtic players had remained on the pitch after the referee plus ball had left it. They had had no instruction to do so. He confirmed he had asked a Rangers director to bring the matter of extra-time before his Board the previous Tuesday. Maley made no effort to shield his players from criticism, as he offered no explanation that could be called 'mitigating circumstances'. It was always boss and worker when the chips were down and it would be a foolish player who expected anything else. Jimmy Hay, the Celtic captain, had been in the act of leaving the field when he saw some of his team speaking to the referee. They were, he said, asking him about extra-time. Seemingly, there was a massive communication problem at Parkhead between management and staff! Hay maintained that there was no significant delay in the players leaving after the referee had left the pitch. A member of the SFA disagreed and said that there had been a noticeable delay. The Celtic captain said that no instructions had been given to the players about playing extra time. A Mr A.B. MacKenzie of Rangers told the enquiry that he had later said to Willie Maley that no such request, as he had referred to had been submitted to his board. James Stark, the Rangers captain, said that although he had left the pitch on hearing the final whistle, several of his players remained. Nothing had been said to the team regarding playing extra-time in the event of a draw. One of the linesmen, Mr D. Campbell, said that he was perplexed by the fact that much was being made of the players still being on the pitch after the whistle had gone. He could not understand this as, in his opinion, the players remained, 'not much longer than usual at any game.'

Both Celtic and Rangers had decided that they would ask the SFA to withhold the trophy for that year. They published that petition in the newspapers before giving it to the SFA. Not popular and rather bad manners. At the SFA meeting to investigate and decide what to do in these very unusual circumstances, one member, Mr Ward, said that if they did withhold the trophy, they would be punishing the wrong people. They would be refusing medals to players who had

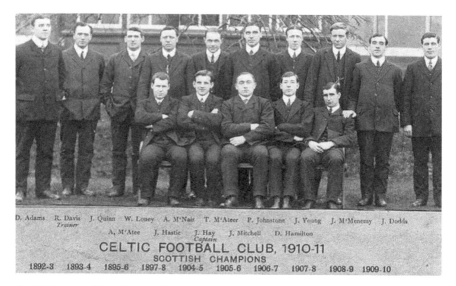

D. Adams   R. Davis   J. Quinn   W. Loney   A. M'Nair   T. M'Ateer   P. Johnstone   J. Young   J. M'Menemy   J. Dodds
        Trainer

A. M'Atee   J. Hastie   J. Hay   J. Mitchell   D. Hamilton
                        Captain

CELTIC FOOTBALL CLUB, 1910-11
SCOTTISH CHAMPIONS

1892-3   1893-4   1895-6   1897-8   1904-5   1905-6   1906-7   1907-8   1908-9   1909-10

fought long and hard to win them. That motion was defeated as was one suggesting awarding it jointly to both clubs. Celtic and Rangers won the day – well, the Boards did! The trophy was withheld. Tom White of Celtic had declared on behalf of both clubs that they would refuse to take part in a second replay if one was ordered to be played. They were prepared to scratch from the competition rather than do that.

Davy Adams and his exhausted teammates went home that day little knowing that they were about to be pilloried and no medal as a consolation. Davy Adams did not have a testimonial of his own but he took part in that for one of Celtic's greatest ever players, Jimmy McMenemy. By this time Davy had had regular bouts of rheumatism and pneumonia coupled with an eyesight problem. He was probably spared the extreme injuries suffered by Dan McArthur because of the simply superb defence he played behind.

1911 saw the beginning of the end of Adams' Celtic career but in the closing game of the 1910–11 season, on 1 May, Celtic took on Aberdeen, the side that had run Rangers a close second in the League Championship. The game was played at Parkhead and the result was a draw. It was reported that although the Aberdeen 'keeper had performed well, the save that Adams made from a Travers header was the finest goalkeeping moment of the game. The game against St Mirren on 2 December 1911 later that year saw the end of one very fine career and the beginning of another. Teammates on that day, as Davy bowed out, Patsy Gallagher bowed in. Such is Fate! Davy had already acquired a public House in Avonbridge and his thoughts had now turned to being a well-respected businessman and his footballing influence given over to the junior game there.

A team is only as good or as great as its confidence in its goalkeeper. That Davy Adams' secure tenure of that position occurred during the ascendancy of perhaps the most consistently great side in the history of the club speaks for itself. A great 'keeper's ability can be reduced to naught by the history books if he has the misfortune to be the last line of defence in a poor team regardless of what heroics he performs. Equally so, the team whose confidence in that last line is sound can spell the death-knell to a goalkeeper's reputation, if that team is overwhelmingly talented. It would appear to be a no-win position for in the last scenario, few opportunities are afforded for praise and the demonstrating of skill as the wizardry of those in front makes all the headlines. As Neil Lennon once said, 'Everybody's only interested in the glamour boys.' Goalkeepers in great sides are consistently overlooked and often given few opportunities to showcase their talents. But injuries and the suspensions of some of the iconic figures in that six-in-a-row side afforded the opportunity for all to see and recognise that these players achieved all that they did by performing as a team where every position mattered, every man a star. Davy Adams retired from Celtic and football to concentrate on running his newly acquired business back amongst his ain folk, secure in the knowledge that he was truly one of Celtic's great goalkeepers.

CAREER:

Appearances: 333
Scottish Cup Medals: 4
Scottish League Medals: 6
Glasgow Cup Medals: 4
Glasgow Charity Cup Medals: 2
Shut Outs: 137

CHARLIE SHAW
(1913–25)

By David Potter

The legendary Charlie Shaw is immortalised, curiously enough, mainly by a song sung by opposition supporters. There were enough songs sung about him by his own supporters, likening him to Bonnie Prince Charlie and 'How can you buy Killarney?' becoming 'How can you buy our Charlie?' (sung also with a great deal of gusto about Charlie Tully half a century later) but it was a song  started by Raith Rovers supporters in Kirkcaldy, then much adapted by supporters of other clubs, which guaranteed that the name Charlie Shaw would be on the lips of all supporters, both Celtic-minded and otherwise, in the halcyon days of the early 1920s when football meant so much to so many people.

It started when a goal was scored by Raith Rovers' John 'Tokey' Duncan, so called for his ability to be in the right place to tap the ball in with his toe. On one occasion, on April 9 1921, Tokey did it twice against Celtic and Charlie Shaw, a rare event in 1921, and some Kirkcaldy songwriters, seizing on the popularity of the officially disapproved of 'Red Flag' – much sung in their triumphant Labour by-election campaign of March 1921 a month previously – changed the lyrics so that they ran:

> *Oh, Charlie Shaw, he never saw*
> *Whaur Tokey Duncan pit the ba'*
> *He pit the ba' right in the net*
> *An' Charlie Shaw sat doon an' gret!*

It was a significant loss for Celtic as well, for it more or less killed what little chance they had of winning the Scottish League that season, but it was overshadowed at the time by Scotland beating England at Hampden on the same day.

Very soon, this song was adopted by supporters of other teams. Dundee supporters claimed that it was 'oor wee Troupie' (Alec Troup), Third Lanark said it was 'Willie Hillhouse' before Rangers supporters said that it was 'Alan Morton'.

New verses were penned – 'Oh, Charlie Shaw, he asked his maw…' and 'Oh, Charlie Shaw, why did you fa'…' – for example, and there was little doubt that until Charlie left Celtic in 1925, he would always be greeted with this song, even at railway stations and in the street. Charlie, as he often did when people tried to rile him, smiled benignly at them.

The point about all this however was that this was such a great compliment to Charlie. Getting a goal past him was a very rare event indeed, and that is why songs were written about such occurrences. It also indicates just how much of a personality Charlie was. It was an age that badly needed heroes and personalities. The avuncular Charlie Shaw did just that.

Charlie was born on 21 September 1885 in what would become the Celtic stronghold of Twechar, not far from Jimmy Quinn's Croy. He was born of illiterate parents James Shaw, a bricklayer, and Elizabeth (Bessy) Smith, who had been married in Clitheroe in England in 1875. Charles was the third of the family, joining Bella and Thomas. He would also have a younger brother called William. He was born at 69 Barrhill Rows, Twechar but by 1891, the family had moved to Kirkintilloch.

Like most boys of that age, he was mad on football, and soon discovered that he had a talent to be a goalkeeper. He was small for a goalkeeper at 5ft 6in, but made his way through the junior ranks with Baillieston Thistle and Kirkintilloch Harp before joining the then senior team Port Glasgow Athletic on18 April 1906. He first played at Celtic Park on 22 December 1906 when he was in the Port Glasgow side who were comprehensively beaten by the mighty Celtic side of that day. Four nil was the score but Charlie was not blamed for the loss of the two goals to Jimmy Quinn and one each to Bennett and McMenemy. Indeed but for Shaw, it might have been a lot more, and Charlie enjoyed the experience of talking to Davy Adams the Celtic goalkeeper, a huge figure of a man, a good six inches taller than Charlie. There was then, of course, as there still is, a goalkeepers' union whereby goalkeepers sought each other out and talked to each other.

He realised something that day. As a small man, he could never hope to dominate the penalty area in the way that Adams did. He was vulnerable to shoulder charging, but fortunately had been nimble enough to avoid the attentions of his friend Jimmy Quinn that day. Charlie realised that he would have to be more agile than other goalkeepers. He would have to train hard. His training regime seemed to work, for Charlie was seldom injured.

By the time that Celtic came to Clune Park, Port Glasgow to play at the end of the season, the destination of the 1907 Scottish League Championship had

51

been decided. Celtic had won it very comfortably, and Port Glasgow were about third from the bottom. There was no automatic relegation in those days, so the game was to all intents and purposes a friendly. Celtic had also won the Scottish Cup becoming the first team to win the Scottish League and Scottish Cup in the same season. The game was played on 4 May before a crowd of about 2,500 mainly exultant Celtic supporters who had travelled there in their brake clubs. They arrived before the Celtic team did, for in one of Mr Maley's rare mistakes, Celtic ended up in Gourock, having taken the wrong train!

It was a fine day, but the game could hardly have started more dramatically. A foul in the penalty box in the first minute resulted in a penalty kick. Up stepped Jimmy Quinn to take it, but Shaw 'with the spring of an acrobat' saved the penalty! The game ended 1–1 with Shaw defeated only by another penalty kick, this time taken by Willie Orr. Shaw was badly injured at one point, seeming to lose consciousness after a knock from Quinn, but he recovered and played a brilliant game, described by his friend Jimmy Quinn as being, 'like Danny McArthur at his best'. Charlie was thus able to claim that the mighty forward line of Bennett, McMenemy, Quinn, Somers and Hamilton had failed to score against him with even one or two of his saves earning a reluctant clap and cheer from the Celtic fans, especially when word spread that this small goalkeeper was a Celtic sympathiser from Twechar.

But his performances impressed someone else in the crowd. Jimmy Cowan, one time Scotland International and generally reckoned to be one of the best half-backs in history with five League Championships and two FA Cups with Aston Villa, had recently been appointed manager of Queen's Park Rangers. He came from Jamestown in Dunbartonshire, and was firmly of the opinion that his fellow countrymen were the best in the world. He had heard stories from various sources of this small but very industrious goalkeeper and was duly impressed by his performance that day. A few days later he offered terms to Charlie Shaw.

It would be a great increase in wages, but the thought of a move to London must have been a little daunting for the young man. But Cowan himself and others had moved to England, and there would be no lack of Scottish people in London. Moreover, no Scottish team seemed interested in him, particularly the one that he really wanted – Celtic, for they were well served by Davy Adams – and Charlie decided that he would take the big step. He was thus almost 22 when he moved to London, to the Southern League team called Queen's Park Rangers, a club situated in northwest London. This was in 1907, and at the same time, the club moved from the Horse Ring as it was called, to the Park Royal Ground, designed by Archibald Leitch, the famous designer of stadia at Rangers, Sunderland, Everton and many others.

Charlie played for QPR 251 times, legend having it that he missed only three games through injury in the six years that he was with them from 1907 until 1913. During that time he was very influential and his goalkeeping much praised and the team won the Southern Football League in two occasions, 1908 and 1912. He was very happy in London, but was possibly motivated to return to Scotland by several considerations.

He would return to Scotland every summer. In 1908 he had a special reason for coming home, for on 3 July of that year in Lennoxtown RC Church, he married Annie O'Donnell of Campsie who was described as a 'printfield marker'. Interestingly enough, Charles is described as a 'bricklayer' not a 'professional football player'. Normally in Edwardian times, there would be a reluctance to describe oneself as a professional football player, which after all, is a very temporary way of earning a living and in any case was not always approved of in 'polite' society. His residence is given as 35 Union Street, Kirkintilloch, not anyplace in London.

He was aware that QPR were a good team, but they were never really likely to win anything significant. The main action in England at this time was the north of the country in places like Newcastle, Sunderland and Manchester. QPR made a few half-hearted attempts to join the Football League where most of the big teams played, (there was no automatic promotion) but the truth was that QPR in north London lacked the resources and the fan base to do consistently well in the Football League. Charlie still aspired to a Scotland cap – he certainly felt that he was good enough to win one, but realised that by 1913 when he was getting uncomfortably close to his 30th birthday, his opportunity had possibly gone. But he was still ambitious.

There was also a residual homesickness and a desire to return to Scotland. Life in the bustling metropolis that London was, was agreeable, but his family still lived in Scotland, and that was where his heart lay. Yet he loved the supporters of QPR as well, got on tolerably well with the management of the club and it was a wrench when the offer came in spring 1913 to return to Scotland.

But it was quite an offer. Even in London, the exploits of the great Celtic team were well known. They had won the Scottish League for six seasons in a row from 1905 until 1910, and although they had lost a little ground to the Rangers team recently, they were still a mighty name, in the same way that Newcastle United were in England at the time. Charlie was also well aware that when he bought his evening paper the first result he looked for was that of Celtic.

Meanwhile, Celtic's great Edwardian team had reached its peak and were in a genteel decline, ironically enough dating from the same time that King Edward VII passed away in 1910. Rangers had won the League in 1911, 1912 and 1913, and

53

although Celtic had won the Scottish Cup in 1911 and 1912, 1912–13 had been a barren season. In particular, goalkeeping had been a problem. Adams had not played since December 1911, suffering from illness and injury. For a while, John Mulrooney, the eccentric comedian, was tried, but he was only a partial success before rheumatism and heart problems restricted his appearances, Bob Boyle was a little short of Celtic class and there was no obvious other candidate until Maley remembered the Port Glasgow Athletic player and Celtic supporter who was apparently seeking a move northwards away from Queen's Park Rangers for whom he had excelled.

Things moved quickly at the end of the season. A sum of £100 changed hands for Shaw's purchase, and Shaw very soon found himself playing for Celtic against Third Lanark in the semi-final of the Glasgow Charity Cup on Tuesday 6 May 1913. The Charity Cup was always played for at the end of the season, and although the proceeds all went to charity, and the players, theoretically at least, all played as amateurs, there was always a certain amount of kudos associated with the trophy particularly in a year like 1913 when nothing else had been won. It would at least give the club and its supporters something to be happy about. After all, 1913 was the club's silver jubilee and it would be nice to win something. 1903, ten years previously, had been the last barren year, but it too had finished with the Glasgow Charity Cup.

A crowd of 6,000 were at Cathkin that night. Mulrooney had played in the goal on the Saturday in the first round against Clyde, but Maley felt that Charlie was worth a go. Very few would have remembered Charlie Shaw from his Port Glasgow days, and the impression was that he might be rather too small to be a goalkeeper. But it was clear from the start that he was acquitting himself well under Third Lanark's opening pressure, the fans particularly liking his willingness to come out of his goal to deal with trouble. Celtic slowly took control of the game, scored through Barney Connolly and Willie Loney to seize control of the tie, and although Thirds scored with a fierce shot near the end (Shaw had no chance), Celtic won the game well.

Press comments were favourable. 'On this showing, Celtic have a gem of a custodian in the man from QPR' says *The Daily Record and Mail* while *The Glasgow Herald* talks about Shaw being 'repeatedly tested' but came out well from the pressure. Another benefit from this game for Charlie was that his opposite number in the Third Lanark goal was no less a man than Jimmy Brownlie, Scotland's goalkeeper. Shaw was thus able to talk to the kindly Brownlie, virtually unchallenged as the best goalkeeper in the country.

He now found himself playing in a Cup Final less than a week after signing for Celtic. He was not the only one either. Johnny McMaster and Johnny Hill had both signed from Dumbarton Harp in the past week, and 39,000 turned up to see a new look Celtic team playing in the Final of the Glasgow Charity Cup against Rangers at Parkhead on Saturday 10 May 1913.

PROMINENT FOOTBALLERS.

C. SHAW,

QUEEN'S PARK RANGERS.

It was also the first day that Shaw, McNair and Dodds played together. The time used to be when old Celtic supporters sitting in the corner of a pub would hold court and tell about the great teams that they had seen and would begin impressively with 'Shaw, McNair and Dodds...'. Sadly they would soon spoil it all by continuing with 'Young, Loney and Hay' unaware, or choosing to forget, that these two mighty troikas never actually played in the same team, for Jimmy Hay had gone to Newcastle in 1911. It was Johnny McMaster who played at left-half that day to supplement the evergreen Sunny Jim and the 'obliterator' Willie Loney whose motto was 'No Road This Way'.

Sadly that was not true this particular day, for Willie Loney was now ageing and lost out on two early occasions to Rangers' Willie Reid who scored twice within the first 10 minutes. This must have been disconcerting, to put it mildly, to Charlie Shaw, playing his first home game and against Rangers at that, and appearing in front of 30,000 fans, probably the biggest crowd he had ever played before. But the defence rallied, tightened up and then the talismanic wee Patsy Gallacher, who had already made an impact on Celtic in his season and a half, pulled one back.

This day, however, was the solitary highlight of Barney Connolly's sadly underperforming career. He equalized in a scramble, and then scored the winner with a 'drive through' past several Rangers defenders and a crashing shot. It was reminiscent of Jimmy Quinn at his best, and had the Celtic fans leaving the stadium singing the praises of their team in a way that they had not done all season. Celtic, at least, had had the last laugh, and Charlie had the opportunity to attend the 25-year celebration dinner with his new teammates and the Glasgow Charity Cup sitting on the table.

The fans and Willie Maley the Manager recalled the almost exact parallel of 10 years ago when the team had had a dismal season but at the very end won the

Glasgow Charity Cup in May 1903 with a new man on board called Jimmy Young who had been signed from Bristol Rovers. Now with three new men on board the same trophy had been won. A supporter claimed in a letter to a newspaper that 'Celtic sign a man on at 2.00 pm and give him a medal at 5 pm!' This wasn't literally true, of course, but the new players were certainly buoyed up by their early success.

For Charlie summer 1913 was a great time. The new season simply could not come quickly enough. Charlie was perhaps even able to grasp the enormity of this club with its massive support and its visionary Manager. Maley was given a cash honorarium for all his efforts at the club – he had been there since the very beginning in 1888 – and he said, 'working for Celtic is a labour of love…it is a very large part of my existence…nothing really matters as much as success, and success is the only thing worth striving for'. With a boss like that, genial, dedicated (almost to the point of obsession), confident and encouraging, Charlie saw clearly that the club had an awesome potential. He had no bad memories of QPR and Jimmy Cowan, but with all due respect to them, Celtic was something totally different.

Charlie was also aware that there was another side to Celtic as well. Although they had more supporters than most teams and had a better relationship with their fans than anyone else perhaps, Celtic fans, when frustrated could turn nasty. Charlie had vivid memories of how the fans turned on the great Dan McArthur who had served the side with distinction winning Scottish Cup medals in 1899 and 1900, but when he had a bad day in the 1901 Scottish Cup Final against Hearts, the crowd had been less than supportive. There is of course no escape for a goalkeeper, for they are blamed for everything. An outfield player can make an error and hardly anyone notices. Goalkeepers' mistakes are often fatal.

Charlie's first full season 1913–14 was a great one in the history of the club. Basically, what happened was that Maley had turned up trumps again. His great Edwardian side had passed its best, and while he retained some of them, notably McMenemy, Young and McNair, he brought it more than adequate replacements for the rest. There was of course the mighty atom, Patsy Gallagher, but there were other shrewd recruitments for the forward line notably the wingers, the earnest young Andy McAtee from Croy with the brawny physique and the legs that looked like those of a billiard table and the occasionally wayward but prodigiously talented Johnny Browning. At centre-half there was the strapping Fifer called Peter Johnstone, and at left half Johnny McMaster 'of the melancholy countenance' but the sturdy tackle.

But at the back were Shaw, McNair and Dodds. Maley himself in a series of articles that he wrote on Celtic in *The Weekly News* in 1936 said; 'Shaw, McNair and Dodds understood each other so well that they developed the pass back into a scientific move of which there have been many imitators but none to equal the originators. It was indeed a spectacle to see either McNair or Dodds passing with unerring accuracy and cheeky coolness the ball to Shaw two yards away with the opposing forwards almost on top of them. That was their method of getting out of a corner, which would in all probability otherwise been fatal'. The pass back, of course, now outlawed since 1993, was a perfectly acceptable means of defence in the 1910s. 'Pass it back to Chairlie' was often the supporters' cry.

But there was more to them than that. McNair, not without cause called 'the icicle' for his calmness under pressure also had the ability to simply be in the right place at the right time. His concentration was intense, and he also took it upon himself to provide cover for the centre of the park as well, if necessary (he had occasionally been a centre-half when Loney was injured) to allow Peter Johnstone to act as an attacking centre-half whereas Dodds was more of the attacking left-back in the way that Tommy Gemmell of a later generation was and Emilio Izaguirre of more recent times. But the important thing was that they all understood each other, and worked together as a team – Chairlie, Eck and Joe, all of them obeying without question the authoritative captain, the fair haired Sunny Jim.

As is often the case with good seasons in Celtic's history, there were a few hiccups early on, notably in the defeat to Third Lanark in the Glasgow Cup semi-final in October. But Shaw was off to a good start to his Celtic career. The first League game of the season, for example, against Ayr United at Celtic Park talks of, 'deafening roars of delight at Shaw's saves' from the 25,000 crowd, and if there had been the slightest doubt about Shaw's ability and popularity with the support, it was dispelled at Ibrox on 25 October 1913 when he saved a penalty-kick.

A crowd of 64,000 were at Ibrox that day, and Celtic were leading 2–0 at half-time. But without both Quinn and McMenemy, they began to struggle in the second half. Rangers piled on the pressure but made no impression on the rock-like back three of Shaw, McNair and Dodds. Rangers scored once, but the goal was disallowed by Mr Murray of Stenhousemuir for an infringement, and in the last 10 minutes, the pressure was intensified. Charlie was there, pointing, gesticulating to his exhausted defenders, and then Jimmy Galt broke away and shot from about 20 yards. Charlie not only got to it, but even brought it down cleanly to the ground without spilling it. Two minutes after that, Rangers were awarded a penalty-kick.

This was now Rangers chance, and the penalty was to be taken by Alec Bennett, the man who had unaccountably jumped ship from Celtic to Rangers in 1908. He was by some distance Rangers best player and it was commonly assumed that he would score this penalty and give Rangers a lifeline. Charlie eyed him unblinkingly, and as Alec ran up to take the kick, Charlie did a little 'sand dance' on his line, then dived to his right to save the kick. The Celtic support behind his goal erupted with joy. Charlie held the ball up for everyone to see, and Alec Bennett, not for the first time nor last time, asked himself why he ever left Parkhead five years ago.

This was the springboard for a great run with 10 clean sheets in a row. They eventually conceded a goal at Stark's Park to Raith Rovers on 13 December, but still won the game, and it was a long time before they conceded another. (The goal, incidentally, was scored by a Raith player called Jimmy Scott who was one of the many who failed to return from the Great War) 'Burglar-proof', 'watertight', 'no leaks', were the phrases used to describe the great defence and questions were now beginning to be asked about whether Charlie might be capped for Scotland in the New Year.

But New Year's Day saw another remarkable game. The 75,000 who attended the packed ground at Celtic Park saw a 4–0 victory for Celtic over Rangers, and left all-enthused about Napoleon McMenemy's great goal, but there was also another saving of a penalty-kick by Charlie Shaw from Alec Bennett, this one long after the game had finished as a contest, and not mentioned as highly in contemporary accounts as his saves from Willie Reid and Jimmy Gordon in the early part of the game.

The good form continued into the early part of 1914. Having laid a few bogeys by winning at grounds like Dens Park and Love Street, they eventually lost a goal and a game to Falkirk at Brockville on 28 February and even then there were extenuating circumstances for Dodds, McMenemy and Browning were playing for Scotland at Celtic Park against Wales. Since losing that goal to Raith Rovers on 13 December, Charlie had gone what is reckoned to be 1,287 minutes (the times are a guess, for newspapers were not specific in their times in 1914) without losing a goal, and that goal scored at Stark's Park was the only one conceded between 4 October and 28 February.

Charlie might have expected a cap that day against Wales – he certainly deserved one – but as he himself cheerfully admitted, the sitting tenant Jimmy Brownlie of Third Lanark was no bad goalkeeper either. He did however get his chance for the Scottish League against the English League at Burnley on 21 March. Indeed it was the Celtic back three of Shaw, McNair and Dodds who represented the Scottish League that day, always giving the impression of 'strength, certainty and resource', as Scotland won an exciting game 3–2. Charlie was not blamed for the loss of either goal, one of which was a penalty-kick. Such was the nature of the man however that when he heard that he was not being picked for the big International at Hampden on 4 April he sent a message of best wishes to the man who got the job and whom he much admired, Jimmy Brownlie.

Not everyone who was alive in 1967 would agree with this, but many think that this was the best Celtic side of them all. This picture was taken on 18 April 18, two days after Celtic had won the Scottish Cup against Hibs. On this very day playing by coincidence against Hibs, they would win the Scottish League as well! Left to right standing; Manager Maley, McMaster, Dodds, Shaw, McNair, Johnstone, McColl, Trainer Quinn; sitting: McAtee, Gallacher, Young, McMenemy, Browning.

The rest of the season was little other than complete triumph for Shaw and Celtic. The Scottish Cup was won at Ibrox after a replay against Hibs on Thursday 16 April, the League was won against the same opponents a couple of days later and then the Glasgow Charity Cup was won with Shaw virtually a spectator in the games against Queen's Park and Third Lanark. He did have one scary moment or two in the first game of the Scottish Cup Final when he needed the knee of Eck McNair to clear a ball off his line in the first half, and then in the dying seconds when Willie Smith of Hibs missed a chance, but the replay was a very one-sided occasion.

He had come far in the last year. He was already a hero with the vast Celtic support, and there was a tour of Europe to look forward to. He had played every single game, and had lost only 14 goals in 38 League games. Not without cause did Celtic fans sing about 'oor Chairlie'. Charlie was a hero, and like most great Celts, the affinity and bond with the support grew and grew.

The tour of Europe in 1914 was a great success. The team played six games in Budapest, Vienna, Berlin and Leipzig, and Charlie played in all six, for there was no other goalkeeper. Had Charlie been injured, Sunny Jim would presumably have taken over the job (he had done this famously once before in 1909). Football on the continent in 1914 was rudimentary with poor pitches and poor referees. There was one nasty game with Burnley the winners of the English Cup, but the other

59

games were light-hearted affairs with Maley keen, as always, to show the best side of Celtic to the Germans and Austro-Hungarians. The hosts for their part entertained the Scotsmen well with food, drink and sightseeing trips, and friendships were made. No-one had the slightest inkling of what was to come when Celtic returned to Scotland at the beginning of June 1914 to enjoy what was generally regarded as a good summer.

The assassination of the heir to the Austro-Hungarian Empire in Sarajevo at the end of June meant little to Charlie Shaw, and as the team returned for training in late July, they were more concerned with the sudden and untimely death of Charlie's immediate predecessor than any talk of a European crisis. This was John Mulrooney, then playing for St Johnstone who had died suddenly of rheumatism. But on Monday 3 August Glasgow was suddenly talking about the inevitability of war, and by the time Charlie arrived for training on 5 August, the country really was at war, not in some far-flung part of the world like Crimea, Sudan or South Africa, but with Germany and Austria where Charlie had made so many friends just a couple of months ago!

Football continued but was severely curtailed. There were no full International games, and no Scottish Cup. The Scottish League and the two Glasgow competitions continued, and for season 1914–15 there were Scottish League Internationals before they too were stopped. A player was not allowed to play on a Saturday unless he had worked in some war-related occupation during the week. And of course there was pressure to join the forces. Such were Maley's connections that he was able to find jobs for most of his fine side, normally in the shipbuilding or coalmining industry. In Charlie's case, he was, 'in sole charge of a business', namely his tobacconist's shop in Bridgeton, not far from Celtic Park, and that was enough to grant him exemption. This was confirmed on 28 August 1916 when he went to a tribunal, and he was given exemption on these grounds.

He would have been happy at that, for the gentle Charlie was no soldier. Indeed he recalled with devastating clarity the goalkeepers of those German and Austrian teams Celtic had played a few months earlier. Charlie had been careful to make friends with the 'custodians' (the goalkeepers union spread over international boundaries) and the thought of having to shoot bullets at them was totally repugnant.

Charlie had two establishments in fact. He had a tobacconist's business in 65 Canning Street, and also a newsagent's shop called the Bookstall at the North British Station at Bridgeton Cross. His advertisements always assured every one of his personal attention and his willingness to 'send out' newspapers, presumably to soldiers in the trenches.

Charlie Shaw is in the middle of the back row of this picture taken apparently outside the front door of the old pavilion at Celtic Park. Manager Maley looks as if he has been caught smoking and has quickly put his arm behind his back!

The first season of the war was in fact a very successful one for Celtic. Charlie had one very bad day in the Glasgow Cup on 12 September 1914 when Celtic lost 0–2 to Clyde. *The Glasgow Herald* is reluctantly compelled to apportion the blame to Charlie Shaw and the credit to Pat Allan (the Clyde centre forward) 'If the Celtic goalkeeper was taken by surprise when he allowed a hook shot from Allan to glance off his hands into the net, it was the turn of the 18,000 spectators to feel amazed when he dropped the ball ever so invitingly at the feet of the same player and made the second goal a certainty'.

This result was reputed to have caused consternation among the forces already in France and Belgium, especially when they heard that the 'culprit' was the previously impeccable Charlie Shaw. It would be a long time before he had such a bad day again. There were other reasons for the defeat as well, for Celtic had a depleted team with injuries and unavailability because of war problems, but Charlie took it upon himself that he would never let Celtic and their supporters down again.

The war was clearly not going to be 'over by Christmas' as the ridiculously optimistic had forecast. Campaigns were launched now and again to get football stopped on the grounds that all these young men should be in khaki, but fortunately the Government felt that football was good for civilian morale. A historian must always be wary of thinking that wartime football was something unimportant. Not so, for it was a great thing for soldiers on leave, the wounded and those working in munitions. If anything, it became more important, for people desperately needed light entertainment to take their minds off the horrors of France and the High Seas. Maley, for his part, was always very conscientious about sending telegrams to the War Office with the results so that soldiers could know how Celtic were doing within about an hour of the final whistle. Footballs were also sent for soldiers to play with.

Season 1914–15 was a great Celtic League campaign. Behind to Hearts for long periods of the season, (Hearts had beaten them at Tynecastle on the very first day, then drew at Parkhead in late January), the team rallied from February onwards and won their games, knowing that Hearts would 'crack' in the face of the onslaught. This in fact happened. Charlie thus won his second League medal and played in every game, but it is interesting to find, on reading newspapers reports, how little he is mentioned. Occasionally we find 'but Shaw was up to the task' or 'Shaw dived at the centre's feet' but seldom are his praises sung.

The reason is of course that he was distinctly under employed. Maley, remarkably, was able to keep the team of 1914 more or less intact while other teams lost men to the forces. There is a myth going around that Celtic only won the Championship in 1915 because Hearts had enlisted en masse for McRae's Batallion. Yes they did, but the Hearts men were still available more or less every Saturday! The real reason for Celtic's success was the excellence of the team with Shaw, McNair and Dodds being suggested as the best defence in Britain and if they could be shipped to France, the Germans would never get through them!

There was also a piece of icing on the cake at the end of the season. Unfortunately, as we have said, there was no Scottish Cup, but Celtic won the Glasgow Charity Cup by beating Rangers 3–2 at Ibrox on the day after the sinking of the Lusitania. Celtic had to work hard to win this game, which sometimes showed signs of getting out of hand. Both of Rangers goals were scored when Celtic were down to 10 men with Patsy Gallagher off injured, but Celtic's defence was outstanding with a clear understanding of each other and refusal to panic when the chips were down. Even when Patsy did come back, he was less than 100% fit, but the strength of the defence radiated confidence and Celtic edged their way back into the game from being 1–2 down. First Browning scored, then McMenemy with a header late in the game. It was Charlie's third Glasgow Charity Cup medal, and they were all on display in his tobacconist's shop a few days after the game.

Seasons 1915–16 and 1916–17 saw Celtic win all three available trophies in each season, and Charlie Shaw played in every single game. That really says it all. The team went from 13 November 1915 until 21 April 1917 without losing a match, and in this period they conceded only 21 goals in 63 games! 'As safe as Shaw', was a common phrase heard throughout Glasgow, and it was at this time that all the stories circulated about Charlie. He went home for his tea in the middle of the game, he did a half hour shift in his tobacconist's so that his wife could go to the other shops, he went to see what was on at the theatre and then, when he came back, he walked round to ask the other goalkeeper if he wanted a hand to keep out McMenemy! Such was the charisma of Charlie Shaw.

He may have experienced some cries of abuse from the ignorant about not joining the Army particularly when he was called up in 1916 but pleaded exemption. This may have been what was behind an incident at Tynecastle in May 1916. The season was over, but Charlie agreed to play in a Charity Match between East versus West for military hospitals. The game had to be stopped when Charlie complained to the referee about being stoned. A few miscreants were removed, but it was not clear whether this was simply sheer hooliganism from the mentally challenged or some protest about Charlie's perceived non-involvement in the war. Certainly Hearts supporters had a bad reputation then, particularly as far as Celtic were concerned – a reputation that has sadly lasted, off and on, for a century. On this occasion the events in Dublin a few weeks earlier possibly added fuel to the already very combustible atmosphere, as far as Hearts supporters and Charlie Shaw were concerned.

Charlie was indeed an unlikely looking hero. He was a man you might pass in the street for he looked so insignificant. And like so many Celtic players, he was sociable, friendly and willing to talk to everyone. He was genuinely appalled at the sort of things that were going on in France and elsewhere, but was very proud of what he was part of at Celtic Park, not least the famous occasion of 15 April 1916 when they played two games in a day, kicking off at Parkhead at 3.30pm, then Fir Park, Motherwell at 6.00pm, won both games and confirmed themselves as League Champions in the process.

Mishaps were few. On one occasion when Celtic were 0--1 down at St Mirren and Charlie joined the attack (this was less rare in the 1910s than it is now) but lost the ball and St Mirren ran up and scored into an empty net. On New Year's Day 1916 at Parkhead Rangers earned an undeserved draw when Eck McNair scored an own goal from an intended pass back past a bewildered Charlie Shaw, both of them misled by a stentorian cry from Sunny Jim 'Ahent ye, Alec' which made McNair think that the Rangers attacker was closer than he really was.

On the odd occasion when Charlie was called into action, he was up to the task. He was never afraid to dive at someone's feet (Maley said he, 'had the courage of a lion tamer'), he retained his amazing reflexes, he could jump up for a ball with remarkable elasticity and most importantly for a goalkeeper he could dive to his left and right when the ball was low. He was simply the best goalkeeper around, now better perhaps than Jimmy Brownlie, and would surely have been chosen for Scotland, if there had been any international games.

By season 1916–17, Charlie found himself the captain of Celtic. It is unusual (though by no means unique) for a goalkeeper to be the captain of a team, but these were unusual times. Sunny Jim Young was badly injured in 1916 and had announced his reluctant retirement from the game in 1917. Charlie was the obvious choice for his reliability and dependability. The self-effacing Eck McNair had serious problems of availability because of his war work and the fact that he had been widowed and left with a family to look after on his own. McMenemy, apparently, did not want the job, so it came to Charlie.

The captaincy proved no sinecure in season 1917–18 as it proved more and more difficult to get a team, and spectators (and indeed players) often arrived at the ground with no clear idea of who was going to be there, such were the demands of war work. This affected all teams of course, and one simply had to do the best that one could. But Rangers were now beginning to fight back, and with so many players arriving on the Clyde to do jobs (sometimes for only a few days), they had, as it were, first pick because they were physically closer and it was easier for a man to finish his shift at 12.00pm on a Saturday and get to Ibrox in time than it was for him to get anywhere else.

This does in no way excuse the defeat in the Glasgow Cup semi-final to Rangers on 24 September 1917. Charlie made one mistake when he dropped a ball and Tommy Cairns was able to tap it in, but the whole team was in chaos for the other two goals. A makeshift half-back line, now of course lacking the inspirational Sunny Jim, was swept aside. *The Glasgow Herald* is philosophical about it, describing Celtic as 'war weary' and 'anxious for peace' for 'football teams, like nations in arms, must in turn give way!'

Charlie would not accept this and working alongside Maley, bent to the task of rebuilding Celtic in almost impossible circumstances. Training was more or less impossible to organise on a team basis and recruitment was even more difficult. Although through his shop and the contacts who came in, Charlie would hear stories about talented juniors being available to play on Saturday. He would pass on the information to Maley, but by the Saturday morning, the man concerned had had to pull out because he was needed for a shift or because transport simply was not there.

Once again an attempt was made in the 'comb out' (as it was called) of winter 1917–18 to recruit Charlie to the Army, but he was classified Grade III which meant that he would be most unlikely to be enlisted. Yet he was not safe, for the losses of manpower continued to be appalling, so all he could do was keep his head down and hope that the long promised victory could come that year. He was very aware of course of what had happened in Russia to the Czar, and his background from Twechar was such that he must have wondered if it could happen in Great Britain as well. Certainly men like John McLean were considered to be sufficiently dangerous to be put away to Peterhead or Barlinnie on various trumped up charges, and Charlie's impression was that the Scottish working class were not going to be pushed much further before they either cracked or (more likely) turned on the middle classes and the war profiteers.

Charlie's form in goal took a decided dip in the early months of 1918, but it was to his credit that the team rallied once again, remaining more or less level with Rangers, and even in March edging ahead of them. But then came the dreadful day of 23 March when Celtic, without Joe Dodds on Army duty in London that day, went down 3–1 to Third Lanark, and an even more dreadful final day of the League season when they could only draw with Motherwell at Parkhead even though Charlie Shaw unashamedly joined the attack in the last few minutes in an attempt to force the winner which would have given Celtic five League flags in a row. At the end it was not to be, and Rangers 2–1 win over Clyde was enough to win them the League.

But there was still a good end to the season as Celtic won a competition called the War Shield Fund Cup, and then for the seventh year in a row, the Glasgow Charity Cup. They beat Partick Thistle 3–0 in the final before 30,000 at Hampden to give the supporters something at least to be cheerful about, at a time when there was little else going on to make them happy.

The following season 1918–19 brought victory (if it could be called that) in the Great War, and the return of the League Championship to Celtic Park. Charlie was still the captain. He played (and played well) in the Glasgow Cup Final of 5 October in a game which Celtic lost 2–0 and, but for Shaw, it would have been a great deal more. But when he came home from that game, he began to feel unwell with a sore head, sore throat and general coldness. It was indeed the Spanish flu, which affected so many people in the last few weeks of the war, and caused Charlie for the first time since 1913 to miss a game for Celtic.

Those who travelled to Kilmarnock on 12 October saw an unfamiliar figure in the Celtic goal. This was a chap called David Syme who played in a 1–1 draw at Rugby Park, and then a dreadful 0–3 defeat at Ibrox. What is significant about David Syme was that his son and grandson Willie and Davie, both became referees without ever endearing themselves to the Celtic support. Willie was the referee in the 1967 Scottish Cup Final when Celtic, en route for Lisbon, beat Aberdeen, and Davie junior managed to send off the wrong man in the awful 1986 League Cup Final before realising his mistake and apologising!

Charlie recovered from the Spanish influenza (many others didn't and Jimmy McMenemy almost died of the illness), the war thankfully ended, and gradually over the winter of 1918–19, things improved for Celtic as men like Andy McAtee came back from the forces. Charlie himself took on a new lease of life as a challenge was made to win the Scottish League. Never was the value of Charlie Shaw more apparent to Celtic than in the run-in when Shaw, McNair and Dodds began to appear more frequently on the team sheets.

Charlie himself was given a game for the Scottish League in the Victory International against the English League on 5 April 1919. A crowd of 65,000 were at Ibrox to see a 3–2 win for the Scottish League, and there were now clear signs that the nightmare of the war was over. But for Charlie there was a Championship to be won. The key game came on Monday 28 April when Celtic were at Tynecastle. Things looked good for Celtic when they were 3–0 up, but then the great Andy Wilson of Hearts scored twice within three minutes, and the revivified Hearts side threw everything at Shaw, McNair and Dodds in the last 10 minutes. But Charlie was their equal, making some great saves, 'despising danger', as he dived at the feet of Wilson and Sharp to keep the score at 32.

The League was won for the 5th time in 6 years on 10 May. It was at Somerset Park, Ayr on a very hot day with well over 10,000 crammed into the somewhat primitive provincial ground. Celtic simply had to win this game, for they knew that Rangers were winning their match against Clyde at Celtic Park (Clyde shared Celtic Park with Celtic during most of the war years) and there was only one point in it.

Once again, Shaw was the saviour for Celtic with two grand saves in the early stages from Richardson and McBain before Andy McAtee scored for Celtic, than after 'more Shavian heroics', Adam McLean finished the job for Celtic who had now won the Scottish League 15 times in its 29 year history!

A minor disappointment came when the team went down to Queen's Park in the Charity Cup, and Shaw himself was disappointed not to be chosen to play in

any of the full Victory Internationals. But he was simply relieved that the war was now over, normality (of sorts) would return next season and he still had a good few years left in him.

'Ten Internationalists and Chairlie Shaw' was the way that Celtic were often described in the early 1920s. The context was usually that Celtic's team was so good that Charlie never had a chance to show that he was International class. The remark was not, of course, literally true all the time, for many of the men who played with Charlie failed to win a cap for Scotland, but it must also be said that there were at least three other reasons why Charlie Shaw did not win a full Scottish cap – and that is without going into the paranoid conspiracy theory of anti-Celtic bias, which has been a constant theme in supporters' conversations over the past 120-odd years!

In the first place, Scotland were well served by three other goalkeepers – Jimmy Brownlie of Third Lanark before the war and Kenny Campbell of Partick Thistle and Bill Harper of Hibs after the war. Scotland tended to do well in the 1920s, winning the Home International Championship more often than not, and frequently the goalkeepers kept a clean sheet. One could not in all honesty say that Charlie was a great deal better than any of the other candidates.

Secondly, Charlie's best years were undeniably during the war when internationals were suspended. Charlie did well for Celtic in season 1913–14 and maintained his good form throughout the war, but by the time that the first full International was played in 1920, Charlie was within sight of his 35th birthday. We know that Ronnie Simpson in 1967 played at that age, but that was very much an exception.

But the third reason was the events of 20 March 1920 when Charlie was given a chance, along with Eck McNair and Joe Dodds to play for the Scottish League at Hampden against their English counterparts. It was Charlie's third game for the Scottish League, but, frankly it was Shaw, McNair and Dodds' worst ever day as they went down 4–0 to the English League, causing an exodus from the terracing in the second half as a result of this poor showing from Scotland. There were other failures as well as Charlie, of course, but the fact was that he had caused the first goal when he had palmed away a shot rather than clutching it, and the ball fell to a grateful Englishman. This effectively killed any chance Charlie had of ever representing his country in a full International. He felt he was good enough, and so did the Celtic fans who watched him, but it was not to be.

For Celtic the first two full seasons after the war promised more than they fulfilled. They won both Glasgow tournaments in both seasons, but failed to win either of the Scottish honours, losing out narrowly twice to Rangers in the League and playing particularly badly in their Scottish Cup games against Rangers in 1920

67

and Hearts in 1921. The fans were disappointed for they felt that they had a great team including a new player, immediately nicknamed 'the boy wonder', in Tommy McInally.

Charlie in his role as captain sometimes despaired of this lad. Tommy had boundless ability and a great desire to do well for the club, but every now and again and often for irrational causes went off in a sulk and either refused to play altogether or played half-heartedly, trying to show off to the fans rather than work for the club. Charlie would frequently take the young McInally aside and tell him that he could be one of the club's all-time greats if only he could knuckle down and work a wee bit harder, swallowing his pride now and again. It wasn't always successful.

Charlie himself continued to play in a way that inspired confidence. The diminutive frame however now had a lot more work to do, for Celtic were far from the dominant force that they had been in 1914 and during the war years. Rangers had caught up and more, and had a fine forward line with men like Sandy Archibald, Tommy Cairns and Alan Morton, although there was one occasion in September 1919 when he brought off one of his best ever saves. This was in the Glasgow Cup against Rangers at Parkhead when Celtic were leading 1–0 and in the last minute Rangers broke through after 'tireless Tommy' Cairns got the better of the Celtic defence and unleashed a fierce drive which Charlie pushed over the bar. Parkhead erupted at such brilliance, and even Cairns patted him on the back.

Diplomatic rather than footballing skills were required by Charlie in a nasty game on Monday 26 April 1920 at Parkhead when the crowd invaded the field to attack the players of Dundee whom they suspected of having lain down to Rangers in a 6–1 beating at Ibrox on the previous Saturday. The suspicions were not entirely groundless given the tactless remarks made by a few of the Dundee players to the Press that it would be no bad thing if Rangers won the League, and *The Dundee Courier* is highly perplexed about this poor performance by Dundee, hinting that things were not entirely straightforward. But the folly of the idiots in the crowd at Parkhead that day became apparent when the game was abandoned as a draw when Celtic might have won.

Shaw, McNair and a few of the Celtic players rushed in to protect the Dundee players and to plead with their supporters that this was no way to behave if the League was to be won. Shaw's influence counted for something with at least some of the hotheads and no player was injured, but Celtic suffered through effectively losing the League by having to concede the game as a draw, and having their ground closed for a spell. Some recompense was given when Celtic won the Glasgow Charity Cup in early May, but Shaw was depressed about these events. He was a Celt and a rebel as much as anyone, but the rule of law had to be respected.

Season 1920–21 was almost a carbon copy of the previous one in terms of achievement, although this time there was no Joe Dodds who had gone for a season to Cowdenbeath, but in 1922, Celtic won back the Scottish League Championship. It was a hard fought tussle with Rangers, and it all came down to a thrilling last day on 29 April when Celtic had to play Morton at Greenock and Rangers were at Shawfield to play Clyde. Celtic were one point ahead.

But Morton were on a high. They had won the Scottish Cup for the one and only time a fortnight previously, and they were a good side, determined to have a say in who was to win the League Championship. The small ground was packed, and the crowd was nasty with frequent fights and arrests, with the creation of the Irish Free State a live and current issue with the crowd. In the circumstances it was difficult to concentrate on the game, but Charlie knew that when Celtic went 0–1 down, and Rangers were still drawing with Clyde, the flag was going to Ibrox. Fortunately Andy McAtee got a late goal, which earned the point to save the day. Celtic now had their 16th flag.

They had done so without Tommy McInally who had had to be dropped after too much clowning in the Cup tie against Hamilton Accies that they had lost. Charlie regretted that, for McInally was such a fine player, but he had a lot of growing up to do. As for Charlie himself he had now won six Scottish League medals, and showed no sign whatsoever of slowing down or getting old. He still looked in photographs like everyone's favourite uncle, and was still revered among the fans at Celtic Park.

Season 1922–23 was indifferent, to put it mildly. Charlie was dropped briefly in the autumn, possibly because he was blamed for the loss of some goals in a 4–3 win over Partick Thistle, but possibly for reasons that were more political in that Charlie was beginning to grumble about wages and conditions at Celtic Park. A young goalkeeper called John Hughes was played, but as one of his games was a 3–1 defeat by Rangers at Parkhead (when only a late Patsy Gallacher goal prevented a total rout) Charlie was soon brought back to the delight of the fans.

The Scottish League was a dreadful disappointment that season, as indeed were the two Glasgow tournaments, but there was more than adequate compensation in the winning of the Scottish Cup. It was Shaw's second Scottish Cup medal, and Celtic's 10th victory, thus equalling the tally of Queen's Park, and the opponents were once again Hibs. (But what a different world since they had last met in the Scottish Cup final of 1914!) This time the score was 1–0, the scorer being Joe Cassidy who had thus scored in every game in the Scottish Cup that season bar one, but it was an undistinguished Final. Hibs played well and in the latter stage laid siege to the King's Park goal to be defied by Charlie Shaw and the other veteran Alec McNair. The goal

BACK ROW—Hilley, W. M'Stay, Gallacher, Gilchrist, Jas. Murphy (No. 2).
MIDDLE ROW—M'Master, M'Nair, M'Farlane, Glasgow, M'Lean, Cringan.
FRONT ROW—M'Atee, J. M'Stay, J. Murphy (No. 1), Shaw, Cassidy, Crilley, Connolly.

Celtic in season 1922–23 with captain Shaw in the front.

had come when Bill Harper was caught in two minds about whether to come out or stay on his line following a long punt up the field and a Joe Cassidy header. Charlie knew how Bill would be feeling and went out of his way to commiserate.

If season 1922–23 was indifferent, the following was simply dreadful. Gates were poor, from time to time there was evidence of serious player discontent, Willie Cringan was transferred for making a reasonable and dignified request about wages and conditions, the stormy Johnny Gilchrist left after a serious disagreement with Willie Maley and the Press frequently said that, but for Charlie Shaw in the Celtic goal, the damage would have been a great deal more.

Only at the end of the season with the capture of the Glasgow Charity Cup once again did Celtic give their supporters anything to be happy about. It was a good win in the Final against Rangers, with Shaw a sprightly veteran, now nearly 39, looking as good as anyone, and still retaining his popularity among the fans who kept on singing their songs like *'We'll rise and follow Chairlie'* and *'Charlie is my darling'*. Yet he must have been aware that time was now against him.

The Celtic side were slowly rebuilding with young players like Alec Thomson, Peter Wilson, Jimmy McGrory and significantly for Shaw, a young goalkeeper from that great Celtic nursery St Roch's called Peter Shevlin was beginning to attract the attention of Willie Maley. This rebuilding was the natural thing to do in the wake of such an awful season as they had just had, and when Shaw did eventually lose his place to Shevlin, it was not necessarily that he had become a bad goalkeeper or that he had lost his popularity with the fans. It was just that his bad games were becoming more frequent, his reactions were slowing down and young Shevlin was performing so well for St Roch's that his claims simply could not be ignored.

Among other things Charlie was famous for his ability to keep calm. Very seldom did he lose his cool on the field, but he did so in a Glasgow Cup game against Third Lanark in an incident involving his erstwhile colleague and protégé Tommy McInally who impeded Charlie from getting to the ball. There may have been something personal in all this, and certainly words were exchanged, but Charlie chased referee Peter Craigmyle all the way to the halfway line to protest. McInally laughed, but Charlie had the last laugh when Celtic won.

The Glasgow Cup Final that year was against Rangers. For Shaw and everyone else, it was a shocker for Rangers won 4–1. It was probably this game that compelled Maley to go for Peter Shevlin, and Charlie played only one more game for the club in January 1925 when he made a mistake in dropping a ball to allow Motherwell a 1–0 victory. He was loaned out to Clyde for a spell in February of that year, but by the time of the famous events in the Scottish Cup in March and April of 1925, Charlie had decided to take a big step in any case.

'The land beyond the wave' had always been a great attraction for the Scottish/Irish community in the early days of the 20th century. The United States of America was huge, and seemed to offer so many opportunities for wealth and jobs. Nevertheless there was a down side as well. The crossing in itself usually took five to eight days, and although navigation had improved considerably over the past 100 years, it was still a long way and the distinct possibility that one wouldn't ever come back. However a team called New Bedford Whalers offered him twice what Celtic did, and he found the offer irresistible and in June 1925, still a month or two short of his 40th birthday, Charlie set sail.

Some supporters were distraught at the loss of Charlie, and went around quoting Robert Burns

> 'A ye wha live by sowps o'drink
> A ye who live by crambo-clink
> A ye wha live and never think
> Come mourn wi' me!
> Our billie's gi'en us a' a jink
> An' owre the sea!'

Even more appropriate was the Jacobite song

> 'Bonnie Chairlie's noo awa

Safely owre the friendly main
Mony's a hert's been brak in twa
Will ye no' come back again!'

But it was clear that Charlie Shaw had done the right thing. He would play there for a good few years, becoming the player-manager of New Bedford Whalers for a spell before he died of pneumonia in New York on 27 March 1938, and the age of only 52. His wife Annie survived him for another 50 years, and was a centurion before she died in 1988.

On 6 April 2013 the Celtic Graves Society appropriately held a ceremony for the great Charlie Shaw in New York. Even though it was far away, it was right that he should be so honoured, for he was a great Celt. His strength lay in his ability to identify with the supporters and for the supporters to identify with him. This was shown in the culture that continually surrounded him – a brake club was named after him, the famous song sung by opposition supporters was a tremendous compliment, as indeed were the many songs that Celtic supporters sang about him. Rumours circulated that he was latterly less than 100% happy with his low wages at Celtic. It is never of course easy for football fans to identify with players wanting more money, for footballers normally earn in any case a lot more than the fans themselves do, but Charlie also felt that the supporters too in the early years of the 1920s did not get a fair deal from society, and he frequently said so. He was, after all, like so many great Celtic players, a fan himself.

The most famous story concerning Charlie Shaw did not involve him directly. Alec McNair was playing golf at Troon and stuck in a bunker. Alec was clearly perplexed and didn't know what to do. Silence reigned in the crowd as Alec thought about the various options. Eventually a voice rang out 'Just pass it back to Chairlie, Alec!' as the crowd burst into laughter and even Eck himself joined in. Everyone knew who was meant, for Charlie Shaw was a national legend.

CAREER:

Appearances: 430
Scottish League medals: 6
Scottish Cup medals: 2
Glasgow Cup medals: 4
Glasgow Charity Cup medals: 9
Scottish League caps: 3
Shut Outs : 240

JOHN THOMSON (1927–31)

by David Potter

'A young lad named John Thomson
From the Wellesley, Fife he came
To play for Glasgow Celtic
And to give himself a name...'

The above song was recorded by Glen Daly sometime in the early 1960s, but it was a lot older than that. It was written very soon after John's death on 5 September 1931 (no-one seems to know by whom) and sung by supporters at games and on buses throughout the 1930s, 1940s and 1950s. It is heard less often these days, but often an older supporter will be urged on buses and at functions to sing the song of the saintly John Thomson.

Most football fans know the bare bones of the tragedy of John Thomson who died at Ibrox in the Old Firm game on 5 September 1931. It is very easy to become sentimental about John – for there was a great deal to be proud of in this young man – and often cynics say that he was not as good a goalkeeper as he was made out to be, and that his early death was no bad thing for his subsequent reputation. But they are wrong. As even the most cursory of glances at newspapers of the time will make clear, John Thomson was widely and correctly reckoned to be the best goalkeeper in Great Britain at the time of his death, and had he lived longer, who knows what he might have ended up doing in terms of shut-outs, medals for Celtic and caps for Scotland?

As far as Celtic were concerned, it all started on the unlikely ground of Glebe Park, Brechin in a Scottish Cup tie in early February 1927, and a certain Wattie Gentles of Brechin City was the indirect and unwitting catalyst to Scotland's greatest ever romantic story. Celtic beat the local side 6–3, but what upset Manager Willie Maley was the loss of these three goals, and the apparent loss of confidence and form in the present incumbent Peter Shevlin. Brechin actually scored first that day through a miskick from Gentles which Shevlin was slow in getting down to. 'Get to that ball a little faster, Peter!' was the cry from the exasperated Willie McStay, the captain, as the blue-coloured Brechin side celebrated, Celtic fans cursed and swore, and the referee Mr Leishman of Falkirk pointed up field to indicate that the Angus men (who were better known for their cricket than their football) were ahead.

A team with Jimmy McGrory and Tommy McInally on board was always likely to beat part-timers from the provinces and they duly did, but then in the last ten minutes, Brechin pulled two back with local hero Wattie Gentles (himself, it was said, a Celtic sympathiser) scoring twice and Peter Shevlin not looking at all happy. Maley was even less happy, considering correctly that the loss of three goals to someone like Rangers or Motherwell might have been fatal in the context of the game. He decided for the next week that he would blood this young reserve from Fife who was doing so well for the reserves and at training, John Thomson. He had just turned 18, but reports about him were consistently good.

The next game was in the Scottish League at Dens Park, Dundee on 12 February 1927. John's elevation to the team was not made public beforehand, and two fans who had missed the loudspeaker announcement and came in late at the far end were amazed at how well Shevlin was playing. As Dundee bombarded the Celtic goal even more, Shevlin seemed to be having the game of his life, far faster, far more agile than normal and he even seemed to have lost a bit of weight. A goal was conceded, however, near the end of the first half when Shevlin seemed to misjudge a lob from Willie Cook. It was only when the teams changed ends and they got a closer look that the supporters realised that it was not Shevlin at all, but a new unknown goalkeeper called John Thomson.

Celtic, in spite of Thomson's first half misjudgement, won that game 2–1 and Thomson was retained for the next game – a pulsating 3–3 draw with Hamilton on the Wednesday afternoon, followed by a return to Dens Park, this time in the Scottish Cup where Celtic turned on a thrilling performance to beat Dundee 4–2. A crowd of 38,000 saw Celtic earn the 'encomium' of the large crowd, according to *The Glasgow Herald*. Thomson had a good game, not being blamed for the two goals and saving once or twice from ex-Celtic favourite Joe Cassidy, now in the twilight of his career with Dundee. Cassidy's successor Jimmy McGrory scored for Celtic as did Adam McLean, Alec Thomson and Willie McStay.

Thomson was now established as Celtic's number one goalkeeper, and very soon earned the love of the support. He was still young, very handsome and won the hearts of the young female supporters and the more elderly matrons whose feelings were more maternal than lecherous. He was not married and famously did not smoke cigarettes (he would do so later, it was claimed) or drink alcohol. Perhaps it mattered more in the 1920s than it does now, but he was not a Roman Catholic either. Nor did he have any known Irish connections. He was a member of the Church of Christ sect back in his home village of Cardenden, Fife.

He had been born in Kirkcaldy at 74 Balfour Street on 28 January 1909. John was the fifth child born to Jim and Jean Thomson, and sometime after John was born, the family moved to the village of Bowhill, near Cardenden to the northwest of Kirkcaldy. His childhood had been uneventful, comparatively untouched by the Great War, and he grew up liking football, as everyone from the mining community did. He became a goalkeeper for his school team and eventually began to play for a team called Wellesley Juniors. There is a story, difficult to substantiate but widely believed, that his reflexes once prevented a fire when he was about six or seven years old. He was at a birthday party, and the fun got a little out of hand and someone knocked an oil lamp from a table. Had it hit the ground, the house might have gone on fire, but the young John dived and caught the lamp before contact was made.

Current League champions Celtic signed him, according to legend, at Gallatown in Kirkcaldy at a tram terminus in October 1926, as John was changing trams to take him home to Bowhill. It was the famous scout Steve Callaghan who did the signing, having watched him that day, but the tip-off came from another Thomson, (no relation) Celtic's famous inside forward Alec or 'Eckie' who was also a Fifer and who had played for the same team.

John was thus not yet 18 when he went to Glasgow, a big, bad city to any young lad from Fife, but also the centre of the universe as far as football was concerned. It was thriving, bustling, full of energy and life, but also teeming with humanity and all the social evils associated with a huge overcrowded, industrial metropolis. But John had settled well at Celtic Park, befriended originally by the kindly Alec but he soon also took a liking to the man whose goal scoring exploits were already attracting the attention of the footballing Press – James Edward McGrory, scorer of the famous winning goal in the 1925 Scottish Cup Final.

But there was also Tommy McInally. Tommy was an insecure character who needed to be the centre of attention, and was able to achieve this aim through his eccentric behaviour or his brilliant play. Now in his second spell with the club, McInally had won the League for Celtic last year when he toed the line, but wasn't always as popular with his teammates as he was with the fans. But he took to John, and once John learned to cope with his perpetual joking and clowning, the pair formed a friendship. This friendship of two totally different characters would

75

survive even Tommy's bizarre activities, which led to his downfall next year. The McStay brothers were no great fans of Tommy McInally, but as long as the team was doing well, they tolerated him.

John was wise enough to understand the undercurrents of what was going on, and loved the companionship, particularly the Glasgow patter of McInally, which could take the heat out of any situation. The Manager Willie Maley was stern, but authoritative and knew a great deal about football. He had a tendency to talk about the past, but he loved comparing John with 'Dan', 'Davie' or 'Charlie', the three great goalkeepers (McArthur, Adams and Shaw) that he had seen in his life. He encouraged John, often seeking him out for a quiet word before a game or after a game, stressing how much he loved 'the Celtic' who were indeed his whole life and expressing the hope that John and others would do the same.

Having stayed in the team all through March, John was very soon in the big time. March 26 1927 saw Celtic in the semi-final of the Scottish Cup against Falkirk at Ibrox, and Falkirk had one very special player. This was the great Patsy Gallacher, reckoned by those who saw him to be the best of them all. The bulk of his career had of course been with Celtic, but now at the age of 36, he was playing for Falkirk. Some Celtic supporters felt that he had been let go too early, for he still had some years left in him, and they startled the conductor of the community singing before the game by singing the Jacobite anthem 'Will You No' Come Back Again?' with rather more fervour than the conductor expected!

For the young John, a crowd of 73,000 might have been an intimidating experience but this was a calm and cool performance from the young Fifer. Falkirk, prompted by the ageing but still marvellously talented Gallacher, created loads of chances but Thomson was there to save his side on many occasions, and then early in the second half, Adam McLean scored the only goal of the game. It was by no means Celtic's best performance of the season, but then again semi-finals, with so much at stake, are seldom good games. What is absolutely essential of course is a good, levelheaded goalkeeper. If Celtic didn't know it before, they knew it now. The consensus of opinion among the Celtic fans was that; 'we've loast Patsy, but we've goat a goalie'.

Three weeks later on 16 April 1927, he found himself in the Scottish Cup Final. The opponents could hardly have been more familiar to John – it was East Fife, whose players were all known personally to John in the tight-knit mining community that Fife was. It was less than a year since the General Strike and the miners, deserted by the TUC and the other unions, had been on strike till the autumn of 1926 when they had been literally, in some cases, starved back to work. Fife was still suffering from the vindictive triumphalism of the owners, but this was a day out. East Fife were still in the Second Division and no-one really gave them much chance, and John was uncomfortably aware that, had he not been playing for Celtic, he might well have been on the terracing supporting East Fife.

And sign of the times, the game was to be broadcast on the 'wireless', as the radio was then called. The Scotland versus England game of a fortnight previously had been broadcast as well. It was not a huge success – neither in terms of the quality of broadcasting nor in the result (for England won) – but it was considered worth repeating. Thus even the Fifers who could not afford to go to Glasgow had a chance to listen to the game, although wireless ownership was still mainly the province of the wealthy, the cranky or the pretentious. A few ice cream parlours in Methil, however, had a wireless rigged up with loud speakers for their customers.

If John was nervous – and it is hard to imagine him not being a little edgy before a Scottish Cup Final – then he was not the only one, for McGrory had been injured by a nasty, vengeful Falkirk side in the League game after the semi-final and young John McMenemy was drafted in. John was of course the son of Jimmy McMenemy the great 'Napoleon', but like John, he was young. Even against mediocre opponents like part-timers from Methil, a youngster would get nervous before a Cup Final. Fortunately McInally clowned in the dressing room to ease the tension, and old hands like the two McStays had seen it all before.

East Fife scored first! A cross, which floated between McStay and Thomson was headed home. Whether it was John's fault or not was hard to say, but naturally everyone does blame the goalkeeper, and more importantly, the goalkeeper blames himself. Fortunately Celtic equalized soon after, and stayed well on top for the rest of the game, winning 3–1, with McInally enjoying himself by showing off and deliberately missing chances so that East Fife, who had won the affection of the Celtic crowd, were not totally humiliated.

Celtic had now won the Scottish Cup for the 12th time, and John Thomson had come far since his debut in February. A Scottish Cup medal in his pocket and a growing reputation as one of Scotland's more promising goalkeepers. Not only that, he was personable and much loved by the Celtic support, of whom there were an astonishing amount, as John discovered when the bus was driven through the crowds back to Maley's restaurant. Used to poverty and deprivation, as he thought, in the Fife coalfield, John nevertheless was taken aback by the scale of it all in Glasgow. But he was proud that he had played his part in cheering them up, at least for the one night.

John was exactly what a great deal of youngsters aspired to be in the 1920s – good looking, smart, abstemious and charming. No mother would have objected to her daughter bringing home someone like John Thomson. He was also a very humble sort of boy. He loved being back in his native Fife that summer, talking to his friends and relations. It is often said that in a small village any success will bring with it a touch of jealousy. This may be so, but it was difficult for anyone to nurture any kind of negative feelings for a boy who was so clearly one of their own, particularly this diffident, shy, self-effacing youth.

He was also humble enough to realise that he still had a lot to learn about goalkeeping. He knew that although he may have done well this season, there were still a few goals that he had conceded that he ought not to have done. He needed to work on his training, his agility and increasingly, he realised, his concentration. The big crowd must not be allowed to distract him. He had a job to do for his team, the Celtic, a team whom he had not grown up loving but for whom he was beginning to develop an affection. These supporters who turned up to watch him were not rich people. They had suffered terribly in the Great War, and the troubled twenties. They deserved something to cheer about.

He was aware that there was more to goalkeeping than simply ability. He was agile with very fast reflexes, but that was not enough unless the goalkeeper concentrated. He must shut out the noise of the crowd, pick up which players on both sides were having a good game, whether the centre-forward was good in the air, whether he was a good two-footed player...and so many other things. Like everything else, there was more hard work and application required than sheer natural athletic ability – but that was an essential as well.

John's next season was less successful for the club, but it was no disaster for this young and developing goalkeeper. He played in every game with 18 shut-outs out of 48, and seldom do newspaper reports criticise him for the loss of a goal. He had a good side in front of him, and but for a fatal misjudgement on the part of the Manager with his storm petrel Tommy McInally, it would have been one of the better seasons in the history of the club.

A marker was laid down as early as October when Celtic won the Glasgow Cup. It was a fine day and 84,536 appeared at Hampden to see the as yet unbeaten Celtic take on Rangers in the Final. The Glasgow Cup was a very prestigious trophy in the 1920s as the huge crowd would indicate. Fine play from McInally saw Celtic take the lead, then they added to it before half-time with Thomson hardly having touched the ball. Things were different in the second half with Celtic facing the wind, and the strong Rangers forward line of Archibald, Cunningham, Fleming, McPhail and Morton throwing everything at the tiring McStay brothers and the young McGonagle at full-back.

But John stood firm. Time and time again the Celtic supporters behind his goal burst into sustained applause as he dived at the feet of forwards, punched the ball over the bar and leapt like a cat to save the shots which rained on him. Rangers did score late in the game but by that time they had shot their bolt and were themselves exhausted. The Celtic fans were in no doubt about who their hero was that day, and Bob Hamilton in the Rangers goal had no hesitation in offering his congratulations at the end. *The Glasgow Herald* talks about Rangers forwards being. 'baffled and discouraged by the very fine goalkeeping of Thomson' and 'the personality of the game was undoubtedly Thomson, the Celtic goalkeeper, whose judgement, ability and agility can scarcely be over-praised'.

Similar praise is heaped upon the 'daring and enterprising' John Thomson about the New Year's game at Parkhead on 2 January 1928 as Celtic beat Rangers 1–0, but then John a fortnight later had what can only be described as a watching brief as Dunfermline Athletic were crushed 9–0 with Jimmy McGrory scoring eight of them! Things looked good for Celtic, and Thomson was even beginning to be talked about as a possibility for representative honours as the team prospered, secure in the knowledge that they had behind them a goalkeeper who would certainly not let them down.

But Tommy McInally let Celtic down. He disappeared after a Scottish Cup game at Keith, re-appeared and was allowed back into the team, but then took a large dose of the huff when some teammates, Thomson included, paid a practical joke on him at the Seamill Hydro, phoning and pretending to be a newspaper reporter. McInally walked out, and this time stayed away. Without him and with the earnest but considerably less talented young Frank Doyle in his place, the team still did well, and by the end of March, were well placed to win both the Scottish Cup and the Scottish League.

But then Maley made his big mistake. To the delight of the fans but to the horror of his teammates (including the young John Thomson), McInally was allowed back. The team then lost two dreadful games in Lanarkshire to Motherwell and Airdrie the next Saturday and Holiday Monday – effectively costing them the Scottish League – and then the Scottish Cup Final to Rangers. Things might have been different if Celtic had scored first, or if John had saved Meiklejohn's penalty – but he had no real chance – but then Celtic collapsed and lost 0–4 with McGrory off form, and McInally giving little impression that he was even caring. Long before the end, it was obvious that Rangers' 25 years without the Scottish Cup were coming to an end.

For John, this was a terrible game. Just as 12 months previously, he had been in a great Scottish Cup Final, he now had to cope with what Maley called 'the bitterness of defeat' as distinct from the 'fruits of victory'. He was not held responsible for the goals, but the disillusion of the fans was tangible and obvious. They did not blame John – indeed he, Alec Thomson and Peter Wilson were the only ones who earned pass marks – but they were puzzled and angry. McInally was transferred to Sunderland in the summer and this time he never did come back. More surprisingly and disappointingly, Adam McLean went with him.

But John's career was still on the up in summer 1928. There was more talk about representative honours, even though he was still many months short of his 20th birthday, and there was also a great deal of speculation about a transfer to England. Herbert Chapman of Arsenal made no bones about his desire to sign Jimmy McGrory and often added 'and that young goalkeeper as well', but that was not likely to happen in either case, even if Celtic did need the money. John was a Fife miner at heart, and even Glasgow was far enough away from his comfort zone, let alone London!

John, like all good goalkeepers sought out the society of other goalkeepers. He remained on friendly terms with Bob Hamilton of Rangers, for example, and made a point of talking to the best goalkeeper of the day, Jack Harkness of Queen's Park, who would presently sign for Hearts. Jack was Scotland's goalkeeper. Indeed in 1928, Jack had played on the last day of March in what was Scottish football's best game to date, namely the Wembley Wizards game in which Scotland had beaten England 5–1. Harkness and Thomson, even though rivals for the Scotland job, would remain firm friends. Thomson would, of course, take over from Harkness, but Harkness was at this time the more experienced man and Thomson was very happy to learn from him. Unlike some hotheads on the terracing and not a few even in his own dressing room, Thomson realised that not everyone who played for a different team was an enemy! They were football players and could learn from each other.

There would be one famous occasion when Celtic were playing Hearts at Parkhead. It was winter (15 December 1928), frosty and early dark. In those pre-floodlight days, there was a natural desire for the game to be finished in daylight and for the large crowd to disperse similarly before darkness fell. The referee therefore ordered the players to remain on the field at half-time and have a quick cup of tea, rather than go off and waste time. So the Celtic players stayed in a circle with Willie Maley berating them, Willie McCartney did likewise with his Hearts men, the referee talked to his linesmen…but there was a fourth group as the two goalkeepers John Thomson and Jack Harkness sat down on the grass with a cup of tea in their hands and discussed the finer points of goalkeeping! Possibly they talked about other things as well – like the injuries to Jimmy McGrory and Barney Battles – or even if they were going to the pictures that night! Would the arrival of the 'talkies' make any difference to cinema audiences?

Thomson had already had one success that season. It was another Glasgow Cup medal. This time it was Queen's Park who were the opponents, and it was this game which really drew attention to John Thomson as a goalkeeper who was something special. In truth, it was not a great Celtic side, nor was it a great Celtic performance on this occasion, but Celtic won their second Glasgow Cup in a row thanks to some brilliant goalkeeping, which even had *The Glasgow Herald* purring with pleasure.

The Glasgow Herald often finds it hard to hide its sympathies for Queen's Park, and there is more than a hint of frustration in its account of the game when it says that only Thomson prevented the Amateurs from gaining a lead that would have been, 'deserved, decisive and substantial' with a brilliant performance in the first half. 0-0 at half-time became 2-0 at full time when Thomson continued to defy Queen's Park and Celtic were able to score twice through McGrory and Gray. Some accounts compare Thomson to a cat for his ability to leap, and another likens him to a contortionist for his apparent ability to turn in mid-air.

The comparison to a contortionist came after a game against Kilmarnock at Celtic Park in September 1928. Celtic won 3–0 but the talk on the way home was about one save by John Thomson from Peerie Cunningham of Killie. Bruce Swadel of the *Scottish Sunday Express* was astounded. 'Cunningham hit the ball in such a way that it seemed certain to go for the right hand post. Thomson dived for it in that direction. Almost on the instant he divined his mistake. The ball was travelling towards the left hand post. Thomson twisted, literally in mid-air, hurled himself across the goal and got the tips of his fingers to the ball to turn it round the post'. Jimmy McGrory in his account of the same save says, 'We stood open-mouthed'.

It was hardly surprising that international recognition came his way after those spell-binding performances. He was chosen for the Scottish League to play the Irish League at Firhill on Wednesday 31 October 1928. A crown of 15,000 watched a rather one-sided game won 8–2 by the Scottish League and Barney Battles of Hearts (and posthumous son of the late Barney Battles senior of Celtic) scored five goals. John may have been at fault for the first Irish goal scored early in the game – perhaps nerves at what was a big occasion – for he didn't clear the ball properly, but for the rest of the game, he was virtually a spectator. The important thing, though, was that he was considered good enough to get another chance in the game against the English League at Aston Villa the following Wednesday.

If the Glasgow Cup Final opened people's eyes in Scotland to the excellence of John Thomson, this Inter-League game did likewise for the rest of Great Britain. The Scottish League were sadly outclassed, and it was only due to John Thomson that the score was kept at 2–1, as he, time and again defied men like the great Dixie Dean of Everton, Ernie Hine of Leicester City and Joe Hulme of Arsenal. Once again he started badly, showing a little uncertainty, but his second half performance had the Birmingham crowd spell bound. *The Sunday Express* in reviewing the game a few days later says that,' The Villa Park grandstand echoed and trembled to a sustained outburst of applause which went on for minute after minute,' as the Brummies showed their appreciation of the young Scottish goalkeeper.

He continued in the same good form for Celtic, and he needed to, for this was by no means a great Celtic side in season 1928–29. Still suffering from the 0–4 defeat in last season's Scottish Cup Final, which was allowed to dominate the psyche of the club (one can compare the 5–1 beating at Ibrox in 1988 in this respect) for far too long, and with Manager Willie Maley showing more signs of being more interested in the building of the new stand than what was actually happening on the playing field, Celtic drifted. McInally and McLean were never adequately replaced, and a particular disappointment was the defeat in the Scottish Cup semi-final on 23 March 1929 to Kilmarnock at Ibrox with only the 'masterly saving' of John Thomson in the Celtic goal keeping the score down. Ironically, Tommy McInally had travelled from Sunderland, who had no game, to come and watch Celtic from the stand on that day!

The season thus ended on a low note for Celtic, and for John there was personal disappointment in that he was not chosen for any of the full Scotland Internationals that season. Jack Harkness was still the incumbent, a good friend of John's as well, and it was hard to be jealous or angry particularly when Scotland won all three games, confirming that they were the best team in the world at the moment. The close season tour saw Sandy McLaren of St Johnstone in the goal – again a good goalkeeper, but by no means superior to John, although it has to be stressed that in 1929 with foreign travel in its infancy, it was no great deal. The Scotland side was full of youngsters in what would have been known in later years as a 'development' team.

Once again John returned to his native Fife for the summer. He had by now met a young lady called Margaret Finlay, but there was as yet nothing serious and he would smile and use clichés like 'just good friends' when her name was mentioned. He was still young, for he had only turned 20 in January, and in any case his football still meant a great deal to him. Like many other Celts from a mining background, notably Jimmy Quinn, he was well aware that the alternative to a career as a professional football player was by no means as pleasant.

Another man from Cardenden, the poet and playwright Joe Corrie, sums up coalmining thus

> 'Crawlin aboot like a snail in the mud
> Covered wi' clammy blae
> Me? In the image o' God?
> Jings, but it's laughable tae!'

Summer 1929 was also the time that Maley tried to sell McGrory. He had already tried to do so in 1928, but this time he tried a little harder. McGrory famously refused a king's ransom to sign for Arsenal, and rumour had it that John Thomson might have been included in the deal as well. John would certainly have also refused for no other reason than that he didn't fancy London. John would have decided to stay in Scotland. Apart from family considerations, he had built up a great relationship with Celtic and their fans. Some who should have known a lot better tried to use religion as an obstacle between Celtic fans and the youngster from the evangelical background. 'They'll try and convert ye,' he was warned. But in saying that, they showed that they understood neither Celtic, nor John Thomson nor even the game of football, which was and indeed remains the one true religion of Celtic fans.

But the new 1929–30 season was not a good one. The new stand was opened at the start of the season amidst a fanfare of trumpets, but there was little else for Celtic fans to cheer about. The recession was starting to bite and attendances were dropping at an alarming rate as Celtic began to struggle. McGrory was still scoring the goals, some of them brilliantly with his head, but the team generally failed to produce the goods, never more so than in the Glasgow Cup Final against Rangers.

In the first game on 12 October before a remarkable crowd of 76,000 Rangers were the better team, but Celtic were rescued by John Thomson who managed to save a penalty kick from Davie Meiklejohn in a reprise of the events of 1928s Scottish Cup Final, except that this time John saved it, while the Celtic end erupted in appreciation. The replay on the Wednesday in dreadful conditions of wind and rain still attracted over 40,000, but this time the fine Rangers team simply took control and even the brilliance of Thomson failed to prevent a 0–4 defeat with the Press reports mentioning that only John Thomson, Peter Wilson, Peter McGonagle and Jimmy McStay were 'shown to any advantage'.

Indeed it was a bad day all round, for the Scotland team to play Wales was announced that day as well, and John might have hoped to win his first International cap at last, but sadly for John his old same friend Jack Harkness was still the goalkeeper. John was nominated as reserve, which was some consolation, but it was hard for him to escape the depression which enveloped Celtic Park and indeed Scotland as the winter approached.

He did however retain his place for the Scottish League in their game against the English League on 2 November. Jakey Jackson of Partick Thistle played against the Irish League, but Thomson was in goal at Ibrox for the game against the Englishmen, which cheered up all Scotland. It was a 2–1 victory in an absorbing contest on which he; 'distinguished himself with masterly saving of shots from Hine and Brook', earning tremendous plaudits once again from the English Press with even *The Times* and *The Guardian* compelled to acknowledge some 'fine Scottish goalkeeping'.

But it was a rare moment of happiness that winter. Wall Street had now collapsed, as the saying went. This meant that America was in economic depression and the slump spread steadily to Europe as well, causing further widespread misery, unemployment and poverty. Celtic gave their fans little to cheer them up with another defeat to Rangers, further reverses to teams like Motherwell, Partick Thistle and Morton and the 1930s opened with three defeats to Rangers, Queen's Park and Aberdeen. Words like 'crisis' were freely used, and people joked that there were only two attractions at Celtic Park – one was the new stand, and the other was John Thomson.

And things got worse for John. On Wednesday 5 February 1930 in a defeat at the hands of Airdrie at Celtic Park, John was taken off after only seven minutes after a collision with Jimmy Muir of Airdrie in which *The Glasgow Herald* tells us prosaically; 'his jawbone had been fractured'. In fact it was a lot worse than that, for he had also sustained a double fracture of the collarbone, a broken rib and had lost two teeth. Manager Willie Maley fulminated, 'He was on the ground when he got the kick that did the damage. He had dived for the ball. My people are very sore about the inaccuracies published. He was not on his feet when injured'.

Maley seems to be implying that there was something deliberate about the injury inflicted, but whether that was true or not, it meant that John was now out for a couple of months, thereby losing his chances of International recognition against England at Wembley and, with all due respect to his deputy John Kelly, Celtic missed him badly. They went out of the Scottish Cup in a shocking performance against St Mirren in mid-February and although League form rallied to a certain extent, the team were well out of everything by the time that John came back to loud and sustained cheers at the end of March. Some people, notably his brother Jim, might have advised him that his severe injuries were a warning about how dangerous a game football was, but as John kept reminding himself, it was a lot safer than coalmining.

The disastrous season finished however on a high note. The team regained a little self-respect in the Glasgow Charity Cup when, even without the injured McGrory, they held Rangers to a 2–2 draw. 35,467 on a fine day saw an unlucky Celtic performance – for they did enough to win – but then possession of the Charity Cup was decided, incredibly, by a toss of the coin, for even the counting of corners after extra-time could not split the teams. McStay and Meiklejohn tossed the coin on the field after the game, but it was Meiklejohn who raised his arms in triumph. Thus although Rangers won a quadruple of trophies that year, at least one of them was not won through playing football.

But John had other things to think about, for he had at long last been picked to play for Scotland! It was a strange match, however, for it was in Paris against France, and it was on a Sunday. It would have been interesting to know in view of John's religious background, whether any of his family objected to that, pointing to the precedent of Eric Liddell in 1924 who refused to run on a Sunday in the Paris Olympic Games. John clearly didn't object, for it was his chance to play for Scotland. It was a curiously low key International, for it was the first time that Scotland had played France, and in any case in 1930, the sporting world was far more interested in how the Australian cricketers, with this young man called Bradman, would do in England.

The weather was fine at the Colombes Stadium in Paris on Sunday 18 May, and Scotland won 2–0 with a goal in each half from Hughie Gallacher. The Parisians were mightily impressed by the Scotsmen, (although some disappointment was expressed that they did not wear kilts!), and particularly by the athletic goalkeeping of John Thomson at one save in particular when he dived to punch a shot from eight yards to safety. Words like 'mon dieu' and 'formidable' were heard. It was a fine Scottish win, and the Scotsmen stayed in Paris for another week where they were much feted by the French crowd who were slowly being won over to the great game of football. Life might have been different for John if Scotland had entered the first ever World Cup held in Uruguay that year, but that was maybe several steps too far for the conservative and stuffy Scottish establishment of 1930!

Season 1930–31 was famous for many things, not least the now unanimous opinion that John Thomson was a great goalkeeper with few equals in the world, either in Scotland, England or anywhere else. The season also showed the gradual development of a great Celtic side. Still lacking a little in consistency to challenge Rangers in the Scottish League, they managed nevertheless to win two trophies and to convince their supporters that they were on the way back. Peter McGonagle was now a fine left-back and Chick Geatons was now a left-half with the talent to supplement the passing ability of Peter Wilson on the right, while up front Peter Scarff had now developed into a good inside-left and partner to 'Happy Feet' Charlie Napier. Two other Thomsons, the wayward and occasionally delinquent Bertie and John's good friend, the kindly Alec, made up the right wing.

That the team was on the way back was proved by the capture of the Glasgow Cup on 11 October 1930. 71,806 were at Hampden to see Celtic beat Rangers 2–1 even with the disadvantage of having Bertie Thomson sent off. The game was an unpleasant one with fouls and a few crowd disturbances, and Bertie Thomson was distinctly unlucky to be the only person to be sent off as Buchanan, Gray and even Meiklejohn fouled persistently. Napier and McGrory scored for Celtic, but then

Rangers pulled one back after a McGonagle error and the last few minutes were desperate ones for the Celtic defence. John Thomson saved several times from Alan Morton, and on one occasion almost gave his supporters heart failure when he ran out of his box to kick the ball away from the advancing Jimmy Smith.

But if it wasn't a good game of football, it was certainly a great triumph for Celtic, and for John Thomson who had now won three Glasgow Cup medals. A couple of weeks after that, he was at Ibrox playing in his first full Scottish International on home soil as Scotland drew 1–1 with Wales. Wales might have won, but Thomson tipped a late drive over the bar in a game that rarely rose above the mediocre. *The Glasgow Herald* is of the opinion that the two goalkeepers, Len Evans of Cardiff City and John Thomson of Celtic were the best men on the field.

A trip to White Hart Lane in London followed for the Scottish League against the English League. This was on Guy Fawkes day, 5 November 1930, and metaphors about fireworks, crackers abounded as far as the Englishmen were concerned with damp squibs and, 'failing to catch fire' used freely about the Scots. The score was 7–3. Frankly, it was a dreadful Scottish performance with a few hints in some newspapers that some of the Scotsmen had enjoyed the social life of London the night before rather too well. But not John Thomson.

The Glasgow Herald clearly looking for some balm in Gilead says; 'against this brilliant English line J. Thomson played the game of his life. His goalkeeping was superb despite the fact that he let through seven goals. His handling was secure, his anticipation reminiscent of J. Brownlie (*the legendary goalkeeper of Third Lanark in the 1900s*) at his best and his daring was thrilling to watch. Thomson defended his charge all through with courage, skill and bulldog tenacity, even when it was obvious that every man on the Scottish team was outplayed, outclassed and leg weary'.

The winter was then spent with Celtic consolidating their growth, sustaining the occasional reverse in the Scottish League, but doing well in the Scottish Cup. Aberdeen were despatched 4–0 in the quarter-final and Kilmarnock 3–0 in the semi-final with Thomson hardly called upon. The team that Celtic had to play in the Final were the strong going Motherwell, a team which, under the excellent management of John 'Sailor' Hunter, were beginning to impress and whose left-wing pair of Stevenson and Ferrier were particularly prominent.

But before the Final on 11 April, John had another very important date at Hampden. This was against England on 28 March. He had played against Ireland in February – another dull 1–1 draw – but this was 'the' International, which everyone dreamed of playing in. And of as much interest to John as anything else was the man who was to be presented to the teams before the start – the Prime Minister, Ramsay

MacDonald! For a Scottish miner, this man was almost a god. Leader of the Labour Party and still having an almost messianic standing in many Scottish working class households, MacDonald had come to the game unashamedly supporting Scotland and perhaps as much in awe of Thomson and McGrory as they were of him.

MacDonald was cheered to the echo, for the Scottish people still believed that he could solve the economic crisis and usher in a new era, but even those cheers were dwarfed by the cries of delight when Stevenson and McGrory scored for Scotland, as the home team won 2–0. Thomson for his part had a quiet and unspectacular game, mopping up everything competently and being lucky on only one occasion when a shot from Crooks went narrowly past the post. Meiklejohn got the better of Dean, and Scotland were worthy winners.

That was good enough, but now came the Scottish Cup Final against Motherwell. The 1931 Scottish Cup Final remains of course one of Celtic's most famous, with the great comeback in the first game when all seemed lost, and then the marvellous performance in the replay. Yet ironically, in neither game did John Thomson distinguish himself. He had, as we have noticed, a habit of starting off badly and nervously, and on this occasion, he conceded two goals in the first 20 minutes – one a slight deflection off Jimmy McStay and the second a far more pronounced one off the same player. He wasn't really to blame for either goal, but there was certainly a malaise hanging over the Celtic defence after the team went 0–2 down, and he deserves a little credit for keeping Celtic in the game as Motherwell applied even more pressure towards the end of the first half and the beginning of the second.

But as the second half wore on, Celtic gradually took control as Peter Wilson and Charlie Geatons won the midfield battle and John was a spectator for most of the second half in the Mount Florida goal in front of the Motherwell fans who contained a few Rangers colours and Union Jacks among them! History knows that Celtic's pressure eventually paid off, and the team earned a replay, the draw being celebrated by the supporters as if it were a victory. The equalizing goal was an own goal caused by a misunderstanding between centre-half Alan Craig and goalkeeper Alan McClory. John, although delighted to be still in the Scottish Cup, was seen to make a point of going to his opposite number and commiserate in the way that any goalkeeper would.

Celtic's victory indeed was not long delayed. On the Wednesday evening, Celtic won 4–2. The impression often given was that this was some sort of easy victory for the Parkhead side. Not so! Celtic were always ahead, but John was again rather uncertain about Motherwell's first goal when he palmed the ball out rather than clutched it, and then with Celtic 3–1 up in the latter stages of the game, he was beaten from 20 yards by George Stevenson's fierce drive. It was at this point that Motherwell threw the kitchen sink at the Celtic defence, but Thomson was up to their challenge, twice denying their great goal scorer Willie McFadyen before Jimmy McGrory eased the pressure by scoring at the other end.

John had thus won his second Scottish Cup medal. The Celtic fans took it on themselves to escort their young hero when he left the Bank Restaurant of Willie Maley where the celebration dinner was taking place in order to get the last train to Fife from Buchanan Street Station. He walked among them, 'just like an ordinary young man', talking about the game, expressing a few regrets about Motherwell whose fans would have been totally shattered by that turn of events on Saturday, smiling politely when he had to field a difficult question about his girlfriend and saying that he was looking forward to the forthcoming trip to America. It was intended, he said, to take the Scottish Cup with them. Life can seldom have been more pleasant for anyone than it was for young John Thomson that pleasant spring evening of 15 April 1931 as the Midnight Mail (as it was called) steamed out of Glasgow.

The season however was not yet over, for Celtic could still win the League if they won all their games and Rangers dropped a couple of points. Celtic beat Airdrie on the Saturday with the Scottish Cup watching and looking itself like a Celtic supporter with its green and white ribbons, but then on the Wednesday night 22 April at Dens Park, Celtic could only register a 0–0 draw, in a game in which both goalkeepers John Thomson and Wilson Marsh excelled. Annoyingly, Rangers also drew that night, meaning that Celtic would have levelled on points if they had won, but the fans of both sides at Dens Park rose to applaud two great goalkeepers as they walked off together, talking in detail about the game.

The season then finished on a note of anti-climax. Celtic beat Leith Athletic very easily 3–0 at Marine Gardens, but Rangers win at East Fife that day guaranteed that Celtic could not reach their points tally. Celtic then lost in the Charity Cup to Rangers on corners, in a game, which reflected little credit on anyone with one or two serious fouls and quite a few players lucky not to be, 'invited to depart the scene'.

But these things paled into significance in comparison with the capture of the Scottish Cup, still in 1931 considered to be the most important trophy of them all. That the team finished second in the Scottish League and also won the Glasgow Cup was adduced in evidence that Celtic were on the way back. They would surely now go to America, spread the gospel of Scottish football in, 'the land of the free' and then return next year to win more honours. John Thomson was a vital part of that team. Celtic clearly had the best centre forward in Scotland in Jimmy McGrory and few doubted that John Thomson was anything other than the best goalkeeper in the world.

Close season tours to America were becoming more common by 1931. Celtic had been to Europe on several occasions but this was the first time that they had 'crossed the pond'. There was certainly something romantic about the idea of seeing the nation, which, through the word of cinema, was now beginning to dominate the cultural life of Great Britain, but life was not always glamorous. The crossing took at least five days (the Caledonia sailed on 13 May and reached New York on 22 May), the sea could be choppy and once they got there, football had to be played on sub-standard pitches in intense heat with decidedly sub-standard referees and opposition which did not always understand how the game should be played. Football or soccer was by no means, as yet, a high profile game in the USA or Canada.

John was a particularly popular guest. He was attractive to the younger girls, of course, but also with the older ones who felt maternal about him for he was so charming, well brought up, well mannered, vulnerable and far from home. He remained, if not totally abstinent, at least temperate with alcohol and was always interested in the sights of New York and other places that they visited.

John was the only goalkeeper taken, so he played in all 13 games before the team returned at the end of June. It was however a great experience, for Celtic were well treated with many dinners and lavish hospitality provided by people of Scottish or Irish descent. And with them was the Scottish Cup, carried in a shopping bag, and shown to the many ex-patriates of Scottish and Irish extraction. On 31 May Celtic played and lost on Rhode Island to a team called Fall River. John was very impressed by his opposite number that day, a man called James Kennaway who preferred to be called 'Joe'.

Both men were in a certain degree of awe of each other. Thomson because Kennaway had been so impressive that day, saving comfortably shots from Bertie Thomson and a few headers from Jimmy McGrory, while Kennaway himself could not understand why the man now regarded as the world's greatest goalkeeper could be so shy and self-effacing. They talked for a long time after the game with Kennaway saying that he would love to come to Scotland or England someday to try his luck there. It was a remark full of dramatic and tragic irony.

Thomson returned to his native Fife in early July for a brief holiday with his parents and family before the start of the new season. His thoughts for the new season would centre on keeping his place in the Scotland goal and winning as many games as

89

possible for Celtic. Like everyone else at Celtic Park, he was aware that Celtic had last won the Scottish League in 1926, and that the champions for the last five years had been Rangers. Another year, and they would equal the feat set between 1905 and 1910 when Celtic won the League six times in a row. Thomson had met quite a few of that great side, including his counterpart, Davy Adams, as well as Jimmy McMenemy and Jimmy Quinn who remained on friendly terms with Maley and the rest of the team. He was aware of how proud and jealous they were of their six League Championships in a row. So Thomson reckoned we must get the better of Rangers. When do we play them? Ah, yes, he thought as he read the fixture list – 5 September at Ibrox.

'On the fifth day of September
Against the Rangers club he played
From defeat he saved the Celtic
Ah! But what a price he paid!'

Celtic approached this match unbeaten, and their supporters were beginning to nurse a few hopes that a challenge for the Scottish League might at least made and sustained. They had drawn a couple of games against Aberdeen and Third Lanark. Third Lanark had looked the better side on the Wednesday evening immediately prior to the game, but John had held his defence firm and Celtic had managed a 3–3 draw. Rangers too were off to a good start in the Scottish League. They had beaten Falkirk 2–1 on the Wednesday night with the newspapers full of praise for Bob McPhail and their new Ulster centre-forward Sam English.

All this had been going on with a major political upheaval in the background. The Prime Minister Ramsay MacDonald whom John had met at the Scotland versus England International in March had been persuaded to form a National Government, which included the Conservatives and the Liberals to deal with the economic crisis. Many members of the Labour Government which had been in power until August 1931 refused to serve in this so called National Government which was in fact little other than a Conservative one under another name. To John and others of his background, it was nothing short of betrayal, and the working class was struggling to come to terms with all this.

But football was still the main concern. *The Glasgow Herald* on the morning of the game says that; 'Many people will learn with regret that Sam English, the Ibrox centre-forward, is unfit to play. Smith comes into the front line once again...' It is not uncommon, of course, for newspapers to get things wrong as they try to predict the make-up of the team, but there can be few occasions when a newspaper could have got something wrong with such devastating irony. English did indeed play in what was his first Old Firm game.

The day was hot and sultry with a hint of thunder in the air as the teams came out. Celtic started off defending the Broomloan Road end of the ground. John Thomson in his red jersey was soon in action as Rangers pressed for an early goal. But there was no great incisiveness in their play; any more than there was in Celtic's and the first half wore on with everyone saying that the game needed a goal to spice things up. Nerves clearly played a big part as well, and the 45 minutes came to a close with defences well on top and both goalkeepers, John Thomson and Jerry Dawson, having good games.

> 'The teams earned a cheer as they left the field for their rest
> With Celtic's young keeper far brightest and best.'

Maley's half-time team talks were usually brief and to the point. He said little that day. He would have wanted a win, but a draw would be a reasonable result at Ibrox, for he knew that this was not a Cup tie, merely a rung on the ladder towards the Championship. It was still very early in the season. Possibly better to settle for a draw if we had to, even though he knew that it was contrary to the natural attacking traditions of Celtic and of his own inclinations. With McGrory up front, there was always the chance of a goal being scored, and with a fine goalkeeper like John Thomson at the back, you always felt comparatively safe. Let's see what the second half brings, he told his players before he left to talk to the Directors of both clubs in their exclusive suite.

The second half was just about five minutes old when it happened

> 'The ball runs on the centre
> And John runs out and dives
> The ball rolls past but John lies still
> For his club this hero died.'

The newsreel footage shows quite clearly what happened, and how Sam English immediately realised it was serious. He was himself injured but limped over to John and called for help. A few minutes later John was carried off. Everyone realised that it was serious but no-one appreciated how bad it really was. It certainly looked as if he was suffering from concussion, but the less intelligent behind the goal at the Copland Road end wondered in raucous ignorance what all the fuss was about. Famously Davie Meiklejohn went over to them and waved his arms up and down to persuade them to desist. Those who write romantic history say that Meiklejohn stilled the storm. In fact, his success was only partial and temporary. He does however deserve some credit for trying.

John died at about 9.30 pm that night in the Victoria Infirmary without ever regaining consciousness. It was a depressed fracture of the skull. Never has Celtic FC had a sadder day than 5 September 1931.

The aftermath was long and painful. The scenes at his funeral at Bowhill Cemetery, Cardenden have been well documented, producing scenes, which even the tragic history of the Fife coalfield would find hard to parallel. A stone was erected and it is much visited by football fans from all teams. Every September there is a five-a-side tournament for local youngsters in John's memory, and full marks are due to people like Alex Burns and Mark Cameron who keep his memory alive.

It would be nice to say that the tragedy of John Thomson brought Celtic and Rangers supporters closer together, and to an extent, that was true, but it wasn't the whole story. The other tragic hero in this story was of course the luckless and totally innocent Sam English who was frequently barracked, and not only by Celtic supporters. Famously, John's parents wrote him a letter absolving him from blame, and no intelligent person really felt that he was responsible.

At the enquiry Maley made his infamous remark, 'I hope it was an accident'. This remark was unfortunate and tactless but must be seen in the context of the other things that he says. He was sitting in the stand some considerable distance away, and did not have a clear view. Indeed no-one really did, for it all happened so quickly.

There is a myth that the rest of the game on 5 September was played out with everyone aware that John Thomson was going to die. That cannot be true. Yes, it was a serious injury and yes, all the Celtic players and supporters would have been worried about him, but they could not have known just quite how serious it was. Head knocks were not all that uncommon and were frequently recovered from. Indeed, although in recent years we have had a few tragedies on the football field, the wonder often is that, when one considers the amount of football that is played all over the world, fatalities, like those of John Thomson, happen very seldom indeed.

> '*I took a train to Parkhead*
> *To the dear old Paradise*
> *And when the players came out*
> *Sure the tear came to my eye.*
> *There was Scarff and James McGrory*
> *In the team for which he played*
> *But a famous face was missing*
> *From the green and white brigade.*'

The effect that this tragedy had on Celtic was significant. Maley himself seemed to go into a shell of depression, becoming more and more abrasive, morose and melancholic in direct contrast to his cheerful, geniality and bonhomie in his heyday before the Great War when the great side of Jimmy Quinn and Jimmy McMenemy were in their pride, and when Young, Loney and Hay dominated the centre of every park in Scotland. Although an effective replacement in Joe Kennaway was eventually found for the goalkeeping spot, the team who might have challenged for the Scottish League that season virtually imploded with the added tragedy of Peter Scarff who took ill and eventually died in December 1933 of that scourge of the 1930s, tuberculosis. It would take some time for a good Celtic team to re-emerge.

It was just the luck of John Thomson and of Celtic that such a thing happened to him at the age of 22. It was as tragic as any of the deaths in France 15 years before and as tragic as the astonishing and chilling amount of disasters that continued to happen in the Fife coalfield. Some two months after John's death, the same Bowhill Cemetery saw another massive funeral when 10 men lost their lives in the Bowhill Pit disaster of 31 October 1931. John was by no means the only person to die young, but that hardly made it any easier.

In the aftermath of his death, there was almost an industry of writing songs and poems in his honour. Some were maudlin, some were extreme in their intensity and some were sheer doggerel, but there is one written in broad Scots by a man called James Dingwall of Leven;

> 'As guid a chiel a ba'
> Has answered noo his maker's ca'
> Ower the vale he's gane awa'
> But if Death wad tak a ransom
> We'd gladly gather ane an' a'
> Tae bring back Johnny Tamson.'

CAREER:

Appearances : 188
Scottish Cup medals : 2
Glasgow Cup medals : 3
Scotland Caps : 4
Scottish League Caps : 4
Shut Outs : 64

JOE KENNAWAY (1931–39)

by Marie Rowan

Joe Kennaway arrived in Scotland from the USA and immediately took the field as Celtic's goalkeeper. Kennaway was no unknown quantity to Celtic – no 'I've watched a video of him and he looks the part' signing. Celtic had suffered at the big Canadian's hands and it had not been forgotten. Forgiven, yes, when it suited Celtic. The club had finally achieved an ambition held by Willie Maley for decades, that of taking the club across the Atlantic and boosting Celtic's profile amongst the emigrants who had flocked to see Celtic while still at home. A tour in May and June of 1931 was arranged whereby Celtic would play a number of games in the Eastern states of the US and also in Toronto, Canada. The season just finished had seen them win the Scottish Cup and the Glasgow Cup, missing out in the Glasgow Charity Cup by corners to Rangers. They had also finished the League in second place to Rangers, just two points adrift.

Wherever they went in both the US and Canada, they were feted by the Irish as poignant reminders of home. One of the teams they met was called Fall River from Massachusetts and they were defeated 0–1. Celtic had actually played very well, but the forwards had been thwarted time and time again by the Fall River goalkeeper, a young lad called Joe Kennaway, a Canadian. Months later, when Celtic's iconic player, John Thomson, died, Maley was reminded that the reason for the unexpected defeat by Fall River had been the outstanding performance of the goalkeeper. No effort was spared in bringing him to Paradise.

Kennaway had been born in Montreal in 1905 to Scottish parents. They had emigrated to Canada where all their children were born. Both of Joe's parents were from Dundee but it was to the West of Scotland that he brought his skills after having distinguished himself both in Canada and the USA. As football had a huge following in Scotland, it was hardly surprising that this enthusiasm for the game continued amongst the immigrant population of Canada and their offspring. Kennaway was with his team, Montreal CPR, when he was capped by Canada against the USA in New York on 6 November, 1926. Unfortunately Canada lost 6–2 but over twelve years later, in September 1938, it was the Rangers goalkeeper who repeated Kennaway's dubious honour of picking the ball out of the net six times with Joe this time watching from the safety of the Celtic goal during a 6–1 rout.

The following year, 1927, Joe joined Providence who played in the American Soccer League. The unusual act of transferring an entire team occurred and thus Kennaway, in May 1931, found himself playing for Fall River against the famous Glasgow Celtic. Despite their formidable line-up and recent successes that season, the pride of Glasgow's East End failed to score even once and were beaten by Fall River by one goal to nil. Kennaway's performance was simply outstanding and it lingered in the memory of the right Celtic officials. Montreal CNR were graced by his presence during the close season and it was while he was with this club that Joe suffered the ignominy of conceding ten goals. 10–0. The entire team had had a very bad day at the office! Even assuming that the defence in front of him was worse than useless and the forwards no better, it was perhaps a little ungentlemanly of the England touring side whom they were playing to notch up such a score when there was nothing at stake. That score could and should have had all the hallmarks of Joe Kennaway's blossoming career hitting the buffers. If perseverance and self-belief are necessities for a good goalkeeper to have in his armoury, Kennaway was obviously destined for great things. Fortunately it was Celtic's memory of their own Kennaway experience that was remembered and the 10–0 drubbing possibly unknown. Negotiations were duly opened and quickly concluded and the good ship *The Duchess of Richmond* brought a great 'keeper to replace John Thomson at Celtic Park.

Joe Kennaway ran out for the first time as Celtic's goalkeeper on 31 October 1931. His baptism was an away fixture against Motherwell at Fir Park and what a thriller it turned out to be! The excitement that Saturday was near fever pitch, it was Fir Park for thrills not Firhill. All eyes were on the man who was newly arrived from across the Atlantic and as the third Celtic keeper in a matter of weeks, sceptics were eyeing him critically from the terracing. Fall River? Where's that? A friendly? What's that? What did it really tell them about Kennaway's ability? They were about to find out and the new lad on the block would find himself representing Scotland at international level within two years. Not a bad answer to their questions.

All eyes might have been on Joe Kennaway, but Charlie Napier was to supply all the finesse further up the pitch. It was a game full of contentious refereeing, so bad was it that during one incident, Peter Scarff received a pass when he was in such an obvious offside position that the nearby members of the Celtic team stopped and waited for the sound of a whistle that never came. Scarff didn't. He resumed his run but sent the ball past from just a few yards out. The purists among the spectators gave him great credit for what they took for a sporting gesture as the referee had obviously erred, but whether it was that or Peter simply muffed his shot, the Celtic forward-line kept a discreet silence on the matter. Napier was a workhorse in both attack and defence. His first was the result of incredible astuteness in forcing his way through gaps in the Motherwell defence that did not actually exist. His second goal was such that Jinky Johnstone's admiring legions would have made their approval known in the loudest possible fashion. With the Motherwell defenders on top of him, it was suggested that nothing short of hypnotism had been used by Charlie as he sent one of them one way and the other in the opposite direction. Napier finished off this display of feinting by calmly walking the ball into the net for Celtic's second goal.

Kennaway was also having a busy baptism and he equalled his opposite number's tally for picking the ball out of the net although he had made a heroic save just before the first one as a shot rocketed towards his goal. The new bhoy managed to turn it away as it sped homewards. It was a game of four goals and high excitement coupled with thrilling incidents. Celtic's right-back, the soon to be Irish internationalist Willie Cook, somehow managed to have the ball land in the crook of his arm after Ferrier had shot at goal. Penalty! No way! Willie had never as much as moved his arm and Kennaway was perhaps just a little disappointed that he had not been allowed to display his penalty-saving prowess. It was one of the few correct calls Mr Leishman of Falkirk made that day. But incidents were plenty where the Celtic fans could see the mettle of their Canadian signing. 'Celtic's New Keeper Shines!' was the headline and it was not wrong. Kennaway leapt to clasp a shot from Murdoch, the Motherwell outside-right, and while doing so, he swung his right arm round so that his outstretched arms were pointing to the back of the net.

Although some thought a goal should have been awarded, those nearest asserted Kennaway was still a good deal distant from the goalline. Joe was praised for his safe hands and impressed all fans of both sides that day with his speed both on the ground and in the air. The highly critical newspaper pundits of the day thought that at this very early stage of his Celtic career, the lack of familiarity between the backs and their goalkeeper was probably the reason for his lack of judgment as to when to come out. As it was his first game for the club, they were unanimous in predicting that particular area of expertise would be quickly addressed and fixed. They also predicted, and it came to pass, that Kennaway was going to be a personality in Scottish football.

Joe Kennaway completed his first season with no medals to show for all the effort a team languishing under the devastating loss of goalkeeper, John Thomson, under the worst possible circumstances had made. The heart had gone out of the team although the players struggled along valiantly. The intense scrutiny Celtic goalkeepers even of today must endure must be difficult to live with. John Thomson's iconic figure and still vibrant memories of his legendary abilities must be daunting to those who have occupied his position down the generations. Joe Kennaway had to remain focused in an atmosphere of constant comparison as the first permanent replacement for that favourite son where he actually had no chance of ever rising above that memory and emotion. It speaks volumes for the man himself that he handled it all with dignity and respect for the supporters and fellow professionals' feelings. He was lauded and appreciated in his own right but he wasn't John Thomson.

Season 1932–33 saw Celtic still in the doldrums and not only did they finish a disappointing fourth in the League, they also failed to win both the Glasgow and Glasgow Charity Cups. But a sliver of light shone through the gloom as the team fought its way doggedly through the various rounds of that greatest pick-me-up of the day, the winning of the Scottish Cup, which is, incidentally, the oldest football trophy played for in the world today. The early rounds saw a determined Celtic defeat Dunfermline Athletic by the healthy margin of 7–0 and Falkirk 2–0. Kennaway missed the Falkirk game through injury and likewise the quarter final 1–1 draw with Albion Rovers. The replay, though, saw him once again restored in goal and a 3–1 home victory saw Celtic on their way to Hampden Park and a contest against Hearts for a place in the Final. A goalless draw and another replay, this time a 2–1 victory, and Kennaway and mates had a very real chance of picking up a much coveted Scottish Cup medal if all went well against Motherwell, the team Celtic had beaten in the 1931 Final and who had turned the tables on the Bhoys the following season.

In Celtic's first decade, poverty was grinding, starvation rife and the hope of a better future struggling valiantly to remain alive. In the very beginning of organised football in Scotland, it was the Holy of Holies, the Scottish Cup that nurtured any hope still lingering in the breasts of all the working classes regardless of race or religion. It was the only means of escape from reality in those times. The 1930s were better but not by much, with disease and unemployment forever present. It is difficult to imagine how Joe Kennaway viewed the massive responsibility that was his as the last man standing when, if he gazed around him at the crowd, he would realise he was being invested with the dreams of the larger part of the massive 102,339 crowd that day 15 April 1933.

Although great football was not on display that day, courage and dogged determination was. On a very slippery surface, it was the men in green and white who coped better, bringing all their power and expertise to the fore. They moved like the Celtic teams of earlier days, combining to create as many opportunities as they could against a Motherwell side that was in no way living up to its reputation of being a sweet-moving side. Celtic's greater guile, though, did not leave Kennaway standing idly by and a mix-up in their own goal area almost cost them a goal before the game had hardly got underway. A Motherwell free kick taken by Murdoch found George Stevenson with McFadyen well placed and Celtic looked as if they were about to go 0–1 down. With evidently no chance at all of saving, Kennaway, by some miracle, dived out and won the ball. His trials were not over, though, for McFadyen yet again kicked a scorcher and the ball flew towards Kennaway's left-hand post. But Joe succeeded in getting a hand to it at full stretch and diverted it past the upright. The Celtic goalkeeper was on a roll now and his next save left all the sports writers present in shock. It was generally agreed that it was one of the most remarkable saves ever. It was Motherwell's Stevenson's turn this time to have a go. His ferocious shot smashed off Kennaway's hands and zipped upwards in front of him and over the bar. A seemingly impossible save, massive relief and jubilation on the terracing. There were indeed moments in the Hungry Thirties when life was worth living. All the near misses were at the Celtic end in the first-half and Joe Kennaway was definitely the reason Celtic were still in the game as the half-time whistle blew on a 0–0 score.

The second half saw Celtic stamp their supremacy at last on the game that had almost got away from them. Jimmy McGrory chose the third minute after the restart to complete a move from Bert Thomson who had sent him a brilliant pass from the bye-line through several Motherwell defenders and Celtic were now one goal up. It was the Motherwell goal that was now under siege and Kennaway's opposite number had to pull off some great saves to keep his team in the match, Charlie Napier giving him a few heart-stopping moments. At the other end, Motherwell's tries were easily fended off by Joe Kennaway who had that first Scottish Cup medal well and truly in his sights. He well deserved it as his superb saves had kept the game alive for his team until his forwards had begun to make their superiority tell. By now their skilful play had begun to take its toll on what was now a disappointingly lack-lustre Motherwell side.

It was now fourteen wins in the Scottish Cup Final for Celtic. Tom White was presented with the trophy after the game in the Queen's Park reading-room, as there was no presentation in those days in front of the paying fans. He asked how often Celtic would have to win it in order to be allowed to keep it. 'Twenty-one times', was the reply from an SFA official, 'and all victories must be in succession.'

Charity, the raison d'etre for Celtic, was therefore a subject or object close to every true Celtic supporter's heart. The Glasgow Charity Cup had first been won by the club in 1892 by the much celebrated side of the day. It had last been won by the Parkhead Bhoys in 1926 when they beat Queen's Park 2–1 at Ibrox. As they had also won the League Championship that season, they had high hopes of repeating that 'double' as they prepared to take on old rivals, Rangers, in the Final. That first victory had been against Rangers and the score had been 2–1 at Celtic Park. The 1936 Final probably brought back memories to the team of their defeat at the hands of the Ibrox team in 1934 at Hampden Park in the same competition. The past decade had seen Celtic as a team prove to be the essence of inconsistency, which had resulted in a paucity of trophies and titles. If any sort of incentive was needed to defeat Rangers, the fact that the teams were already standing at eight victories apiece in the competition provided it. Neither team wanted the other one to inch ahead and that thought had some bearing on their thinking on the day of 9 May 1936. Celtic were determined to make their tally nine. They were just marginally favourites to win and the message had gone out earlier that in the event of the game being tied on the goals and corner-kicks count-back, there would be a replay on the following Tuesday. It was traditional that the Glasgow Charity Cup-Final closed the season and it fell to two of the Glasgow teams to make the most of this chance to lift the last of the season's silverware. Kennaway, it was noted, had already booked his passage for America and Canada, and was due to leave on the '*Tuscania*', sailing from Yorkhill on the coming Friday. Celtic had toured Ireland the previous week and Joe had been given the honour of captaining the side against Waterford and Cork. The Irish air must have proved a real tonic for Kennaway for his performance in this Charity Cup Final was rated outstanding.

99

The pitch was hard and dry, the wind at Hampden Park gusting. All in all, it was expected to make playing quality, entertaining football difficult. Not so. It was declared a memorable Final and one of the best games of the season. Celtic set off with a bang and within the first minute had won a corner-kick. Buchan, Celtic's inside-right, was unlucky not to score from a very clever piece of play. Minutes later, with Rangers still trying to steady themselves, they were again shaken to the core. McGrory had raced away and his pass to Johnny Crum was flicked on to Murphy. Murphy's shot came off Gray and a second corner was Celtic's within minutes of the kick-off. Celtic definitely meant business. The ball was centred by Murphy and knocked down by Winning. There were loud claims for a penalty but Buchan played to the whistle and his shot crashed off the Rangers' right-hand post. Rangers replied immediately and a shot on goal from Meiklejohn was caught by the swirling wind. Kennaway managed to take advantage of this and within moments, had the ball safely in his arms. Or so the Celtic supporters thought! He was dispossessed amidst a melee of players but to everybody's relief, Turnbull's shot went past. The 63,000 crowd were in full voice as the teams now went head to head. Rangers finally steadied themselves. Smith, their centre-forward bore down on Kennaway's goal. The Canadian tumbled down to save it and while on the roll, flicked it away from his goal. It had now become a fascinating game, both teams at their attacking best, long accurate passing, fast open play, inventive, creative football at its best. Murphy for Celtic was having an excellent game, causing the Rangers' defence no end of trouble. A fine Kennaway save from the ubiquitous Meiklejohn saw the Rangers man, within minutes, win a corner at one end and concede one at the other, such was the speed of the play in this game. The corner was cleared but a hovering Johnny Crum was once more on the ball. His shot was parried by Dawson in goal for Rangers, but was picked up by Delaney who slipped the ball just inside the left-hand post. Thirty-three minutes gone and Celtic were now one goal up. That sparked off both attacks going at full speed but it was Rangers whose efforts bore fruit with just five minutes to go till half-time as McPhail evened up the score. 1–1.

The second-half began with a magnificent save by Kennaway, which had the nerves of the green and white fans jangling yet again. The Rangers forwards had raced up the park from the off and found themselves with the luxury of being able to choose any one of three places to put the ball in the net. But Joe Kennaway had other ideas. McPhail accepted the opportunity afforded to head the ball for glory, but Kennaway cheekily plucked it off his head. The game swung from end to end with narrow escapes for both teams. The fans were certainly getting their money's worth and it was anybody's guess who would emerge victorious. An unstoppable shot from Turnbull brought all speculation to a halt and Rangers were now ahead 2–1, – for all of two minutes. A Murphy cross had Delaney racking up his second goal of the game with a magnificent header. Two goals apiece but Celtic were ahead by six corners to five. A slender but precious lead for if the result were a draw in terms of goals, these corners at the end of the game, would determine the destination of the Cup. Fifteen minutes left to play and the atmosphere inside the ground was electric as one incident followed another, chances were missed, potential deciders saved. Kennaway was hurt saving a ferocious shot from Ross. The tension in no way abated and the pace did not slacken for one moment. With ten minutes to go, Celtic were not only trying to score, but also trying to protect their corner-kicks advantage. A Rangers corner on the right knocked that advantage on the head. Delaney clawed it back and everything was frantic with Rangers attacking and Celtic desperately trying to maintain the status quo. But the great Jimmy Delaney was not one for dwelling amongst the ranks of the desperate. With only three minutes remaining, Delaney accepted a pass from Crum, cut in and calmly lobbed Dawson to put the Bhoys ahead. The Celtic supporters went berserk – a little premature maybe for those still dancing with delight, for they missed a glorious McGrory special a minute later. From ten yards out, Jimmy McGrory swung round and his right footed shot beat Dawson and Celtic were 4–2 up when Mr Hutton blew his whistle seconds later for the end of the game.

All in all, it had been a splendid, action-packed Final. The teams were perfectly matched, had given their all despite having to cope with the hard surface and the wind. The game had looked as if it was likely to be decided by corner-kicks but Delaney's opportunism and McGrory's ability to make something out of nothing spelled the difference between the two teams and sent the Glasgow Charity Cup on its way to Celtic Park. Delaney's Old Firm hat-trick was destined for the history books and pub quizzes. Of a very good Celtic attack, Crum was outstanding as were Kennaway and Lyon in defence. Joe could now catch that boat with another medal in his luggage to show the relatives across the Atlantic.

This particular Scottish Cup Final was to bring Joe Kennaway a second Scottish Cup medal having already won one in the 1933 victory over Motherwell. It would be interesting to know if his reaction to being hit by a deafening wall of noise as the teams emerged from the tunnel was

C. Geatons, R. Hogg, J. Kennaway, J. Morrison, W. Buchan, G. Paterson
J. McMenemy, J. Delaney, J. M'Grory, W. Lyon, J. Crum, F. Murphy, W. Maley
Trainer   Captain   Manager

the same as his teammate Willie Buchan's. Buchan had said he was terror-stricken. This game, which took place on 24 April 1937, is legendary for the size of the crowd that day at Hampden Park, which was well over 146,000 as Celtic faced Aberdeen to try and win the Scottish Cup for the fifteenth time in the club's history. With the habit of lifting youngsters over the turnstiles, it is thought that the crowd probably numbered over 150,000.

The game was a showcase of fair play and sportsmanship and neither side let their club or fans down. It was described as a 'meringue' of beautiful football and thrilling incidents with Celtic the pre-match favourites, but not by much. Celtic appeared to be much more composed in their play than Aberdeen, less likely to buckle under pressure, more likely to keep going in periods when things were not going their way. Aberdeen allowed their frustration at times to negate good play when times got rough while Celtic stayed with it in times of adversity. The worst culprits for this, surprisingly enough, were Aberdeen's more experienced players.

Celtic spotted the Aberdeen weaknesses early on and made the most of this knowledge. Buchan and Crum repeatedly pulled the Aberdeen left- and right-half out of position to allow their teammates room to exploit the gaps and send them through plenty of passes unhindered. Buchan was at his brilliant best, constantly changing tactics and bamboozling his opponents. Second guessing means moments too late in counteracting. His inside-left, Crum, had it off to a fine art, too, if in a slightly less colourful way, but it was noted that it was just as effective. Joe Kennaway had a really fine game, some terrific saves, one of which in particular had both Celtic and Aberdeen fans still talking about it weeks later. He had jumped up from down on the ground in time to clutch a shoulder-high shot from Beynon, the Aberdeen outside-right, who had looked certain to score.

Eleven minutes into the game, Buchan shot at goal. The ball was deflected by an Aberdeen defender and Johnstone in the Aberdeen goal managed to get his hands to the ball and stopped its progress into the net stone dead. Crum, never one to refuse a gift like that – a ball lying just a foot from the woodwork – ran in and tapped it over the line as Johnstone lay prostrate. Jubilation in the Celtic ranks turned to horror when, moments later, Aberdeen ran up the pitch at the restart and equalised. Beynon, Aberdeen's best player that day, had raced towards the Celtic goal, crossed to McKenzie who then passed to Armstrong and got the Celtic defence on the turn eluding Kennaway. Joe had no time to cross the goal before the Aberdeen centre-forward slotted the ball into the net. 1–1. Jimmy McGrory was by this time nearing the end of his career but his efforts showed up the fact that the young Aberdeen 'keeper, Johnstone, had class. Unfortunately, McGrory passed up the chance to score with only the 'keeper to beat. He appeared to hesitate a little and the ball ran loose. It was cleared before any serious damage could be done. Murphy, too, had missed a great opportunity in the first-half. Aberdeen tried to bring off the winner but with twenty minutes left on the clock, following a sustained period of attacking by them and great work by Kennaway to thwart them, Celtic's McGrory had other ideas. It was noted that a mini-version of the Hampden Roar was heard. No doubt some 'neutrals' getting carried away. Jimmy, having been responsible for the birth of that sound after scoring a goal against England in 1933, rightly judged he was the one who should be inspired by it. He breasted down the ball with his back to the goalmouth and the Aberdeen defence seemed to join the crowd in watching this manoeuvre. They looked on while he got it under control and admired the way he passed it to the feet of the incoming Celt, Buchan. Buchan collected it in his stride, ran on and then fired a low shot that hit off the inside of Johnstone's left-hand before travelling on at an angle across the goalmouth and finally landed in the net. Aberdeen were now 1–2 down but not out. To their credit, they never stopped trying and were hoping to at least earn a replay. But Celtic were now comfortably in the driving-seat and a Celtic team in a Cup tie playing at their best and most confident are almost impossible to defeat. Celtic now had the measure of Aberdeen's mistakes and capitalised on them and the final score was 2–1 in their favour. Thus Celtic's Canadian goalkeeper Joe Kennaway, not only had the satisfaction of knowing he had had a very good game, he had another much coveted Scottish Cup medal to keep his 1933 one company. It was a game played in the finest traditions of Scottish football and the referee and linesmen were roundly congratulated for their first-class handling of it.

At the function later, the Celtic one not the official SFA one, which was held in Willie Maley's restaurant, The Bank, the players were congratulated by legendary players of Celtic's great teams of the past. Jimmy Quinn, Patsy Gallagher, Jimmy McMenemy and Joe Dodds all probably regaling the gathering with tales of past victories and perhaps the odd defeat. No doubt Joe Kennaway had more than a word or two with John Kelly, a true veteran of Celtic's birth as Kelly had played in goal for the famous 'Snow Final' on 2 February 1889. Kelly had also watched Celtic lose the Glasgow Cup Final to Rangers on 12 October 1935 along with Dan McArthur and Davy Adams. An audience to make Kennaway a little anxious, perhaps. The official function was held in the St Enoch Hotel and Tom White had to be there so a brief appearance at The Bank had to suffice. Aberdeen supporters occupied other parts of the premises wearing their black and gold and, it seems, they were hoping to be allowed to touch the Scottish Cup despite its being draped in Celtic's green and white ribbons.

Celtic with the Scottish Cup of 1937. Kennaway is second from the left beside Jimmy McGrory.

Celtic with the Scottish Cup of 1937. Kennaway is second from the left beside Jimmy McGrory.

Any excuse for a football tournament in Scotland and to celebrate the 1938 Empire Exhibition was as good an excuse as the country was going to get in those depressed days. Also the opportunity to see, compare and appreciate the standards reached by the best teams in Scotland and England was one likely to fire the football-mad Scots with delightful anticipation. The fact that it was held during one of the wettest summers on record, barely diminished the enthusiasm. The Empire Exhibition was being held to showcase the best of manufacturing and cultural aspects of life in the Empire and, hopefully, to attract substantial amounts of inward investment. Royalty of the first water would be in attendance and Kennaway, Crum and fellow-players were more than willing to turn out to match themselves against the best in the land. Their 'subjects' were also more than willing to turn out to pay homage to their Celtic heroes. Bellahouston Park being the Exhibition venue, the football tournament was to take place in the nearest stadium. As Ibrox Park was no more than half-a-mile distant, Rangers' ground was where it would all take place. The trophy was an eighteen-inch replica of the superb Tower of Empire (Tait's Tower), the tallest building on the site. Mr Tait was the principal architect of the exhibition and the Art Deco style was well to the fore. It was indeed a feast for the eyes. The players of the winning team were to receive miniatures of the silver trophy, the runners-up, medals. It was to be a true celebration of football as the leading teams of both Scotland and England were being pitted against each other. The teams were Celtic, Aberdeen, Hearts and Rangers from Scotland and Brentford, Everton, Chelsea and Sunderland from England. Arsenal, the English champions were unable to compete due to a previous engagement. When they discovered that fixture had been cancelled, they alerted the Exhibition committee but were told that they were too late to be included in what was now being billed as the British Championship.

It is no exaggeration to state that but for the superb goalkeeping of Joe Kennaway against Sunderland, Celtic's first opponents and Hearts, their next one, the stunning Empire Exhibition Trophy which so graces the boardroom at Celtic Park today would be resting elsewhere.

The tournament opened for Celtic with a game against Sunderland, the previous season's FA cup winners, on 25 May 1938. A good crowd of 50,000 saw a fascinating game between two highly competitive teams, Celtic's line-up being the same one that had beaten Rangers 2–0 earlier that month in front of a crowd of 40,000 in the Glasgow Charity Cup Final. A goalless draw saw the two very evenly matched teams head for the dressing-rooms at half-time with great expectations of a finely balanced contest expected as Sunderland had gradually entered the fray in earnest as the clocked tick by. Raich Carter for Sunderland did not disappoint and a terrific header saw Celtic's nerves almost shattered as it headed for the corner of the net. Only a phenomenal save from Kennaway in the Celtic goal saw the score remain level. It was destined to remain on a knife-edge when the final whistle was blown as Celtic threatened to open the scoring. Extra-time saw both teams stepping up a gear with Sunderland almost snatching victory in the second half before another incredible effort by Kennaway thwarted Sunderland's left-winger Burbanks. A goalless draw signalled a replay the following evening.

Injuries to Delaney and Carruth saw Matt Lynch and Malcolm MacDonald in the team and once again Celtic survived due to the brilliant goalkeeping of Kennaway. Eventually Sunderland opened the scoring in the first-half through a Saunders goal and Celtic heeded the wake-up call with Crum scoring to let Celtic go in at half-time level on goals. Two goals within ten minutes of each other in the second half by Divers put Celtic into the next round. The very wet evening had resulted in a poor crowd of around 20,000 but they had seen a contest where Celtic had dominated the 1937 FA Cup-winners.

An all-Scots line-up it was, as Celtic took on Hearts on 3 June. Celtic were much refreshed after their week's rest but Hearts had only had two days off after their match with Brentford. Against all odds, the pre-match favourites, Celtic, were completely outplayed by a Hearts team replete with Scottish internationalists. Once again, only the formidable goalkeeping of Celtic's imperturbable Joe Kennaway allowed them to survive Hearts' domination. For the third time in this very important and prestigious tournament, Kennaway exhibited the hallmarks of a Celtic great and kept his team in the competition. A Johnny Crum goal in the sixty-fifth minute eased the tension for a very short period until the relentless Hearts attacks resumed with renewed vigour. Kennaway not only survived this pressure, but excelled in rebuffing wave after wave of opposition assaults on his goal, ably assisted by a determined Celtic defence. When the final whistle sounded, this 1–0 result in Celtic's favour put them into the Final and a game against a brilliant Everton side who had just defeated Aberdeen 3–2 having already seen off Rangers.

The contest between two excellent sides was eagerly anticipated and both teams did not disappoint on the day. The amazing Empire Exhibition trophy was the prize and from inside Ibrox Park, the Tower of Empire itself could be seen in all its stunning architectural grandeur on a hill in nearby Bellahouston Park. This building, which had originally been intended to remain as a permanent feature in the park when the exhibition was closed and the other buildings dismantled, was removed as the Second World War began, its position being too close to the River Clyde with its shipping and shipyards, arousing fears that the building could be used as a navigational aid to enemy aeroplanes. It was indeed a great loss to the people of Glasgow.

The game was a feast of football for the 82,653 who turned up to see that Final on 10 June 1938. Everton's team was replete with household names but every man and

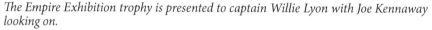

The Empire Exhibition trophy is presented to captain Willie Lyon with Joe Kennaway looking on.

his Celtic-supporting granny could also fire off the renowned players in the green and white. This team was famous for their skill, teamwork and attacking prowess. This late 1930s side was one of the few truly great Celtic teams and the favoured Celtic close-passing, skilful, attacking style of play was second-nature to Delaney, MacDonald, Crum, Divers and Murphy. Heroic goalkeepers were, of course, just as much a tradition of the club and Kennaway saw it did not lapse. Once underway, he came yet again to Celtic's rescue as the great Tommy Lawton, through the defence and about to score, saw his effort thwarted by the man who was undoubtedly the hero of Celtic's tournament. Kennaway dived, with no thought to his own safety, right at the feet of the Everton and England player and thus kept not only the ball, but Celtic's hopes in the competition alive. It took a period of extra-time to settle the destination of the Empire Exhibition Trophy after a goalless ninety minutes.

Celtic dominated this, taking full advantage of Everton's injury problem on the right wing. Within seven minutes, Johnny Crum accepted a pass from Divers and his rocket-like shot from fifteen yards out settled the trophy's destination. Crum treated the fans behind the goal to a Highland fling. Perhaps Malcolm MacDonald, whose family hailed from South Uist, had indulged in a bit of coaching beforehand. Ecstatic crowd, ecstatic team and the trophy joined the League Championship one in the boardroom. A long time later, Johnny Crum said it was the support of the Celtic fans that night that he would never forget. They were loud in their backing for the team right from the kick-off. Johnny suggested two reasons for that in addition to their natural inclination to rally behind their own team. Did the Scotland versus England card come into play plus the fact that Everton had played in blue? Definitely food for thought. Johnny Crum has his name inextricably linked with the Empire Exhibition Trophy and rightly so as the tournament was, in fact, looked on as something of an unofficial British Championship decider. But Celtic would never have made it through the various rounds and into that crucial period of extra-time if it had not been for the repeated brilliance of their goalkeeper, Joe Kennaway.

The headlines were Celtic 6, Rangers 2. Had this game been played in recent years, the DVDs would have been flying off the shelves. An earlier one in 1895–96 season was won by Celtic by the same margin. This one in 1938 is a surprisingly forgotten 'demolition derby' with a bit of the Celtic penchant for pressing the self-destruct button thrown in when the supporters least expected it. Willie Maley's six-in-a-row greats were first and foremost a team and that's what the Celts were that day in September, 1938. The Bhoys won 6–2 that glorious day and that made it three victories over Rangers on the trot that season of 1938–39. It was written that that day the men in blue had proved that it was possible for eleven of them to

The Celtic team of 1938.
Back Row: Geatons, Hogg,
Kennaway, Morrison, Crum,
Paterson:
Front Row: Delaney,
MacDonald, Lyon, Divers,
Murphy.

run around and still look as if they were standing still. Having won the League and the Empire Exhibition Trophy, all in 1938, it seemed to the Celtic fans that things could simply not get any better. But that afternoon at Parkhead it did – with a vengeance. The score did not reflect the terrible and inexplicable collapse of Celtic for twenty minutes of the second-half and that's when Joe Kennaway, the penalty-saver specialist, came into his own. But the penalty given was for Celtic and Joe looked on merely as a very interested spectator.

The team that was facing Rangers was the one that had beaten Everton in the Final of the Empire Exhibition tournament on 10 June 1938. Malcolm MacDonald, that most superlative of footballers, settled any Celtic nerves when he opened the scoring in the nineteenth minute. Celtic's second came as a result of Johnny Crum's complete mastery of Woodburn, the Ranger's centre-half. Crum's neat flicks and the dazzling interchanging of positions by the Celtic forwards were completely out-foxing the Ibrox men. Crum passed to MacDonald and Calum raced through to the Rangers' goal. Woodburn took the feet from him inches outside the 18-yard line. Before the free-kick could be taken, both players were booked for what the papers termed an 'ungentlemanly scene'. Lyon came up to take the kick. Delaney, once described as a top-grader in opportunism and of high courage, caused a diversion by running towards the line. The Rangers' wall broke to stop him and Lyon took full advantage of the resultant gap and crashed the ball into the top of the net. Celtic's third came from a penalty some five minutes before half-time. When the Rangers' goalkeeper, Dawson, had safely defused another Celtic attack on his goal and had the ball safely in his hands, Woodburn charged the incoming Delaney from behind. Willie Lyon, the Celtic captain, made no mistake with the penalty-kick and it was 3–0 to the men in the green and white.

Half-time came and went and then suddenly Celtic found they were in a contest for Smith of Rangers who had been very poorly supported in the first forty-five minutes found himself the darling of his team's fans as he opened the scoring for Rangers after McPhail had seen his own effort hit off the Celtic cross-bar. Now, having completely outplayed the opposition, the Celtic players were the victims of Smith catching the rebound. He put his foot out and slotted the ball away out of Kennaway's reach. Within fifteen minutes of the restart, a brilliant mazy run by Kinnear, Rangers' outside-left, ended with a pass to Thornton, their inside-right and he just swept it cleanly into Celtic's goal. Joe had thrown himself at the ball but failed to make contact with it. As he lay prostrate, Thornton shot it over his head and into the net. Three up and coasting had become 3–2 and the Celts were left wondering how it had happened and what should they do next. Celtic, stunned and struggling, answered the latter of those questions by stepping up a gear or two. The indecision vanished as quickly as it had appeared and the now-confident and high-flying Rangers side were put back into their place as the next goal was the result of the ball landing slap bang in the back of their own net and not Celtic's. With an equaliser looking imminent, Murphy, Crum and Delaney broke through the Rangers defence. Crum – some reports say Murphy – almost on the bye-line, lobbed the ball across the Rangers' goalmouth and Jimmy Delaney, with a magnificent flying effort, almost stole the ball from Dawson's hands and blitzed it into the back of the net. A magnificent goal and almost every Celtic player tore up the pitch to congratulate him. But Joe Kennaway, ever mindful of his responsibilities, stayed on his goalline. There would be no lapses laid at his door. 4–2 and Rangers were not only down but out. From here on in, Celtic were once more supreme and they knew it. They could do no wrong. Malcolm MacDonald was in his element. In a fight, there was no greater man, as history had proved time and time again, than a Highlander. Just to rub it in, Malcolm completed his hat-trick forthwith.

The Celts that day, but for that near-fatal spell of almost total collapse, came away with all the credit and all of the points. A handsome win against Rangers had been achieved yet most newspapers were more focused on that lapse than on the superlative play of the team overall. Not so the fans. That they had won at a gallop was the impression on the terracing and every man in the team a hero. Kennaway came in for special congratulations as he had held fast in the storm that had attempted to engulf him shortly after half-time, no-one blaming him for the two very good goals Rangers had scored. MacDonald's goals were declared gems and Delaney's sensational. But for that short spell, Rangers had been out-thought and out-played by a truly great team performance by Celtic.

Only two years after leaving the US to play in goal for Celtic, Joe Kennaway found himself playing on the international stage for the land of his forefathers.

Having had to withdraw from the Scotland versus Wales international match at Cardiff at the last minute due to illness, Kennaway was quickly back on international duty. In November of the same year, 1933, he took his place in the line-up as the Scotland team faced the might of the hugely talented Austria. The crowd swelled to 62,000 and they had turned up not only to cheer on their own boys but also to wonder at the skills of a team they had heard so much about. They certainly got their money's worth. The result was a 2–2 draw and Celtic's Kennaway came out of it with great credit. It was a bit of an international baptism of fire, for the Austrians more than lived up to their reputation as sublime footballers with terrific ball-control, uncanny ability to change positions and the ability also to find their man both quickly and accurately. Joe Kennaway was to become very familiar with this type of play as Crum, Buchan and the others in the Celtic forward-line in front of him in that wonderful Celtic team of the late 1930s displayed these qualities time and time again. Joe was not the only Celtic player in the team that evening as Peter McGonagle lined up at left-back in front of him.

Recognition of Kennaway's talents by those running Scottish football, at least by the Scottish Football League at the time, came early as Joe was chosen to represent the Scottish League against the Irish league at Ibrox on 19 October 1932, exactly one year after he had landed in Liverpool on his way to Celtic Park and only one day short of his debut for Celtic. He was in fact the only Celtic player chosen for the game as presumably it was reckoned that the Celtic team of John Thomson's day were still suffering psychologically from his death.

The game itself was an unusual one, very quiet and unadventurous, especially the Scots, to such an extent that the frustrated home supporters amongst the 11,000 crowd actually began to cheer on the Irish who were that day, wearing white shirts. The whole game had an unusual quality about it. Boyd of Clyde, however, livened up the proceedings when he opened the scoring after 35 minutes but it was well into the second-half before the next goal came. Kelly, for the Irish team, on making a wonderful run, ran past three Scots, passed to Devan of Coleraine who scored as Kennaway came out in an attempt, 'to retrieve the failure of his colleagues' as one commentator put it. The Scottish League team suddenly woke up – wonder what Kennaway said to them – and by the time the whistle sounded for full-time, Boyd had added a second to his tally and Telfer and Stevenson one each. A 4 – 1 victory but the Irish took a great deal of credit for their display of tenacity especially by their half-backs. All told, a very satisfactory Inter-League debut for Kennaway

It was on 10 February 1934, that Kennaway made his next appearance in an Inter-League game. This time Joe faced the English League team again at Ibrox and he must have wondered why, with Jimmy McGrory and company beginning to demonstrate their skills once more, he was one of only two Celtic players in a team replete with six from Rangers. Perhaps the venue had something to do with it. An incredible crowd of 60,000 turned up to see the game.

A draw would have been considered a good result for the Scots before the game and that was what the journalists from Scotland were hoping for. Their opponents were thought to be more than capable of defeating them. After the game, though, and a 2–2 draw, the Press were of the opinion that but for an appalling decision by the referee, Mr Dougray from Glasgow, the Scottish League team would surely have won.

The English League took the lead through a ball that had been almost a foot over the line. It was too fast for Kennaway to save. Then the Scottish attack took over and Simpson equalised. The teams had been playing for only eleven minutes and yet two minutes later, a brilliant left-footed drive from the English League inside-left gave Joe no chance at all. The shot was so fierce the ball finished up wedged tightly in the back of the net near the iron stanchion. A goal neither Beresford the scorer nor Joe Kennaway were very likely to forget. Both attacks had great shots on goal, Nicholson for the Scots hitting the post and Bastin for the English League one that struck the crossbar. At half-time, Scotland were down two goals to one.

Eight minutes into the second-half, McPhail took a throw-in from Brown, his Rangers' teammate, and proceeded to score a terrific goal. Having accepted the ball from Brown on his head, McPhail dropped it and wheeling round hit it low past the diving Sagar in the English goal. It was now 2–2 and that was the score when the whistle was blown for full-time.

A sports journalist wrote on the Monday following the match that, 'Joe Kennaway must come out well on the credit side. Several of his masterly saves roused the crowd. The Celt must be considered as a certain for further preferment.' (*Daily Record 12 February 1934*) No doubt Joe must also have been pleased that his teammate at Celtic, McGonagle was judged to have fully justified his selection.

October 1934 proved to be a very busy month for Kennaway as he represented the Scottish League twice, once against the Irish at Firhill, Partick Thistle's ground, then against the English League in London. It would seem that the honours in football are like bananas – they come in bunches.

First up was the one versus the Irish League at Firhill in Glasgow. This time 8,000 were there to see a Scottish victory as the home team beat the Irish 3–2. It was a very wind-swept day and the rain had drenched everybody and everything in Glasgow. But those brave souls who had braved it all saw a thrilling ninety minutes of football. The stand was, as always, bulging with football officials and Press from all over Scotland. It was noted that the ground had been taken over by the League for the game and unfortunately, the hospitality or lack of it which that organisation provided, bore no resemblance to that usually on offer by Partick Thistle FC. What the folks from Ireland and England thought of that was made quite clear especially by the Irish reporters who were used to a much more traditional Scottish reception.

The after-match talk was of Joe Kennaway's outstanding display, which was universally thought to have guaranteed him a Scotland cap. Elsewhere, it was noted that Dawson, the Rangers goalkeeper, had played well in a friendly against Manchester City at Maine Road. It was suggested that as Kennaway had, 'so distinguished himself' during the Irish game, the selectors would have a hard time choosing the goalkeeper for the internationals. A Celtic player up against a Ranger? Poor Joe. No chance!

Joe Kennaway's Final Inter-League appearance came later that month at Stamford Bridge, the home of Chelsea FC, in London, when the Scottish League played the English League on 31 October 1934. This time Joe was joined by two other Celts, McGonagle and Napier, and the game was played in front of a crowd of 20,000. The Scots went 1–0 ahead after only 15 minutes but Brook levelled the score before adding another to make the Final score 2–1 to the English League.

Kennaway was still signed for Celtic for season 1939–40 and had played half-a-dozen games for the club when war broke out and the final game in the Scottish League was played on the 2 September 1939. Although football was not closed down, the League was reformed into smaller, local ones and Celtic suffered a sudden lack of interest in taking it all seriously. Although the organisation of the game had changed for the duration of the War, the game was as popular as ever. As it had when Celtic had first entered the footballing arena, the game provided a much-needed diversion from the tensions of life. Other clubs retained their competitive edge and accepted the offer of the services of some of the greatest footballers in the UK when these men were stationed nearby. Celtic refused most offers and that decision to allow other clubs to build up their expertise for the future, put Celtic the best part of a decade behind the other Scottish teams when peace finally came.

Joe Kennaway left for his native Montreal in 1940 and was not idle for long. He combined working for Vickers with playing for their football team. One of Celtic's greatest ever goalkeepers playing for his works team? That information would have been greeted with astonishment in Glasgow. But Joe's activities were still of interest to his massive Celtic fan-base and a report appeared in the *Glasgow Weekly News* on 21 September, 1940, stating, 'Our old friend, Joe Kennaway, is all set to show the football fans 'over there' how sound a 'keeper he still is. Joe has signed up for SA Healey FC of New York.' Kennaway eventually became the football coach for Brown University of Providence in 1946 and remained there till he retired in 1959.

Joe Kennaway had sailed from Canada to play for Celtic at a very difficult time. John Thomson's massive reputation and tragic end and the affection in which he was held by the club's supporters all combined to make it an incredibly difficult task for his replacement. But by September 1939, Joe could with confidence claim, 'I came, I saw, I conquered.' Kennaway, Hogg and Morrison – a back three dreams were made of and which will surely reverberate down the generations as one of the greatest ever.

CAREER:

Appearances: 327
Scottish League Medals: 2
Scottish Cup Medals: 2
Glasgow Cup Medals: 1
Glasgow Charity Cup Medals: 3
Empire Exhibition Winner's Trophy: 1
Scotland Caps: 1
Shut Outs: 75

WILLIE MILLER
(1942–50)

by David Potter

It was a cold day at Pittodrie in 1980 the week between Christmas and the New Year. Celtic were sliding to a fairly comprehensive defeat, unable to get through the excellent Aberdeen defensive pairing of Alex McLeish and Willie Miller. The Main Stand at Pittodrie was, agreeably and harmoniously, populated with fans of both persuasions, but when the Dons supporters in other parts of the ground took up the refrain of 'There's only one Willie Miller', the douce middle class Aberdonians joined in. Indeed he was a fine player, but my elderly and venerable companion had to disagree.

'No, he's no the only Willie Miller. I remember anither wan – and he was a damned sight better than ony o' them twa!' he said jabbing his aged fingers in the direction of both goals where stood the excellent Pat Bonner and the equally worthy Jim Leighton. He was referring, of course, to the Willie Miller who had played in the Celtic goal in the 1940s. He was as good a goalkeeper as Celtic had ever had, but paradoxically, won no major medal for the club.

Robert Burns said to the mountain daisy in his famous poem of that name 'Thou's met me in an evil hour'. Similarly, it could be said that Celtic and Willie Miller met each other in an evil hour. The Second World War had almost run three years of its course when Willie made his debut for Celtic in August 1942, having previously played for Maryhill Harp. The circumstances were far from auspicious.

Great Britain had until recently been alone against Nazi Germany. In midsummer 1941 Hitler had invaded the Soviet Union, and Britain now had an ally (of sorts). In December of the same year the Japanese obligingly bombed Pearl Harbour and Britain then had another (and a far more wholesome one) in the United States. But the outlook was still grim with everything that Britain tried coming to naught, and the sinking of ships in the Atlantic causing particular concern. Rationing was in full force, and although Glasgow retained its sense of humour and general vibrancy (indeed with all the English, American and Commonwealth soldiers and sailors based on the Clyde it was even more alive than normal), the place was gripped with fear of what might yet happen. Apart from Clydebank in 1941, there had been no serious bombing in Glasgow, but everyone was apprehensive. The Army had already been badly defeated in Dunkirk in 1940 and now there was every chance that the Army in Africa might yet be lost to Rommel's Afrika Korps with their Panzer tanks.

Football struggled in these circumstances. Full-time professional football was not allowed and all players had to be doing some war related work as well as playing football. Teams were not always easy to select because players might be unavailable at the last minute, or might be delayed by the problems of war transport. The Scottish Cup had been shelved for the duration, and the Scottish League had become the Southern League as far as Glasgow was concerned. This was to prevent teams having to make long journeys to Dundee and Aberdeen in difficult wartime circumstances where everyone was deterred from travelling with the phrase 'Is Your Journey Really Necessary?' Clearly it was not felt necessary in 1942 for Celtic to play against Aberdeen.

It would be wrong however to suggest that football was not a matter of importance. This was emphatically not the case. There had been a few attempts to stop football altogether in 1939, but rightly the Government allowed it to continue for morale reasons, and so that there would be a degree of normality in a difficult situation. In fact, the game sometimes assumed undue importance in the eyes of some fans, probably because people needed to have their minds taken away from the horrors all around them. If a soldier, sailor or airman was worrying about Celtic, he was not, for a short while at least, terrified of the next bomb, bullet or torpedo. There was simply no escape from modern warfare whereas football, like the cinema, did proved a momentary relief and escape. Making up for the loss of the Scottish Cup, local competitions like the Glasgow Cup and Glasgow Charity Cup flourished, and Junior football from whence sprung young Willie Miller, positively boomed.

BBC Radio played a great part in the propaganda war. Famously of course it told everyone to fight them on the beaches and elsewhere, but it was also a vehicle for informing soldiers and sailors about the football results with news from important games awaited with as much interest and enthusiasm in places like Cairo and Gibraltar as they were in Glasgow and London. But the news was not always good for those of the Celtic persuasion.

115

Celtic were in the doldrums. The reason was possibly still Willie Maley who had resigned, retired or been paid off (depending on one's take) in January 1940, but whose influence pervaded everything at Celtic Park. Maley is rightly called the man who made Celtic, and the years immediately after his departure showed how much the club still needed him. Indeed, he should really have been pensioned off with honour in 1938 after the Empire Exhibition Trophy triumph of that year, and a successor groomed to take over.

Instead the club gave him an honorarium but made him pay the income tax on it! Maley became bitter, was ill frequently in season 1938–39 and after a bright start, the team collapsed. Maley should have been replaced before the war. As it was, when he did go in 1940, the club ignored the claims of Jimmy McMenemy who had been an excellent trainer under Maley and had, in practice, run the team, and went for Jimmy McStay who had been a great centre-half and captain under Maley. However, it was beginning to be apparent by the start of the 1942–43 season at the time when Miller joined the club, that Jimmy McStay was not a great manager. It would have been interesting to see him having a chance in better circumstances.

Rangers read the situation in 1939 as well as Maley had understood such things in 1914. Most of their players were found jobs in war-related industries on the Clyde, whereas Celtic simply allowed things to drift. To be fair to McStay, there was a general half-heartedness from the Directors as well, and Celtic paid the price for all this incompetence on the field. 1941 was not a great year at Celtic Park, and had included a period when Celtic Park was closed following some disorder from Celtic supporters at, of all places, Ibrox Park.

Willie Maley, now a frequent attender at Cathkin, Hampden and even Ibrox was not slow to tell anyone who was prepared to listen just what exactly was wrong at Parkhead. His diatribes and fulminations were naturally laced with anecdotes of his great teams with the occasional maudlin and lachrymose reference to those he had lost like Peter Johnstone, Peter Somers, Peter Scarff, Sunny Jim and of course; 'goalkeepers come and goalkeepers go, but the more I think of goalkeepers, the more I think of our genius, John Thomson.

Joe Kennaway had returned to Canada soon after war broke out. Celtic had struggled to get a goalkeeper to replace him. There was now however at Parkhead a young man who had the potential to be just as good as John Thomson. Willie Miller had been born in October 1924, had played for Woodside Secondary, then St Rollux United BB, then St Rollux YMCA before signing for Maryhill Harp in early January 1942. He was of average height, but very lithe and supple. He was also one of those players who was very fond of a joke and a bit of banter with his teammates most of the time, but whenever a game was in the offing, became totally focussed and obsessed with the idea of guarding his goal.

He was thus only 17 when he made his debut. He was meant to be playing in the first game of the season on 8 August to cover for the sitting tenant Willie Culley who had concussed himself in a pre-season friendly, but Miller himself fell ill with tonsillitis and could not play, compelling Culley, concussed or not, to play instead. Miller's first game was thus two weeks later on 22 August 1942 against Hamilton Accies at Celtic Park in what was called the Southern League. Celtic's third game of the season finished up like the previous two, a 2–2 draw.

This one was different however in that Celtic were 2–0 up at half-time, and the crowd were delighted in the form of the team with the new goalkeeper looking as if he could fit the part. The goals had been scored by the great Jimmy Delaney and by Pat McAuley, probably the only two Celts worthy of the green and white jersey that day. Malky McDonald, an outstanding success in the late 1930s, particularly in the Empire Exhibition Trophy of 1938, was still around but his form had been disappointing, and the second half ruthlessly exposed Celtic's defensive weaknesses as Hamilton scored twice. Although *The Glasgow Observer* says that Miller was; 'helpless against the two shots that beat him,' he nevertheless, 'pleased the Parkhead fans highly'. The same newspaper also criticises the ineffectual forwards with, 'only Delaney in the least dangerous'.

Axiomatic to the rest of the season was the first meeting with Rangers on September 5 1942. It was at Ibrox in the Glasgow Cup semi-final, and although Celtic fought hard and took Rangers to extra-time, nevertheless it was Rangers who won through 2–1. Miller had nothing to reproach himself for, however, being described as, 'daring and magnificent' and performing some 'miraculous saves'. It was an unlucky defeat, but a defeat nevertheless, and Celtic now did what they have often done at other times in the wake of a defeat from Rangers, namely they went into freefall, losing to Morton, Motherwell and Hibs.

The young Miller thus had loads of practice as the team was generally overrun, but one of the things that kept the supporters going was the ability of Willie who sometimes revealed a maturity 'way beyond his years' and kept the score down to respectable levels. Celtic had, 'as much control over their own destiny as a drifting log,' said one unkind journalist, and things were as low at Celtic Park as they had ever been. The support dwindled, as one might expect, but there was still a residue of loyalty and defiance. Miller is on record as saying that he was impressed by the support who never failed to cheer him on, hoping against hope that the corner might one day be turned.

In fact things got a little better for the last few weeks of 1942, although the word always used was 'inconsistency'. Celtic's management simply lacked imagination. They might have, for example, used a few 'guest' players, but for reasons that looked like nothing other than sheer obstinacy, refused to do so. Matt Busby, for example, an unashamed lover of Celtic, a Scottish internationalist and great wing half for Manchester City, was available to them and said so publicly on many occasions, but they ignored him. In addition, many great English players like Tommy Lawton were from time to time available to play for a Scottish team and would have loved a chance to play for the Celtic team who, it might have been argued, were still the Champions of Great Britain following their famous success in the Empire Exhibition Trophy of 1938. Lawton had played in the Final of that trophy, and knew what Celtic were all about. But Celtic failed to approach him.

Often youngsters had to be tried, but the circumstances were against any chance of a development policy or anything like that. Football, as we have said, still was important but by now in late 1942 was losing out in public consciousness to the mighty events that were happening in North Africa where the Eighth Army were sweeping in triumph over Egypt, Tripolitania and Libya and rightly earning praise from Winston Churchill and indeed the rest of the world, for it showed that the Germans could be beaten. In addition another German army was increasingly isolated and trapped around Stalingrad in the Soviet Union and would by early 1943 be compelled to surrender after sustaining horrendous losses.

In such earth-shattering circumstances, it was hardly surprising that the development of Willie Miller in the Celtic goal was not much noticed or commented upon. Another momentous event, the implications of which were not noticed until later, was the appearance of a young man called John or Jock Stein playing his debut for Albion Rovers against Celtic in a 4–4 draw in mid-November 1942. But most perceptive Celtic fans noticed with approval, that although goals were being lost at an alarming rate – four to Dumbarton at Boghead, for example – the goalkeeping skills of Miller were enough to limit the damage that might otherwise have been sustained.

There was the occasional good result as well. On 7 November, Celtic beat Hearts 3–0 at Parkhead to cheer up the faithful and there were times that with Jimmy Delaney in good form and young Pat McAuley hinting at what he might achieve, some supporters believed that good times were not all that far away, especially with young Miller showing such promise at the back. But the majority of the time, disappointment was the order of the day with the support shrugging their shoulders and heading home along London Road, wallowing in nostalgia about

Jimmy McGrory and Peter Wilson of a decade ago, and Patsy Gallacher and Jimmy Quinn of the more distant past.

And nothing could have prepared either Miller or the Celtic support for the cataclysm which would occur at Ibrox on 1 January 1943. The 8–1 defeat remains one of Celtic's darkest days, showing quite clearly to all concerned the nature of Celtic's futile and pusillanimous resistance to Rangers. But although Rangers were the better team, there were extenuating circumstances. Miller had been crocked (perhaps deliberately) early in the game and was powerless to reach some of Rangers goals. One of Rangers goals was blatantly offside, and Malky McDonald and Matt Lynch were sent off for pointing this out to the referee.

It was however a very dark day in Celtic's history and it was perhaps as well that so many of the support were far away at the time, involved in far more momentous affairs. The hammering, bad though it was, does not appear in official records because it was indeed a wartime game, and the record victory in a Celtic versus Rangers game is of course the 7–1 in the Scottish League Cup Final of 1957.

The rest of the 1942–43 season was an irrelevance as far as Celtic were concerned with further defeats in the League and the new League Cup, and the impression given that Celtic were, as they would be in the early 1960s and the early 1990s, transfixed, as it were, like a rabbit in the glare of a car's headlights whenever Rangers were around. This, Miller realised, was a learning experience, and a good one too, for such was the nature of the Celtic defence that he was permanently in the game, and there is no better way for a goalkeeper to learn his trade than in a bad team, and this in 1943, Celtic undeniably were.

But then suddenly in May something happened. Some nine months previously apropos of the success at El Alamein Winston Churchill had said. 'a bright gleam has lit up the helmets of our soldiers'. Now something similar happened to Celtic supporters who unexpectedly and without warning began to walk about Glasgow with their heads up and their shoulders back, talking animatedly about their team. Those in Africa, the Far East and on ships in the Atlantic were suddenly able to do likewise, for Celtic won the Glasgow Charity Cup.

The soldiers in Tunis in particular had reason to be doubly happy. The Germans (about a quarter of a million on them) were surrendering to the British at places like Cape Bon on the tip of the peninsula, the victory parade was held on 20 May 1943, and back in Scotland on 22 May, Celtic, before a good crowd of 25,000 beat Third Lanark 3–0 to win the Glasgow Charity Cup for the 24th time, a record. It was an indication of what Celtic could have done and could still do, even in the extenuating circumstances of wartime. The triumph in Glasgow was quickly reported to Tunis by the BBC World Service, and a great night was had by the Celtic supporters, some of whom believed with ridiculous optimism that the whole war would soon be over and that they would soon be back home seeing Jimmy Delaney and this young goalkeeper that fathers and sisters kept writing about in letters – Willie Miller.

He was of average height perhaps, had dark hair, a pleasant smile to supporters if he met them on the street, but he was not a man you would have immediately picked out as a Celtic football player. He was of course very proud to be a Celt, and even more so to have won something. He knew that Celtic were a team famed for their magnificent goalkeepers, all of whom lasted a long time. He knew all about Joe Kennaway, Charlie Shaw and of course the tragic John Thomson.

The Celtic success in the Charity Cup was, of course, just a flash in the pan, for the team then subsided pitifully in the Summer Cup, but Miller was entitled to feel that he had had a good season. He had now served his time as an engineer, and clearly in Glasgow at that time, there were vacancies for men of that skill. He was therefore unlikely to be called up, and thus would be able to continue to play for this team that was beginning to mean so much to him. Even at the tender age of 18, he was aware that Celtic supporters, who still turned up in admirable numbers to see a mediocre team deserved something to cheer about, as did the soldiers on leave, the war wounded and even the older men who still appeared at Parkhead bearing the scars of a previous conflict.

Season 1943–44 saw a slight improvement in Celtic's League performances, and there was a rare event for the wartime Celtic. That was a victory over Rangers. This occurred in the Southern League at Ibrox on 11 September, a few days after half-hearted Italy surrendered to the victorious Allied troops who were invariably greeted as heroes by the Italian population who shouted things like, 'tedeschi non buoni' (the Germans are no good) and, 'f*** Mussolini'. Far away from that at Ibrox, Willie Miller inspired Celtic to their rare triumph.

Rangers expecting a re-run of their 8–1 triumph of New Year's Day, threw everything at Celtic and Miller for the first quarter of an hour, but Miller was magnificent, saving fierce drives, tipping balls over the bat and round the post, and revealing a tremendous amount of courage as he dived at the feet of Torry Gillick and Jimmy Duncanson. Such however was the fecklessness of Celtic's attack that they needed an own goal to score the only goal of the match, then spent more or less the rest of the game defending deep!

A new aspect of Miller appeared that day, and that was his leadership qualities. All good goalkeepers need to dominate their penalty areas and tell their defenders where to go and what to do. This, Ronnie Simpson, with all his experience excelled at. Here, Willie Miller, still not yet 19, took a grip of the Celtic defence telling legends like Bobby Hogg and George Paterson where he wanted them to be, who to mark and what to do. To their credit, the experienced veterans did what they were told, and full-time came with Rangers in despair about how they could manage to have so much of the play, and fail to beat the Celtic defence.

The Celtic fans in the 30,000 crowd celebrated disproportionately, as they always did with their scarce victories in these lean times, and the press had no doubt at all who was the architect. *The Glasgow Herald* is very happy to single out Miller on the Monday as Glasgow now began to radiate optimism with the news of Italy's surrender and the headlines about the British soldiers continuing to pour into the 'soft underbelly of Europe', as Mr Churchill described Italy.

The problem was that although Miller could stop most goals, he could not run up to the other end and score them! For example, a game at Tynecastle a couple of weeks later saw Miller once again winning all sorts of plaudits by his performance, but the game finished a 0–0 draw, for Celtic simply could not find a free scoring centre-forward to take advantage of the brilliance of Jimmy Delaney. For a support who had seen Sandy McMahon, Jimmy Quinn and Jimmy McGrory, this was hard to take, but there was little doubt that the Celtic tradition of good goalkeeping as established by men like Dan McArthur, Charlie Shaw and John Thomson was being carried on by the lithe, energetic figure of the young Willie Miller. Once hostilities were over, there seemed little doubt that Miller would show the world just how good he was. It was indeed a shame that so many supporters were unavoidably overseas and were thus unable to see the development of this fine 'keeper.

Celtic's reasonable start continued to be just 'reasonable'. Miserable defeats in the two Glasgow competitions and mediocrity in the Southern League meant that Rangers once again were triumphant. Teams like Morton and Hibs were good, and had the occasional fine performance, but Scotland lacked a sustained challenge from the only club that was likely to put any consistent pressure on Rangers, namely Celtic. Because of that, football was so much the poorer.

Seasons 1944–45 and 1945–46 were much the same. The fall of Rome, D-Day, the Battle of the Bulge, VE Day, the victory of Labour in the General Election and the dropping of the atom bomb in Japan all passed with Celtic irretrievably (apparently) in the doldrums. Press reports about Miller, however, continued to be good. New Year's Day 1945 saw Celtic win 1–0 at Ibrox. The prospects of an early victory in Europe and the visible decline of the menace of the Luftwaffe allowed the authorities to relax the restrictions on attendance, and an astonishing crowd of 70,000 turned up to see the game. George Paterson scored the only goal of the game early in the second half, but the man of the match was once again Willie Miller who time and time again defied the Rangers forwards and even at the end earned a grudging round of applause from the Rangers season ticket holders in the main stand.

Celtic won a Cup of sorts a couple of days after VE Day in May 1945, beating Queen's Park by counting corners at Hampden. It was called the Victory in Europe Cup. Miller once again was praised for his performance by all concerned. It did at least give the supporters something to be happy about, for once again Celtic had broken the hearts of their supporters with all sorts of miserable performances in the League and the Glasgow trophies, as well as the new tournament called the Southern League Cup which would, at the resumption of normal peace time seasons, become the Scottish League Cup.

Miller may also have noted with wry amusement that goalkeeping seemed to be becoming an occupation for the very young, for, at the beginning of June 1945, Queen's Park had fielded a 14-year-old called Ronald Simpson, and there were still people saying that he himself, now almost 21, was still young, and had a lot to learn. Indeed he did, but he had proved a quick learner.

The manager was changed in summer 1945 when Jimmy McStay was replaced by Jimmy McGrory, but any feel good factor quickly evaporated with a poor start to the 1945–46 season and the feeble transfer of Jimmy Delaney to Manchester United in February. The team continued to be mired in mediocrity, and although the servicemen who returned in 1945 and 1946 were less than impressed by the team in general, they soon agreed that in Miller there was something special in the Celtic goal.

Season 1945–46, although the nation was now at peace, was technically another wartime and unofficial Scottish football season. There was still no Scottish Cup – for reasons that are hard to understand, for there was an FA Cup in England – and any Internationals were unofficial ones. At the end of the season there was a Victory Cup to replace the Scottish Cup. The replay of the semi-final against Rangers became notorious when two Celtic players were sent off by a drunken referee, but that tends to obscure the performance of Willie Miller in Celtic's goal in the first game.

James E. Handley who wrote *The Celtic Story* in 1960 was there that day and says; 'For the occasion Miller, the Celtic goalkeeper, donned the mantle of his great predecessor, John Thomson. Repeatedly in the air and on the ground his anticipation was superb and time and time again he repelled shots that he could not have been faulted for missing. In the opening seconds he lifted a ball from the feet of Thornton and thereafter he was invincible. In rapid succession he defied Thornton again, Waddell and Duncanson. Thornton's shot was a rocket that was hurtling to the top left-hand corner of the net. Miller, stationed almost at the opposite post, rose like a bird and touched it over the bar. In his wonderful work, he had the solid support of Hogg, Mallan and McAuley...'

The Glasgow Herald, normally little given to effusive praise of any player says; 'Miller's uncanny anticipation of the flight of the ball, whether in the ground of in the air, had to be seen to be believed... Celtic can thank Miller for earning them a replay'. *The Sunday Post* says that Miller was; 'a 'keeper in a million...a golden Miller', whereas *The Sunday Mail* talks about; 'salmon-like leaps', and 'more thrilling saves seen in 90 minutes since before the New Year', whereas *The Glasgow Observer*, rabidly pro-Celtic, as always, says that Miller was; 'the darling of stand and terracing', adding slightly more improbably; 'and not among Celtic supporters only'.

Sorrow was expressed when the replay, controversial and nasty, saw Rangers win through, for it was felt by everyone that Miller deserved a great deal better than what he was getting in terms of success in a team which was, frankly, poor by any standards, let alone those of Celtic. It was now hoped that with the return of official football for the 1946–47 season, Celtic might begin once again to take life a little more seriously.

Alas! No, the 1946–47 season was another poor one and a major disappointment for all those who had dreamed of a brave new world. It was happening in other respects. The Labour Government of Clement Attlee and Nye Bevan were determined to make a change to working class life – and oh! how the middle classes squealed with their cries of over-taxation, poverty and austerity. In fact, for most people things were a lot better than they had been before the war. But there was no sparkle from Parkhead in spite of huge crowds and eager fans.

The new League Cup tournament was one that Celtic would take a long time to come to terms with. In 1946–47 although they had a couple of good results when the section had more or less been completed, they could not get the better of the emerging Hibs side who would soon be the only team to challenge Rangers. Celtic departed the Scottish Cup at the first time of asking to a good Dundee side at Dens Park, even a late McAloon goal failing to spur the team on to earn a replay, and worst of all was their feeble performance in the Scottish League. They finished 7th, a distant 14 points behind Rangers and below teams like Partick Thistle and Morton. The story is well documented of how on a Wednesday evening in early September 1946, Celtic went down badly 4–1 to Third Lanark at Parkhead. The fans were far from happy and had gathered outside the front door to vent their displeasure and to demand change and the spending of money to buy more players. It is not clear whether Miller was sent out by the craven management to appease the crowd or not, or whether he was simply going home after the game, but in any case, Willie Miller emerged and; 'stilled the storm', saying a few things about how the players were equally upset by the poor results, that work was in progress to build a better team and that the support of the fans was much valued. Such platitudes had the desired effect for while some walked with Miller to 'escort' him to his tram, others simply dispersed to wait for better days. It would be a long wait, however.

Funnily enough the team did not do too badly against Rangers in the two League games – a desperately unlucky 2–3 defeat at Parkhead in September, and a creditable 1–1 draw at Ibrox on New Year's Day 1947, but the season was summed up by what happened the day after. With the support all buoyed up and turning up in large numbers to Parkhead, Celtic collapsed miserably 5–1 to Aberdeen! The best chance of a trophy came at the very end of the season in the Glasgow Charity Cup when they reached the Final against Rangers at Ibrox. On a terrible night with the pitch a quagmire after heavy rain, Rangers won 1–0 in a game that *The Glasgow Herald* says that the highlight was; 'the brilliant goalkeeping of Brown and Miller'. Amazingly the game attracted 40,000 and equally amazingly, at least half that amount were supporting Celtic even in spite of the awful season they had had.

Celtic supporters clutched at straws, but they were hard to find. A young red head called Bobby Evans was impressive, and there could be little doubt that Willie Miller in the goal was the best around, arguably in the opinion of the neutral press, a shade better than his friendly rival, Bobby Brown of Rangers and the two Johnstones of Motherwell and Aberdeen.

The thing about Miller as well was that he was respected and loved by supporters and players of other clubs. He received his fair share of shoulder charging (as all goalkeepers did in those days) but he was never a goalkeeper who would invite a charge by holding on to the ball for too long, or by staring provocatively at a forward when he had the ball in his hands. In one game against Partick Thistle at Firhill in November 1946, a sadly outclassed Celtic team went down 4–1 to a good Thistle team, but Miller, though badly injured and possibly even slightly concussed, stayed on the field to keep the score down, even in an obviously lost cause. At full-time the whole Thistle team converged on him in wonder and awe to congratulate him for his pluck, as one or two of his own teammates helped him off the field. This brave and possibly even foolhardy performance earned him universal praise.

The season was also characterised by the awful winter in February and March, (*The Glasgow Herald*, middle-class to the core, seems to think it was all caused by the Labour Government!) but for Miller there was more than a little compensation in the international recognition that he was given on four occasions. The first was in the very first full international after the war at Wrexham on 19 October 1946. It was not a great occasion for either Miller or Scotland, but the word 'ignominious' used by *The Glasgow Herald* is a bit harsh for a 3–1 defeat. Miller was disappointing. He is not blamed for any of the three goals, but he did on two occasions fumble the ball in the second half, but neither occasion 'proved fatal'. Bobby Brown of Rangers was chosen for the next International against Ireland.

But it was the afternoon of Wednesday 12 March 1947 that was arguably Miller's finest ever performance. This was the League international between the Scottish League and the Football League (or in common Scots parlance, the English League). The game was played in between heavy falls of snow but the pitch was good. In spite of it being a Wednesday afternoon and in the face of Government disapproval (the Government would have preferred everyone to be working!), a crowd of over 84,000 turned up at Hampden to see the game. Many more were disappointed that the game was not even on the radio, and they were therefore dependent on evening papers or the 6 o'clock news on the Scottish Home Service.

The English League won 3–1 with Stanley Matthews proving why he was called, 'the wizard of the dribble' in a classic display. Raich Carter lately of Sunderland but now Derby County and Wilf Mannion of Middlesbrough were also at their peak, and the England side was at least as good as the one which would win the World Cup twenty years later. Indeed they were probably better. But *The Glasgow Herald* says that Miller was outstanding. 'There was one Scot, however, who earned the highest possible praise. Miller gave a magnificent performance. In addition to performing the normal goalkeeping duties, he three times risked himself by diving headlong at an opponent's feet to save certain goals. Each time he was injured and on the last occasion had to be assisted from the field. Fortunately he was able to return after five minutes absence, during which time Husband kept goal, and for all the splendour of Matthews the biggest cheer of the afternoon was reserved for the gallant Celtic 'keeper'.

The last sentence is significant. It was often felt by those of the Celtic paranoia persuasion that Scotland crowds were 80% pro-Rangers and did not take kindly to Celtic players in the team, particularly if he were, as here, taking the place of a strong Rangers candidate in Bobby Brown. This claim was not entirely without foundation, one feels from time to time, but clearly it was not universally true and certainly not so on this occasion. Good football has always been more important to the Scottish fan than narrow sectarian considerations, and this was clearly a piece of excellent goalkeeping. He was a curious sight as well as he walked off with his head, 'wrapped in a bandage that looked like an Indian turban'.

125

The late Bob Crampsey, a man with unsurpassed knowledge of football, was even more extravagant in his praises of Willie Miller than *The Glasgow Herald* on this occasion. In an essay on goalkeeping written in 1963, he said that the best display of goalkeeping and certainly the most courageous was this game. 'The Scottish side was very weak, and it was confidently expected we would be thrashed; that we weren't was due entirely to Willie Miller. Time and time again the white shirts sliced through the Scottish defence; time and time again Miller hurled himself at their feet with reckless gallantry. Eventually and inevitably he

went down and didn't get up; he was taken off, had stitches put in his forehead, and returned – not to go on the wing, but back into goal where his first act was to dive headlong at the feet of Westcott of Wolves the English centre who was clean through. We lost 3–1, but the Hampden stand knew enough about courage to rise to the bandaged Miller at the end as he came wearily off'.

Following this game, Miller was a certainty for the goalkeeper's spot in the full Scotland team to play at Wembley on 12 April. He thus became the first Celtic goalkeeper ever to play at the famous stadium, and he didn't let Scotland down. It was difficult for Scottish fans to be optimistic about their country, but they attended in great numbers, about 30,000 according to some accounts (giving a lie to all the talk about poverty and austerity, incidentally) and left with their heads held high after a creditable 1–1 draw.

Miller had no chance with the goal scored, and on one occasion had a save that had the radio commentators and all of Wembley, not to mention Raich Carter himself amazed and astounded. Carter looked offside as he ran in on goal, and the Scottish defence stood still expecting the flag. No flag came and Carter fired from eight yards fully expecting to see the net bulge and the crowd erupt. But Miller had not stopped to appeal for offside and leaped acrobatically to turn the ball past the post.

The country needed something to cheer them up, and that game did the trick. Prime Minister Clement Attlee, a hero naturally to men like Willie Miller, was introduced to the teams before the game. He was an insignificant little man who frequently was not recognised on the London tube trains, even by those who had voted for him! He smoked a pipe and loved cricket, although with a fondness for all other sports as well. Well known for his laconic style of speaking, and although an Englishman, he was particularly keen not to upset the millions of Labour voters in Scotland, so when asked on the radio what he thought of the game, Clem said, 'Both teams played well'.

Miller also played another game for the Scottish League that season, a 7–4 win over the Irish League in Belfast at the end of April. Losing four goals does not make one think that he had a great game, but as the team won, no-one really cared and Miller was chosen for the tour of Belgium and Luxemburg with the full side in May. He was even touted by some people for a place in the famous game of Great Britain versus Rest of Europe, but it was Frank Swift of England who was given the nod. But the European tour would give him a great deal of compensation. It cannot be underestimated just how big a thing foreign travel was in 1947, particularly when the particular part of Europe he was going to had until very recently been a warzone and had been under occupation. The young Miller still only 22, may well have been overwhelmed by the experience. He did not have his best game against Belgium at the Heysel Stadium as Scotland went down 1–2 – he allowed the second goal to pass under his body but that must be balanced against the many other fine saves that he had – but the game against Luxemburg was a 6–0 win for Scotland and one of the quietest games he had had for a long time.

Miller was happy in 1947. His team were not doing well – nor was there any sign that that was going to change in the foreseeable future – but his form was good, and he retained his popularity with the fans who needed a hero. An unfortunate clash with a Dundee forward at Dens Park early in the 1947–48 season saw him carried off. As a direct result, Celtic lost 4–1 and exited the League Cup. He recovered fairly quickly for the rest of the season, however, and his hero status stayed for a while because he was picked for the two Scotland Internationals in autumn 1947 – two defeats to Ireland and Wales and for all three League Internationals that season – two victories over both Irelands and a creditable 1–1 draw at Newcastle against the English League. Miller had played well in that game, which England might have won if they had taken their chances or been able to beat the inspired Willie Miller.

But for some reason (perhaps, 'his form in recent weeks has not been all that convincing', as *The Scotsman* put it) Miller was not chosen to play at Hampden against England in April 1948, his place going to Ian Black of Southampton, a choice that did not meet with universal approval particularly as Scotland lost 2–0, and Black's habit of punching the ball out rather than clutching it frequently got

Scotland into trouble. Black was dropped for the next game, his place going to the excellent Jimmy Cowan of Morton, and Miller never again played for Scotland.

Celtic had not had a great spring in 1948 – in fact for the whole season they had been inconsistent at best and downright poor at worst, and slowly the realisation dawned on Scottish football that the unthinkable might happen and that Celtic might even be relegated. Yet they had had a good Scottish Cup run, having lost to Morton only in extra-time in the semi-final. However they approached their last League game at Dens Park on 17 April, knowing that a defeat might put them in great danger of relegation depending on how other teams fared.

Yet those who relished that prospect, and gloated in the possibility that Celtic might be in next season's Division B were more than a little out of touch with reality. Celtic, contrary to what the paranoid supporters might think, were actually not unpopular with the rest of the teams in Scotland who appreciated the huge crowds that travelled all over Scotland to watch them. James E. Handley in *The Celtic Story* gives the erroneous impression that all of Scotland were wishing Dundee to win, and even Gerry McNee who ghostwrites for Jimmy McGrory in *A Lifetime in Paradise* repeats the myth that Dundee were on a huge bonus if they managed to sink Celtic, claiming improbably that McGrory was told this at a funeral! Leaks however from the Dundee dressing room a few years after the game told a totally different story. In fact, even if Dundee had won, relegation would not have been guaranteed for Celtic. It would have depended on the performances of other clubs in the relegation zone, and in any case, the whole game was a bogey, for Dundee wanted Celtic to win.

A rat was smelt in certain quarters when Bobby Ancell, Dundee's left back and an honourable man, was not playing. Clearly he wanted no part in the charade, and another Dundee player admitted in later life, that if he had had to, he would have scored an own goal. Nevertheless Miller and all the Celtic players were not necessarily aware of all this, and must have travelled to Dundee on that day in a considerable state of apprehension. In any case, the problem with any attempt to 'fix' a match is that, it cannot be guaranteed to work.

Celtic, one could argue, saved themselves in any case by playing Bobby Evans at right-half, having deployed him ineffectively all season in the forward line, and by Jocky Weir finding some belated good form and scoring three goals, the last one of which, after some suspicious weakness in the Dundee defence, saw an eruption of Celtic joy that had not been seen for a decade. Miller, who had turned down the chance to go full-time earlier this season, was relieved if not actually delighted by this turn of events. Had Celtic been relegated, Miller might well have considered offers to go elsewhere. Certainly quite a few English teams had been very impressed with him.

But he stayed with Celtic in Glasgow. It was indeed a funny time in world history. A casual glance at newspapers of the time (particularly the right-wing ones) will give the impression that the British people were suffering from dreadful poverty, deprivation and repression by a Government that imposed so many restrictions on them. Not only that, but the world was on the verge of another even more dreadful war with the Russians poised to invade Western Europe. In fact, the opposite was the case. The Russians continually rattled sabres about Berlin, but emphatically did not invade, and the lot of the working people in Great Britain, although constrained to a certain extent by rationing, in fact was steadily improving. The National Health Service was launched in summer 1948, and suddenly children became healthier. Unemployment virtually disappeared, and a start was made to knock down the evil slums where disease and illness flourished.

Season 1948–49 saw a bright start for Celtic with the promise that the tide had been turned, but sadly it did not last. Celtic had signed an Irishman called Charlie Tully for £10,000 from the now doomed Belfast Celtic, and he looked a talented player. Proof that he really was something special came on 25 September when Celtic beat Rangers 3–1 in a League Cup game at Parkhead which prompted the refrain; 'Boden, Paton, Weir and Tully – The men who ran the Rangers sully', sully being the Scottish way of saying 'silly', and it rhymed with Tully! Yet Rangers had scored first, when Miller made one of his rare mistakes early in the game by dropping a ball for Findlay to stab home.

He rallied immediately after that though, having a great game as he repelled more Rangers attacks, and by half-time, Celtic were ahead and finished the job in the second half. But that glorious day was then capped by the winning of the Glasgow Cup on the Monday. Before a crowd of over 87,000 (it was a Monday Holiday, but even so, that was an astonishing crowd for the Glasgow Cup) Miller defied the strong autumnal sun, the capricious breeze and the talented Third Lanark forward line, which included man like Jimmy Mason and Bobby Mitchell, for long periods. One particular piece of acrobatics amazed all the Press. Jimmy Mallan, Celtic's left-back, was attempting to clear when the ball rebounded off a Third Lanark forward and was heading to the goal over Miller's head until he leaped backwards and tipped the ball over the bar.

The Celtic End at Hampden simply erupted at such brilliance, but the joy was even greater when Willie Gallacher (son of the famous Patsy) scored once and Jocky Weir twice to win the game for Celtic. When referee Mr Livingstone signalled full-time to indicate that Celtic had won their first trophy since the Charity Cup final of 1943, the stadium was rocked by the delirium and relief that Celtic could actually win something. Celtic fans had, of course, a new darling in Charlie Tully, but he had to share the honours with goalkeeper Willie Miller who had had two fabulous saves in addition to the one already described. Bobby Mitchell, who would later go on to become a hero at Newcastle United, said that he had never faced a better goalkeeper than Willie Miller on that day. A couple of days later on Wednesday 29 September, Miller was at Ibrox playing for the Scottish League against the League of Ireland in a rather one-sided 5–1 win for Scotland. Thus in the space of five days, had Miller been involved in three victories at each of the three large Glasgow grounds!

The Monday night was one of the few occasions in that era that there was any singing and dancing in the Celtic heartlands of the Gorbals and Garngad. Such was the fanaticism of the support in that era, but it was a false dawn. Celtic then collapsed in the League Cup, conceding five goals to Clyde and four to Hibs before losing to Rangers at Ibrox on the day of Rangers' famous publicity stunt when they invited no less a person that Eamon de Valera, hero of the 1916 rebellion and in some ways the father of modern Ireland, to Ibrox to see them defeat Celtic. Celtic then more or less disappeared for the rest of the season, collapsing in the League (although this year avoiding the humiliation of being listed among the potential relegation candidates) and exiting the Scottish Cup to the incredulous Division 'B' side Dundee United at the then primitive Tannadice Park.

Miller did however on 6 November 1948 win another Scottish League cap on a victorious but painful occasion in Belfast against the Irish League. He won great praise for his many dives at the feet of the Irish forwards and on one occasion sustained a very bad injury to his rib cage. It did not seem to be all that bad at the end of the game, but the pain intensified on the boat home, and Miller had to go to Glasgow's Royal Infirmary for an X-Ray on his return. Nothing was broken but the pain was such that he then missed a game for Celtic and the full international against Ireland at Hampden on 17 November.

Things began to go badly for Miller after the whole team had a real shocker in a 4–0 defeat at the hands of Rangers at Ibrox on New Year's Day 1949. Worse than that for Miller was the emergence of a genuine threat to Miller's place at Parkhead. This came in the shape of Johnny Bonnar whom the club had signed from Arbroath in August 1948 and who was given a few games in the first team towards the end of the season. This came after Miller had a dreadful game in an encounter against Hibs at Parkhead, misjudging the easiest of shots, a miskick from Gordon Smith, and then looking as if he might have done better with the next Hibs goal as well. On such occasions, Parkhead would lapse into an introverted silence. There was no booing or catcalling as would happen with other unfortunate Celtic goalkeepers, for Miller remained a hero.

130

Yet as a result of these unfortunate lapses, Miller was given a rest, and although he was brought back before the end of the season, Miller's Celtic career was now very much on the slippery slope. In the very last game of the season – an unlucky defeat to Partick Thistle in the Glasgow Charity Cup final – *The Glasgow Herald* says that' 'Miller, his confidence restored, is now once again a very fine goalkeeper', but that was one of the few pieces of praise that we find about him at this time.

His decline was somewhat masked by other more extraordinary evens which took place in the autumn of 1949. These events are well described in Tom Campbell's *Celtic's Paranoia...All In The Mind?* They involved some scarcely believable happenings, which included a blatant kick in the stomach of Charlie Tully by a Rangers player, and a boycott by Celtic supporters of another Rangers versus Celtic game. Miller was still in the Celtic goal for these games, but failed to win a cap for any of the Scottish representative games that autumn.

Celtic had allowed themselves to be affected by these awful events and, although there was the occasional good performance when people like Charlie Tully, John McPhail and Bobby Collins were on song, by the turn of the year the team in general were still failing to raise their game to what was required with Miller in particular looking badly at fault for some at least of the goals conceded to East Fife in the middle of December. All this time he had been under pressure from Johnny Bonnar who was consistently earning good reviews in the reserve team, and Celtic had even gone to the length of signing yet another goalkeeper in George 'Sonny' Hunter a few days before Christmas.

It was Hogmanay 1949 however, which saw his last Celtic game. He was injured, but his removal from the first team might have been coming anyway. It was a 4–2 defeat before a crowd of over 44,000 at Tynecastle. Miller (and Celtic) had a poor game, but Miller also hurt his hand in a goalmouth scramble, apparently his hand having been stood on by a Hearts forward, and this ruled him out of the next game, which was the New Year's Day game against Rangers at Parkhead. John Bonnar took his chance and played well in an honourable 1–1 draw so that even when Miller recovered, Bonnar retained his place.

Many supporters were distressed to hear of Miller's transfer to Clyde on the eve of the 1950–51 season, with Miller apparently much moved by the letters of support that he received from Celtic fans at his departure. We now fast forward the action to 28 April 1951 to a happy Celtic Park for the last game of the League season. The Celtic fans, about 40,000 of them were all cheerful, for the week before Celtic had won the Scottish Cup, their first major national honour since 1938, and songs of triumph were in the air. But they also were welcoming back two old Celts.

The first was the grand old man of Celtic, Willie Maley, 'the man who made Celtic' who had celebrated his 83rd birthday a few days previously and who had now settled the feud that he had had with the club over the past decade. He was given a huge ovation as he took his seat in the stand. The Scottish Cup draped in green and white ribbons was then brought out to another great ovation, but it was a sign of the affection in which Willie Miller was still held by the Celtic faithful that the ovation given to him when Clyde ran out was no less than that given to Maley and the Scottish Cup! Miller was visibly affected by the extent of his welcome.

The game itself was a poignant and indeed important one as well. It mattered little to Celtic but it was far from an end of season friendly for Clyde. They had to win to avoid relegation. Frankly Clyde had a very poor side, and with Celtic on the crest of a wave, they should have been hammered. That they weren't was due to two things. One was an understandable reluctance of Celtic to kill off their East End friends and neighbours, and the other was the outstanding performance of Willie Miller who defied John McPhail and Jock Weir time and time again, until late in the game Bobby Collins managed to get one past him. The reaction of the fans was a strange one. There was of course a cheer for their team scoring, but many of them were also distressed at Miller losing a goal after having defied them for so long. Miller's distress was doubled when he trooped off the field to discover that Morton, Airdrie, Third Lanark and St Mirren had all won, and that Clyde were, as a result, relegated.

It was therefore a sad return to the ground that he had grown to love, but Willie played on for Clyde for about four years. He had one good season for them in 1951–52 as they won the Scottish League Division 'B', the Glasgow Cup and a share in the Glasgow Charity Cup. The Glasgow Cup campaign was remarkable, for not only did Clyde, managed by ex-Celt Paddy Travers (whom many thought should have had the Celtic job before McGrory) beat Rangers on the way to the Final, they also managed to beat Celtic in the Final on Monday 24 September 1951 at Hampden before a large crowd of 70,000. Miller was deceived by the goal scored by Sean Fallon, but made up for it with some remarkable saves as Celtic piled on the pressure trying to equalize after Clyde had scored twice. At one point he was injured and had to leave the field with a head knock and returned with his head covered in bandages. As a footnote, incidentally, Clyde arrived for this game in a Celtic Supporters Bus after their own transport had failed to turn up!

After leaving Clyde he played for Stirling Albion for a spell before joining Hibs as a cover goalkeeper in 1954 until he eventually retired in 1956. He was still only 32, not old for a goalkeeper to retire, but then again retirement did not mean as much to Willie as it would have for other players, for he never was a full-time football player. He worked as an engineer then ran a tobacco shop and also at one point was the licensee of a public house in McAslin Street which he called 'Willie Miller's Bar'. It was often said that the reason why he was such a good goalkeeper was because he never had football as a full-time career. He was of course a professional, but a part-time one. During the war, there was no such thing as a full-time footballer, and quite a number of wartime players decided to keep it that way when peace came. It was of course an era of full employment, so a player could quite easily work in his daytime job, train in the evening and turn out for his club on Saturday afternoon.

He was therefore under no constant pressure to perform. He could afford to take risks. The same argument used to be used about County Cricketers in that the amateurs could afford to be cavalier and take risks as distinct from professionals who had to be aware of the source of his livelihood and not do anything that would jeopardise his career. So, in football, part-timers could be more reckless and enjoy themselves more.

Courage was something that he never lacked. Many are the reports of him diving at someone's feet, and many were the occasions when he was injured, and really should have stayed off the field, but insisted, against the advice of the trainer, to return, his head often swathed in bandages. There were of course no substitutes in his time, not even for an injured goalkeeper, and if he had stayed off the field, another player would have had to don the goalkeeper's jersey, usually (but not invariably) in the 1940s, a thick yellow polo neck.

It would have to be owned that he did concede a fair amount of goals. But this is

due not so much to his attitude but more to do with the undeniable hard fact that Celtic throughout his career from 1942 until 1949 had a very poor team with neither forwards not defenders anything like as good as 'the Celts of old', whom Maley and older supporters kept talking about. Indeed Celtic's near relegation of 1948 was proof of this. Their 'rescue' was maybe nothing to do with famous match at Dundee (whether it was fixed or not) as the performances of Willie Miller throughout the season. On at least four occasions, an outplayed Celtic side managed to get a draw against

133

a superior side through the excellence of Willie Miller. An outstanding example of this was in December at Easter Road when the great Hibs side (who would win the League that year) poured everything down the slope towards Willie Miller but could only get a draw.

He retained fond memories of his football career and would talk happily to anyone about his time at Celtic, but he was never the sort of man who pushed himself forward to boast about what he had achieved. He was a quiet, modest, retiring sort of man, and that was one of the reasons why he was loved so much by those (not all of them Celtic supporters) who remembered him play. He died on 23 June 2005 at the age of 80. It would have been nice to see an encomium written about him which could have mentioned something about Scottish Cup Finals or League championships won by Miller. He had his fine moments for Scotland, but for Celtic, he just had the misfortune to have come at the wrong time. Yet he brightened up those dark, grim days for Celtic fans.

CAREER:

Appearances: 265
Glasgow Cup medals: 1
Glasgow Charity Cup medals: 1
Scotland Caps: 6
Scottish League Caps: 7
Shut Outs: 74

RONNIE SIMPSON
(1942–50)

by David Potter

The publisher, Thomas Campbell, looked across the desk at the earnest young author. His pleasant, round face smiled tolerantly, as he adjusted his glasses. His desk was covered in manuscripts, designs for new books, letters from lawyers and the picture of his two children.

'Well, I think you have talent, and it's certainly a good story, but I'm afraid it has to be anchored in reality…at least to a certain extent.'

'How do you mean, Mr Campbell' stammered James Robbie, a nervous looking youth, full of idealism but with a reputation among his friends for being a bit of a 'geek' or an 'anorak' with all his knowledge of football facts. He was personable and pleasant, and flattered even that a publishing firm had taken the trouble to read his manuscript and to invite him to talk to them.

'Well, look James, I like the idea of his dad playing for Rangers and him playing for Celtic. Yes, that's good! But it's the other things. Starting off as the youngest ever player in Scottish football at the end of the Second World War, and then becoming one of the oldest Internationalists over 20 years later – well, that is the stuff of Boy's Own, *I'm afraid – and then the other things that you add in. Playing for Great Britain in the 1948 Olympic Games! Then he turns professional and goes down to play for Newcastle alongside Milburn and Mitchell and wins two English Cup medals – yes, that's good and I like your descriptions of Wembley and bringing the Cup home to Newcastle, having been presented with his medal by Winston Churchill and the Queen – but then you have him returning to Scotland to play for Hibs whom he saves from relegation in 1963. OK, then he falls out with his manager and is put out to graze because he wants to go part-time, then he is sold to Celtic for a minimal price as a cover for injuries.*

'So far, this is all possible – a bit unlikely maybe – but then that same manager whom he fell out with at Hibs becomes Celtic's manager, and then puts him in the first team when he expected a free transfer. The team then begins to prosper after a long period of under-achievement – wins everything in Scotland and even the European Cup (some hope!) and your goalkeeper suddenly finds himself playing for Scotland in the team that beats England for the first time since they won the World Cup!

'It gets worse and worse, James. He is laid out by a missile in South America (well, that could happen down there, I agree) but continues playing, winning League Championships before a couple of shoulder injuries put him out of the game but not before Celtic made him captain for the day of his birthday and the crowd sing "Happy Birthday" to him! On his 39th birthday! Come on, James!

'His post-football career is OK. Manager of Hamilton Accies for a spell, goalkeeper coach with Dunfermline, the Scottish representative on the Pools Panel – yes, all that I can accept – and the opening of a sports shop in Edinburgh, but what I really have to draw the line at is when he becomes a City Councillor in Edinburgh, FOR THE TORIES! Come on, James, you can't really expect anyone to believe that, can you? I mean how can you play for Newcastle and Celtic and vote Conservative! When he dies, you have the Corstorphine Road in Edinburgh coming to a standstill for his funeral. James, that's the main road to Glasgow!

'Mind you, James, I like your style of writing, and I'm sure you have it in you to write a good story, but stick to facts, or if you must write fiction, keep your feet on the ground. Actually, I enjoyed the read and I would advise you to keep trying – but sadly, I cannot believe in your goalkeeper – what's his name? – Robert Samson, or something like that? Try writing about a real player – what about Bobby Murdoch or Jimmy Johnstone, perhaps? Keep in touch, James. I'm sure we'll be able to publish something from you some day!'

Ronald Campbell Simpson was born in October 1930. He could hardly have been said to have been a Celt by birth or even by inclination, for his father was no less a man than Jimmy Simpson, then centre-half of Rangers. He was part of the great Ibrox half-back line of Meiklejohn, Simpson and Brown in a phenomenally successful era of Rangers' success. He won five Scottish League winners medals, and four Scottish Cup winners medals as well as playing 14 times for Scotland. He was a 'robust' centre-half in the Ibrox tradition, but he could play the game as well, and certainly understood it. His tussles with Jimmy McGrory were much looked forward to and argued about by the fans of both sides.

It was June 1945 when young Ronnie made his debut. It was a strange time. The war (or at least the European War) had been over for about a month but most servicemen, including Jimmy Simpson, were still in the services awaiting demobilisation and perhaps fearing that they might yet be deployed in serious action against the Japanese in the Far East, or even the supposed Allies of the Soviet Union. Ronnie attended King's Park Secondary School in Glasgow and on a Wednesday in late May had the honour of playing in the goal for his school at Hampden in the Glasgow Schools Final against St Mungo's Academy.

He clearly impressed the watching Queen's Park committeemen. A couple of days later they approached Ronnie's Headmaster, Mr Hodge, about playing him in the goal for them at Hampden in the Summer Cup. Queen's Park's regular goalkeeper Bobby Brown was unavailable, for he was still in the Royal Navy. The circumstances of the time made it difficult to get anyone else, so Ronnie was invited. Thus Jimmy Simpson came home for the weekend that Friday night to discover that his son Ronnie was playing for Queen's Park against Clyde on the Saturday afternoon – but he was also playing for his school team in the morning! On Saturday 3 June 1945, Ronnie Simpson became, as far as can be ascertained, Scottish senior football's youngest ever player.

He played well and the team won and he would now play for Queen's Park for some time. His father was naturally very proud of him, but apparently insisted to newspapermen that; 'they should not lay it on too thick'. Ronald continued to play amateur football for Queen's Park for a few years while working as a clerk after he had left school. He was small but very lithe and agile, and had a good reading of the game so that he could anticipate where there would be trouble.

His first big opportunity to attract headlines came in 1948 when the Olympic Games were held in London. These Olympics became known as the 'austerity games' because of the financial circumstances in triumphant but impoverished London. The Olympics were, of course, strictly amateur and Ronnie was chosen for the squad along with several other Queen's Park players. The team were managed by Matt Busby, then the young Manager of Manchester United whose team had just won the English Cup that year. Great Britain finished fourth. Simpson played in two of the four games, beating Holland 4–3 in one of the sectional games, and then losing 5–3 to Denmark in the third-place Final on a miserable wet night at Wembley. Simpson thus narrowly missed a bronze medal.

Shortly after that, Ronnie was called up for his National Service. Every young man (unless he had a very good excuse) had to serve two years in the Army in the 1940s and 1950s, such was the (groundless but nevertheless widespread and almost hysterical) fear of the Soviet Union or the even more absurd possibility of Germany having a third go at world domination. Cynics saw this as a way of keeping the unemployment figures down, and many were surprised that the Labour Government did not put a stop to it. National Service would last until 1961. Ronnie was based at Catterick in Yorkshire for the best part of two years until 1950. It was not necessarily a desperately unhappy time, for footballers tended to be preferentially treated and he played often for the various Army teams and he was often allowed home at weekends to play for Queen's Park.

But in summer 1950 when he was demobbed, he decided that the time had come for him to try his hand at professional football. He did not travel far from Queen's Park, moving a couple of hundred yards to Third Lanark. Even by 1950, Thirds had seen better days but they still were a strong force in Scottish football and it would not be until the 1960s that the rot of corruption would set in. They would finally go to the wall in 1967, ironically at the very time that another Glasgow team were the champions of Europe! Ronnie clearly played well for his local professional side – for he still stayed near the ground – and attracted the attention of quite a few sides, including Rangers.

Ronnie himself tells a story of how as early as October 1947, Rangers had tried to lure him to Ibrox by offering his father Jimmy a job if he could use his influence to persuade his son to come too! Jimmy felt that Ronnie was too young, and perhaps in any case, an intelligent man, he was beginning to despise the narrow sectarianism of the tyrannical Struth. The offer of the job was in any case withdrawn when Jimmy told Struth that his son would make up his own mind!

Rangers may have tried again for Ronnie when he started to star for Third Lanark, but it was Newcastle United who persuaded him to join them in February 1951. In some ways it seemed a strange decision for Ronnie to make, for Newcastle made it plain that he could not be guaranteed a first team place because they already had an excellent goalkeeper in Jackie Fairbrother. On the other hand, Newcastle were clearly an ambitious side and were traditionally built on Scotsmen. Indeed they had several Scotsmen with them at the time and one ex-Third Lanark man in particular, the pale-faced Bobby Mitchell, generally reckoned to be one of the best left-wingers in the business.

Newcastle attracted astonishing crowds in the late 1940s and early 1950s in a city where football always has been an obsession. The performances on the field tended to be a little disappointing, but that in no way diminished the enthusiasm of the fans. When Simpson joined the Geordies in February 1951, they were in the middle of an FA Cup run which would end in success.

The young Simpson played no direct part in all this but was there with the official party as reserve goalkeeper at Wembley on that day of 28 April 1951 when Newcastle won their fourth FA Cup. They beat Blackpool 2–0, both goals scored by the McGrory of Tyneside, Jackie Milburn. Fairbrother had an excellent game in goal and Ronnie was delighted for the man with whom he had struck up a friendship. This would be a theme of Ronnie's life at Parkhead as well, when he and his rival John Fallon were the best of friends. Goalkeepers, he would often stay, must stick together.

Ronnie settled well in Newcastle in lodgings. He would always love the city, which was, of course, in the 1950s a bustling centre of industry with full employment as the country began to recover from the war. He was fascinated by the passion of the fans, the huge crowds and the great rivalry with Sunderland. Very soon opportunity came his way when Fairbrother was injured in a game at Old Trafford, and Ronnie was given his chance in the 1951–52 season and took it. The Newcastle crowd took a while to warm to him, not because he was Scottish, which would hardly have been a problem given the amount of Scotsmen in the team in any case, but because he was small and slender, and did make the occasional mistake. In addition the form of the team was not very good either, including a 3–0 defeat by Charlton Athletic at the Valley, something that did little to dispel the popularly held view that the Magpies never do well in London. Very soon it was apparent that those who hoped for a League challenge to follow last year's Cup success were going to be disappointed.

There was, however, still the 1952 FA Cup in which Simpson played in every Round. They did not have the easiest of passages and had to beat teams like Aston Villa and Tottenham Hotspur. Blackburn Rovers took them to a replay in the semi-final at Hillsborough and Newcastle needed a Bobby Mitchell penalty kick in the replay at Elland Road to take them back to Wembley for the Final against Arsenal. It was not generally regarded as the best of the FA Cup Finals as Newcastle beat 10-man Arsenal (Wally Barnes was carried off injured) 1–0. The day was dull and enlivened only by Bobby Mitchell's cross for Chilean George Robledo to head home the only goal of the game.

Simpson however had a good game dealing competently with everything that Arsenal could hurl at him, and at full-time he was presented with his medal by Prime Minister Winston Churchill. King George VI had died in February and for some reason it was not felt appropriate to ask his daughter the new (as yet uncrowned) Queen Elizabeth to do the job. It mattered not, for it was a great day for Ronnie Simpson, watched by his proud father, as the Geordies became the first team in the twentieth century to win the FA Cup for two years in a row.

Ronnie stayed as Newcastle's first team goalkeeper for some time after that and had another great day in 1955 when Newcastle won the FA Cup yet again, for the third time in five years. Sadly they have not won the trophy since that day on 7

The young Ronnie is on the extreme right of this picture of Newcastle United with the FA Cup of 1952. The great Jackie Milburn has also taken his shirt off.

May 1955 when Jackie Milburn scored early on with a header, and Newcastle beat a strong Manchester City side 3–1 to lift the trophy.

It had been far from an easy task to reach the Final, with seemingly smaller sides causing some difficulty – a melancholy tradition that lasts until this day at St James Park, with the difference that in 1955 Newcastle eventually emerged victorious. The campaign opened with a long trip to Plymouth and a narrow 1–0 win, then Brentford were disposed of. Nottingham Forest then took three games before Newcastle eventually won through. The Geordies then needed two games against Huddersfield before defeating them. Then there were another two games against York City in the semi-final.

The final itself was probably Newcastle's best game of the campaign, although as in 1952, they were helped by an injury to an opponent, this time Jimmy Meadows and thus Manchester City were obliged to play with 10 men in those pre-substitute days. But Ronnie had a sound game and thoroughly deserved the adulation of the Geordie fans as they returned to Newcastle.

It was often felt, certainly on Tyneside that a Scotland cap might not have been out of the question for Ronnie. But all he achieved were two games for the Scotland 'B' side. Yet he played so consistently well, even after 1955 when the team began to slide, losing in the FA Cup to teams like Scunthorpe and Millwall, and failing through inconsistency to make any real impact on the English League. Vociferous criticism abounded in Newcastle of the team's performances, but usually the 'wee Scotsman' in the goal (he wasn't really all that 'wee' at 5ft 10in – but that is considered small for a goalkeeper) was exempt, for on many occasions he stood between the Magpies and defeat.

1958 on a tour of Romania saw Simpson sustain a serious and career-threatening injury, which he called the 'flaking of the bone' in his leg. His book *Sure It's a Grand Old Team to Play For* gives a horrendous account of the treatment, and it means that he missed entirely season 1958–59, and played only a few games after that in season 1959–60, for he had lost his place to the worthy Bryan Harvey.

Season 1960–61 dawned without any sign of him getting his place back, yet he was now totally fit and too good a man to languish in the reserves. In October a chance came for a return to Scotland when Hugh Shaw of Hibs offered him the opportunity. It was a wrench to leave Tyneside where his wife and family were happy and settled in the west of the city, but first team football was a great attraction, and he moved to Edinburgh, even though his family still lived in Newcastle for a spell and at one point he drove every day from Newcastle to Easter Road for training!

The early 1960s were turbulent times for Hibs. As with Newcastle, their glory days of the early 1950s had clearly passed, and although they had Joe Baker and competed sometimes spectacularly in Europe, they were failing to make any real impact on the competitions in Scotland, as other teams like Dunfermline and Dundee now rose to challenge Rangers, Hearts and that team with the huge potential but little current success, Celtic.

One of Simpson's early games was against Celtic in a Scottish Cup quarter-final in March 1961 when Hibs scored first and were holding on with only minutes to go before Steve Chalmers equalized, and then in the replay at Easter Road, John Clark scored a late winner to the devastation of Simpson. He also played in a few European roughhouses where his calm demeanour helped smooth a few things over, notably in an Inter Cities Fairs Cup semi-final against AS Roma.

But his greatest contribution to Hibs came in season 1962–63 when his goalkeeping managed to save Hibs from relegation. It was of course the season of the big freeze-up from January to March, and when the season resumed with a big fixture pile-up, Hibs began to slide inexorably towards the bottom of the table, with all sorts of protests being seen at Easter Road including an incredible one when the ball landed in the high terracing, and a supporter with a white raincoat picked it up, ran up to the top of the terracing and threw it out of the ground! However, that did little for the cause and the month of April saw the Hibees sink deeper and deeper into the mire towards the unthinkable with clear signs of the Directors becoming more and more desperate. They were too big a team to go down!

A key game came on 11 May when Hibs, in front of a paltry crowd of less than 5,000, eventually beat St Mirren 2–1 to stave off what would have been definite relegation that day. Simpson lost an early goal, but then saved about four or five certain goals before Hibs eventually got two unconvincing goals at the other end. Simpson's performance seemed to turn the tide for Hibs because on the Wednesday night (ironically the same night as the infamous Hampden walkout when 50,000 Celtic fans, almost with one accord abandoned the Scottish Cup Final in protest at a feckless performance by their team) Hibs travelled to Queen of the South and won 4–0. Then in a surreal atmosphere in Kirkcaldy with Raith Rovers already relegated and less than 1,000 present (more or less all of them from Edinburgh), Hibs again won 4–0 to make sure that Clyde, rather than Hibs, joined Raith Rovers in the lower Division.

This was a great achievement for Simpson, but saving a club from relegation is a hollow triumph. Next season, Simpson lost his place to Billy Wilson in goal and it began to look as if his career was over, particularly when on 1 April 1964, Jock Stein arrived at Easter Road as Manager. The two men seemed to have had some sort of disagreement about whether Ronnie could play on a part-time basis, but perhaps surprisingly, Simpson was kept at Easter Road over the summer. His career was going nowhere, however, under Stein's business-like but stern and authoritarian regime, and it was only a matter of time before he signed for some minor club – Berwick Rangers had already shown some interest – but then one day in early September, Sean Fallon from Celtic, needing cover for John Fallon now that Frank Haffey had gone to Australia, phoned his old friend Jock Stein and enquired about Ronnie Simpson. The fee agreed was a paltry £4,000, even in 1964 not very much for a professional football player.

This was indeed a pleasant surprise for Ronnie, but it must also have come as a shock, not least because of his father's connections with Rangers. His father Jimmy was very supportive, however, thinking that this interlude could last no more than a season, for Ronnie was surely going to Parkhead only to cover for injuries. Jimmy Simpson owned a pub in Govan and one imagines might have had to field a few difficult questions about his son! Ronnie duly signed for Celtic and found himself at Parkhead on 5 September 1964 in pouring rain watching Celtic, for the first time in several seasons, beat Rangers. The score was 3–1, but Simpson noted that John Fallon had an excellent game in the Celtic goal. He would not be very easily displaced, Ronnie didn't think.

In view of what happened later on in that season, a few people with the misleading benefit of hindsight claim that Stein deliberately sold Simpson so that a great goalkeeper would be in place when he (Stein) arrived in March 1965. It is a nice idea, but sadly the facts do not back it up, for Stein, at that stage, could not possibly have known what was about to unfold. In any case, Ronnie's career was slowly floundering in September 1964, and all the evidence points to the idea that Simpson, now nearly 34, was at Celtic Park for no reason other than as a short-term cover for injuries, until such time as he found a job outside of football.

Celtic fans could have been forgiven for not being too put out, either for good or bad, about the arrival of Simpson. He was after all only a cover goalkeeper, and John Fallon was currently doing well, one of the few outstanding successes in 1964. But in the game that Simpson watched from the stand, Celtic's play had been first class and there was now talk about the wheel turning and honours returning to Celtic Park after a long absence.

While Simpson watched a few games, and played now and again for the reserves, Celtic reached the League Cup Final on 24 October. To the intense dismay of their supporters, they lost the Final 2–1, narrowly and unluckily, to Rangers. As often happened with Celtic, a defeat by Rangers, felt keenly and deeply by all players, triggered a dreadful loss of form with the hitherto excellent John Fallon by no means unaffected by the general malaise and depression. He had a particularly awful game at Muirton Park, Perth and noises began to be made about how the veteran Simpson might be brought in, at least until Fallon had a chance to regain his confidence.

In the event Simpson's Celtic debut came about in bizarre circumstances and at the most unlikely of venues – the Nou Camp in Barcelona on 18 November 1964 in what was then known as the Inter Cities Fairs Cup! The reason for Simpson's sudden elevation was, presumably, that his experience would stand Celtic in good stead. Predictably Celtic lost, but Simpson played well and retained his place until the New Year. He thus had the misfortune to play in the awful midwinter of 1964 when Celtic were more or less on their knees with some really awful performances including a defeat at home from Dunfermline and a dreadful New Year's Day game at Ibrox in which Jimmy Johnstone was sent off, and Bobby Murdoch missed a late penalty which would have earned the side a draw.

It was generally agreed that Simpson was one of the few successes in this dark hour of Celtic's history, but a defeat at Tannadice (never one of Ronnie's favourite grounds) on 9 January was the death knell for his run in the team, at least for the time being. John Fallon came back for the visit of Hearts on 16 January, and remained in position until the end of the season, playing well and earning plaudits for at least one great save from Alex Edwards of Dunfermline on the momentous day that Celtic won the Scottish Cup to bring to an end the trophy famine.

Simpson was delighted for his great friend John Fallon, but he would not have been human if he had not worried about his own future at Celtic Park. He was now nearly 35, which is old for any football player, even a goalkeeper, but there was now, of course the other dynamic of Jock Stein being the manager. It was no secret that Jock and Ronnie were not the best of friends – indeed it was hardly Glasgow's best kept secret that Stein had been the main reason for Simpson's willing departure from Easter Road – and Ronnie was bracing himself for either a free transfer or a quiet off-loading to some team like Partick Thistle or Raith Rovers, who had shown interest in him.

Simpson describes himself as being, 'like a kid with a giant lollipop', when he heard that he was being retained at Parkhead. Even a fringe player (and he was now part-time) could not fail to be infected by the atmosphere at Celtic Park in that glorious summer of 1965 as Stein repeatedly held Open Days for the Press, and everyone talked in an upbeat fashion about the great future that lay ahead for the green and whites and their huge support who had suffered so much and for so long. Such enthusiasm even reached Ronnie's father Jimmy who was now several times seen at Celtic Park, talking sagely to his old rival but great friend Jimmy McGrory.

But Fallon remained in the goal, and, give or take a few mishaps, did well enough for the team as it qualified for the Scottish League Cup quarter-finals from a difficult section of Motherwell and the two Dundee teams. But then Celtic lost in the Scottish League to Rangers at Ibrox on 18 September. It was a major disappointment for the fans, and John Fallon was the sacrificial lamb, although he was hardly to blame for that particular defeat. It was not, in any case, the end of the world, being one League match out of 34 in the season. The fans however had to be appeased.

But the following Wednesday night saw no Fallon in goal and no Simpson either! The young Irishman Jack Kennedy found himself in the goal for a second leg Scottish League Cup quarter-final against Raith Rovers. It was a totally insignificant game for Celtic had won the first leg 8–1, so it was a good game to give Kennedy an outing, but where did that leave Ronnie Simpson? A journalist saw Jock Stein in a long talk with George Farm the manager of Raith Rovers, and putting two and two together to make five, suggested that a move to Stark's Park was imminent for Ronnie Simpson.

But that was off beam, for on Saturday 25 September, Simpson found himself in the team to play Aberdeen at Celtic Park. He was hardly tested, for Celtic turned on a great performance to beat the Dons 7–1, but from now on Ronnie retained his place, apart from injury for the rest of his footballing career. His experience and general know-how was much needed and much exploited. Celtic's first target in autumn 1965 was the Scottish League Cup. They were, arguably, very lucky to get a draw in the semi-final against Hibs at Ibrox with the Celtic End of Ibrox rapidly emptying when Bobby Lennox grabbed a very late equalizer. No mistake, however, was made in the replay as Celtic ran out 4–0 winners to set up a League Cup Final against Rangers, a game which would be highly significant in the subsequent history of both clubs.

As far as Celtic were concerned, a defeat here, following the defeat in the League a month previously, might indicate that the Scottish Cup success was illusory and that the days of the inferiority complex and the slave mentality as far as Rangers were concerned had not gone, whereas a victory would send out the clear signal to the world that a new era was opening up in Scottish football. Simpson's contribution would be vital.

Celtic did indeed win 2–1 with two penalties scored by John Hughes. Simpson had a great game in spite of being injured early in the second half. He had saves from Jim Forrest, Davie Wilson and John Greig but his greatest contribution came in the last desperate six minutes. Celtic had been 2–0 up but John Greig had scored a fortuitous goal off Ian Young's face, and now Rangers were pouring everything forward to the goal at the King's Park End of the ground where stood most of Celtic's 50,000 support, all anxiously gripping crush barriers, looking at watches and trying to make deals with God.

It was not only the fans who were anxious, for some of the defenders were showing signs of panic. The normally unflappable Billy McNeill was running around like a headless chicken, pointing, gesticulating and showing every sign of losing the place. Tommy Gemmell's swagger had deserted him, Ian Young made a few mistakes, John Clark was looking tired and Bobby Murdoch was far from his composed self. But there was the slight figure of Ronnie Simpson, calm, confident, composed and thumping one fist into his other hand and clearly telling everyone to get a grip on things, concentrate, face the ball and to get through these last few minutes. Jimmy McMenemy of old had passed away during the summer, but it was almost as if his ghost was there with his famous 'Keep the heid, Celtic!' war cry of long ago.

The last six minutes did eventually pass, and it was no accident that many of the players made a beeline for Simpson who now had a League Cup medal to go with his two FA Cup ones from his Newcastle days. His rival for the goalkeeping spot,

John Fallon, was one of the first to put his arms round him when he came off the field. Simpson was now 35 and seemed to be ending his career on a high note, even evading an attack by some young Rangers thugs as Celtic did their lap of honour with the Scottish League Cup.

A new hero entered the Celtic Valhalla that night, but it was only an entrance as yet. A great deal more had to happen. In the stand that afternoon was his father Jimmy Simpson, sitting not far from his old rival Jimmy McGrory and both revelling in the triumph of the new Celtic side and of the goalkeeper with the Peter Pan quality of not, apparently, getting any older. Simpson senior, it was claimed, used words like 'we' and 'us' when he talked about the future of his son with Celtic.

Simpson's reflexes were still sharp, and his ability to get to where he needed to be was still unimpaired, but what stood him in really good stead for the rigours of the game that he had now been playing for more than 20 years was his positional sense which experience gave him. He saw a situation developing and would be in the right position for the shot or the header that was to come.

The rest of the 1965–66 season was an interesting one. The Scottish League was won for the first time since 1954, the Scottish Cup was narrowly lost in a replay to Rangers, and there was a European adventure which ended in failure but which laid down a few pointers for the future. Simpson shared in the 5–1 beating of Rangers at the New Year, the Scottish Cup game at Tynecastle which looked as if it would have to be abandoned because of the overcrowding on the terracing, the trip to the Soviet Union where a combination of bad weather and awkward Russian bureaucracy almost prevented the team from getting back to fulfil their next fixture, and then the bitter night at Liverpool where the much vaunted home side would surely have been beaten if there had been a sharper linesman who could appreciate the sheer speed of Bobby Lennox or if a shot which Ronnie had covered had not been unwittingly deflected by John Clark.

But the League was won at Motherwell and then it was off for a tour of North America in which the reputation of the club was much enhanced and in which his friendship with John Fallon deepened. Another phenomenon, of course, was the relationship with Jock Stein, which had slowly developed from one of suspicion and hostility to one of mutual respect. Stein, it was often said, did not understand goalkeepers. This may or may not have been true, but in any case, Stein took a step back and left Simpson to deal with the goalkeeping tactics. With the supremely talented Jimmy Johnstone, the tactics were often all the lines of, 'You, just get the ball and do what you f***in want wi' it'. With the goalkeepers, he didn't even bother talking to them!

The team were back home from North America in time to see the World Cup at Wembley on TV. It gave Ronnie a chance to recall his great days at Wembley for Newcastle United, but he would hardly have been likely to reckon that he might soon be back there – and that even his international appearance would not necessarily be the highlight of the 1966–67 season!

Words can hardly do justice to Celtic in 1967. They won everything, including spectacularly the European Cup, and Ronnie Simpson played in every game bar one, and never let them down. Oddly enough, this was not one of these 'water-tight defence' seasons that we saw in 2013–14 and 2014–15, for example, for in the Scottish League a total of 33 goals were conceded. Ronnie would be honest enough to admit that some at least were his fault, but the real 'fault' (and that is hardly the right word to use in such a splendid side) lay in the attacking style of Celtic's play that year. Men like McNeill and Gemmell were frequently up the field supplementing the already impressive repertoire of attacking play that characterised that mightily talented side, and this inevitably led to gaps in the defence. So it was no infrequent occurrence to see the team conceding two goals, but this being more than made up for by the five scored at the other end!

The memory remains of Ronnie that season, wearing pants that seemed to come too far up his body and to begin at this elbows rather than his waist, and his yellow jersey, rising above the defence to take high balls, then arriving back on the ground and within a split second running towards the edge of the penalty box to kick or throw the ball up field to a colleague, the whole manoeuvre having taken a few seconds and leaving about five opponents behind the action. He was an absolutely integral part of that great side, and a great favourite of the fans.

It was significant that in the two games that Celtic lost on the domestic front, to Dundee United home and away, Simpson had what was generally reckoned to be poor games. This was certainly true of the game at Tannadice on Hogmanay when Celtic allowed a 2–1 lead to be converted into a 2–3 defeat with Simpson looking badly out of position for at least one of the goals. He was by no means entirely to blame for this, but it was speculated that Stein might give the ever-worthy John Fallon a run in the team. As it was, Stein in fact put the blame elsewhere by changing the full-back pairing from Gemmell and O'Neill to Craig and Gemmell with a few stern words issued to the rest of the defence.

Then in the other game against Dundee United, the circumstances were odd. Celtic had just won the Scottish Cup the previous Saturday, and for this Wednesday night, a crowd of 45,000 were there hoping to see Celtic clinch the Scottish League as well, if they could beat Dundee United. In a game eerily similar to the game at

Tannadice on 31 December, Celtic allowed a 2–1 lead to become a 2–3 defeat, and Ronnie did not look too clever with either of the two second half goals. The cynics who remarked that this was all deliberate so that Celtic could win the League at Ibrox on Saturday were probably wrong – and that thinking does less than credit to Dundee United – but in a splendid game of football in the unremitting Govan rain three days later, Celtic duly won the title with a 2–2 draw – and this time Simpson in the muddy conditions in which he always revelled, was superb! It was a curious game with one spectacular goal and one scrappy goal for each side, but that was enough for Ronnie to collect his first Scottish League medal.

There were at least two other games that season in which Celtic were hugely indebted to Ronnie Simpson. One was the Scottish League Cup Final at Hampden in late October 1966. Celtic had taken a lead through Bobby Lennox in the first half, but even the most fervent of Celtic supporters would have had to admit that Rangers, if not necessarily the better team in any technical sense, certainly enjoyed more territorial possession and the second half in particular saw a great deal of pressure put on the slight figure of Ronnie Simpson in the King's Park goal. It was like 12 months previously in last year's League Cup Final except that it lasted longer, and older supporters would compare it with the Coronation Cup of 1953 when Johnnie Bonnar and Jock Stein defied Hibs' Famous Five.

One incident in particular showed Simpson at his best. This was the time of Willie O'Neill's moment of glory, when with all the defence stranded, Willie charged back to turn a trickling deflection round the post to concede a corner. The grateful and exultant Celtic End then saw Ronnie Simpson ruffle Willie's already receding hair, then turn to the rest of the defence, thump (characteristically) his fist into his other hand and give orders to the rest of the defence about where they should be for the ensuing corner-kick. Even captain McNeill acknowledged Simpson's leadership at this critical point of Celtic history, and did what he was told. The corner kick was cleared, and Celtic went on to lift their first piece of silver for the season in a 1–0 win, and a very significant win it was as well, for it quite clearly told the world that Celtic now *expected* to beat Rangers. The inferiority complex had gone, and as WB Yates might have said, 'All was changed and changed utterly'.

Simpson's other game that changed the course of Celtic history that season was of course the European Cup semi-final against Dukla in Prague. 3–1 up from the first leg, Stein made what turned out to be the correct decision in deciding to defend with only Stevie Chalmers up front. Some say that he had no choice in any case, for Dukla were a magnificent side, but they could not get the ball past Ronnie Simpson that night. Simpson's contribution that evening was not so much his shot stopping and general positional sense, as, once again, the inspiration that he engendered. Men like Willie Wallace, Bobby Lennox and Jimmy Johnstone, by no means natural defenders, grew to their task with the friendly words of encouragement from 'Faither' in the goal, and in the knowledge that, even if all else failed, he would not let them down.

Full-time came, but there was no excessive celebration, for it was more or less straight to the airport to be back in time for the Scottish Cup Final against Aberdeen on the Saturday. This was Simpson's first Scottish Cup victory, and he became one of the few players to have won a Cup medal in both Scotland and England. Celtic beat Aberdeen 2–0 with a Willie Wallace goal on either side of half-time, yet it might have been different, for Aberdeen were no bad side and Simpson's contribution was by no means negligible.

As for his two other great occasions that spring, little need be said that has not been said before. His selection for Scotland in the game against England at Wembley was a little controversial, for there were those who felt that the heart was being put before the head in choosing such a veteran. There were indeed quite a few other more than competent goalkeepers around in Bobby Ferguson of Kilmarnock, Bobby Clark of Aberdeen, Jim Cruickshank of Hearts and a host of Anglos, but Manager Bobby Brown (who of course had known Ronnie in his Queen's Park days of 20 years previously) and who had been a fine goalkeeper himself for Rangers, plumped for the 36-year-old Ronnie Simpson.

If that was what fairy tales were made of, how could you describe the actual game itself? Not all Scottish people necessarily believed that England were deserved World Cup winners the previous year, and here we had a great Scotland team on one of these rare days when both Law and Baxter were on song, becoming the first team to beat the World Cup winners of 1966. In truth, it was not exactly the humbling that it has been made out to have been, for England might just have sneaked a draw at the end, but the 3–2 win was enough to cheer up the whole country and to at least put a temporary damper on those strident voices that had hailed last year's victory with such fervour. To his credit, Kenneth Wolstenholme the BBC commentator praised Scotland and Ronnie Simpson. Some others were considerably less effusive.

At least one part of England was happy as well. This was Newcastle. Their venue of St James' Park had been ignored (while Roker Park and Ayresome Park, the homes of Sunderland and Middlesbrough were deployed) and no Newcastle United man came anywhere close to selection for the England team. There were the Charlton brothers from Ashington, nephews of the great Jackie Milburn, but they did not play for the Magpies, and therefore a sentimental eye was turned to

149

their great erstwhile hero of yesteryear, Ronnie Simpson. Questions were now being legitimately asked of their management on the point of why he had been allowed to go six years previously!

Simpson and the other three Celtic players in that Scotland team – Wallace, Lennox and Gemmell – had of course just played their first leg semi-final of the European Cup against Dukla at Parkhead the previous Wednesday night and were heavily involved in other things, so there was no time to relax. Indeed, Ronnie Simpson, whatever his private emotions and thoughts were, just seemed to take it in his stride. Naturally a shy man who seldom pursued the limelight, he did not seem to realise just what he had done, nor what he was about to do.

The night of 25 May 1967 will of course remain 'etched on every Celtic heart' (in the words of the song) for all time, even when the men who did the deed (sadly only eight out of 11 remain) and those of us lucky enough to have witnessed it, whether in the 'heat of Lisbon' (lyrics from another song) or on television, are all gone. In retrospect it seems remarkable that it all happened, particularly in the context of what had happened in the early 1960s when we had all despaired of Celtic. But it did happen, and Ronnie Simpson played as big a part as any.

His own account of the game is a fine mixture of fact, humour and sheer emotion. He seems to have burst into tears of many occasions in the immediate aftermath, and there is the amusing story of Bobby Lennox at full-time racing past him the rescue his own and Ronnie's false teeth, which were kept in Ronnie's bonnet in the back of the net! And of course there is the moment when Ronnie might have changed Celtic history with his famous back heel!

It was in the first half when Celtic were one down from the unconvincing penalty-kick awarded to Inter Milan. They were pressing forward and the Italians were deep in defence other than the odd marauding raid. Ronnie was well out of his penalty area when the ball came to him and an Italian was charging towards him. Calm as you like, Ronnie back heeled the ball to John Clark! It was an incident which was not much highlighted at the time, for it was dwarfed, naturally, by other more momentous events in that game, but had that not come off, it would have been 2–0 for Inter Milan, and the road back for Celtic would have been considerably more difficult, if not impossible.

Ronnie, like most Celtic players, found it hard to imagine just exactly what they had done. It will remain the greatest ever achievement in Scottish football for all time – it has never been repeated since, although Celtic reached the Final again in 1970 without Ronnie in the goal – and the effects were seismic. The return to Glasgow the following night was in itself a great occasion with people like the

Lord Provost of Glasgow, and John Lawrence the Chairman of Rangers Football Club waiting at the airport to greet them, and even august bodies like the House of Commons and, remarkably to some eyes, the General Assembly of the Church of Scotland (in session in Edinburgh at the time) paying homage to the great Celtic team. It was indeed a far cry from the days of 1965, only two years previously, when Ronnie expected a free transfer! And as if 1967 did not need another honour for Simpson, the Scottish Football Writers Association voted him their Player of the Year!

The worthy John Fallon was given a game in the benefit match for Alfredo di Stefano a fortnight later (and he played well) but Ronnie was back in the goal for the start of the next season, which although a great deal less successful than 1966–67 was no less turbulent and significant with the word Celtic seldom out of the newspapers. There was a great game against Rangers at Parkhead in August to qualify Celtic for the League Cup quarter-finals, but then in the month of September, things took a severe dip with several heads having swollen out of proportion and an anti-climactic exit from the European Cup to Dinamo Kiev caused by what seemed to many supporters to be sheer complacency. At times like these, after a bad result or two, senior members of the team must take a lead, and naturally Ronnie was one of those who was always willing to provide a calming influence.

He also retained his place in the Scotland team, and anyone who had the slightest doubt about his ability was quietened when he saved a penalty-kick against Northern Ireland in Belfast, the highlight of an otherwise dreadful Scotland performance. The Scottish League Cup was won, but then that very night the team were airborne to South America for that turned out to be a total cataclysm for the team. Celtic had beaten Racing Club at Hampden in a game that gave an indication of what we might expect in Argentina. Wiser counsel might have been for the team to withdraw and not to fly to South America, and Ronnie, in particular, would have wished they had done just that, for he was the victim of a brutal and cowardly attack.

The team were warming up for the game in Buenos Aires in front of a hostile crowd. Hostile crowds are of course nothing unusual in South America, but this one was more so than most, and suddenly, Simpson collapsed to the ground, felled by a piece of metal. No culprit was ever found, and detailed investigation revealed that there was a strong possibility, given the mesh that kept the crowd from the pitch, that the missile was thrown from the playing area itself, either by an Argentinian reserve or even a policeman! Nothing was reckoned to be beyond the bounds of possibility in Argentina at that time, for it was the era of repressive dictatorships where the phrase 'human rights' did not seem to exist.

Ronnie could not play in that game nor the play-off game a few days later. Celtic lost the trophy, but worse than that was the loss to their reputation with several players disgracing themselves. The sad fact about that was that it tended to draw attention away from the cowardly attack on Ronnie Simpson, something that, surely, would have provided justifiable grounds in itself for abandoning the game and for Celtic to fly home, as Chairman Bob Kelly apparently toyed with doing. Even the Argentine Press could not condone such thuggery, and were full of condemnation for the attack.

Simpson soon recovered but Celtic took a long time to get over that dreadful trip. Ronnie was able to play in the first game back in Scotland after the return – wearing a plaster on his head in the first game against Airdrie at Broomfield in an insipid 2–0 win. Hardly surprisingly, the team did not play particularly well for a spell after that but they still managed to eke out wins until the New Year. It was at times like that when the influence of Simpson, unseen but ever-present, was crucial in bringing some of the players back to something like their normal best after such an emotional catastrophe that the South American trip had proven to be.

Things took a turn for the worse at the New Year. Ronnie was injured against Clyde on New Year's Day before the game against Rangers at Parkhead, and his deputy John Fallon had a nightmare, thus allowing Rangers to regain the initiative in the League race. Worse came at the end of January when the team exited the Scottish Cup in front of their own fans at Celtic Park to Dunfermline. Dunfermline were a good side, but the Parkhead crowd expected better and this now meant that Celtic were in danger of winning nothing apart from the Scottish League Cup in the season after their greatest ever.

The League Championship however was now also apparently beyond this team. Rangers were two points ahead and did not have to play Celtic again. Celtic were therefore relying on other teams to beat them. Stein (and Simpson) however reckoned that Celtic were still a great side (one does not receive the European Cup for nothing, after all!) and that if they won all their games spectacularly (with the defence, if possible, keeping clean sheets), Rangers would crack and slip up.

For a long time it did not look as if it were going to happen, but Celtic kept plugging away, winning five vital away fixtures at Kilmarnock, St Johnstone, Dundee United, Hearts and Aberdeen, and then Rangers did crack, dropping a point at Dundee United (four days after Celtic had thrashed the same team) and then Morton (while Celtic were winning the Glasgow Cup at Hampden) before finally collapsing against Aberdeen at Ibrox while the Celtic team were sitting in the stand watching the Scottish Cup Final between Dunfermline Athletic and Hearts.

Simpson had thus won three Scottish League medals. He was now nearing his 38th birthday and the question was beginning to be asked more and more about when he was going to retire. But there were still no signs of that – indeed he was still playing at international level for Scotland, and when season 1968–69 opened, Ronnie was still there. Not only was he still there, he continued to be worshipped in song by the Celtic fans who said he was better than the legendary Russian Lev Yashin

> '*Aye, aye, aye, aye*
> *Simpson is better than Yashin*
> *And Wallace is better than Eusebio*
> *And Johnstone is better than anyone!*'

His best friend at Parkhead was still the somewhat surprising one of John Fallon. In other clubs perhaps, there would have been bitter rivalry with conspiracies, back-stabbings, mutterings and leaks to the Press, but not with these two. No-one had been more supportive of Fallon during his nightmare of the aftermath of the Rangers game at the New Year than Ronnie Simpson. They always sat together on bus trips, talked about goalkeeping, cheered each other up, exchanged confidences and Stein, of whom it was always said that he didn't understand goalkeepers, left them to it and smiled tolerantly. He was less tolerant of the fact that both enjoyed the occasional cigarette, but he found that difficult to stop.

The new season started with Simpson, now sometimes called with deliberate ambiguity 'the evergreen' in top form as Rangers were defeated twice in the League Cup, a competition whose Final had to be postponed because of a fire at Hampden. Simpson kept impressing and was still Scotland's choice. Indeed it was playing for Scotland in early November in a World Cup tie against Austria at Hampden that he sustained a leg injury, which turned out to be more serious than it looked at first sight and obliged Ronnie to be off for a few months. John Fallon stepped in and did well, but Simpson was brought back in early January for difficult trips to Aberdeen and Dundee United.

A more serious injury was sustained in a Scottish Cup game against Clyde at Shawfield on 12 February. It was a dislocated shoulder, ironically caused in a clash with a Clyde forward called Jimmy Quinn. Quinn was actually a Celtic player on loan to Clyde, and the grandson of the great Jimmy Quinn of old. Tommy Gemmell had to take over for the rest of the game, and Ronnie was out now for the rest of the season, thus missing out on the remarkable month of April 1969 when Celtic won all three Scottish trophies!

John Fallon was playing excellently in the goal, and it was now being openly asked of Ronnie Simpson whether it was time to bring an end to this remarkable career.

This question was posed with more frequency, particularly when the season opened and Fallon was still in the goal, even though Simpson was fit. Fallon stayed in goal until the end of September 1969 when Stein brought Ronnie back. The idea may have been to rotate the goalkeeping job, but events then sadly took over in a remarkable few days that were effectively the end of Simpson's career.

Simpson was certainly in the goal on 11 October against Airdrie at Broomfield, the day of his 39th birthday. As luck would have it, McNeill was ill with a bad cold, and Simpson was therefore made captain for the day as the crowd all wished him a Happy Birthday, possibly the first ever Celtic player to be feted in this regard. For all that Simpson was not a Celt by birth, his popularity with the support seemed to know no bounds! Simpson's tact and diplomacy were much required that day, for it was a nasty game in the heat of Broomfield, punctuated with fouls and at one point Jimmy Johnstone was laid out in an incident early in the first half which was spotted by the crowd but not by the officials. Simpson was there to stop matters getting any worse.

Two days later Simpson played (McNeill was back as captain) but sustained a repetition of his shoulder injury when he made a great save to deny Alex Ingram of Ayr United. The save probably won the game for Celtic (a narrow 2–1 victory against determined opponents) but it effectively brought down the curtain on Ronnie's footballing career. He was taken off, and Tommy Gemmell again took over in goal to see the game out, but then the very next day (coincidentally, one presumes) Celtic signed another goalkeeper in Evan Williams. With Fallon still around as well, there would be no opportunity for Simpson even when he did recover – and of course at the age of 39, dislocated shoulders are less easy to mend than they are for a younger man.

He stayed on the books of Celtic for the rest of the season, missing out on another Scottish League and Scottish League Cup success, and of course another run to the European Cup Final in Milan, before he announced his retirement on 7 May 1970, the day immediately after Celtic's catastrophic defeat in the European Cup Final to the determined, professional and better-prepared Feyenoord. Simpson was with the party, but the day after that won a seat on Edinburgh Corporation as a Conservative! Clearly whatever he was now going to do, his footballing career was over.

The demission of Simpson was buried under the welter of news about Celtic's sub-standard performance in Milan with a few questions now beginning to be asked about Stein and some of the players. But the career of Ronnie Simpson was highlighted in some newspapers a few days later with quite a few of the journalists, perhaps the younger ones, seemingly staggered by just what exactly this man had achieved in his remarkable 25 years in football.

There was one moment of pure theatre left. In May 1971, a year after Simpson retired, Stein brought him back to come out with the 11 Lisbon Lions for a game against Clyde at Parkhead. This was before all of the Lions left on their different ways. Simpson, of course, was no longer registered and could not actually play in the game, and had to be replaced by Evan Williams, but he did, with the main stand in the throes of substantial reconstruction lead the team out for the last hurrah of the Lisbon Lions.

His involvement in football did not end with his departure from Celtic. Among other things, he was Manager of Hamilton Academical for a brief spell, although he probably was far too nice a man for the brutal world of football management. He sat on the Pools Panel, a body which determined football results in games that were postponed because of bad weather. This did not involve him working every Saturday but he had to be ready to fly to London to be the Scottish representative, and effectively to decide the result of Scottish games.

He was also a goalkeeper's coach for various clubs, notably Dunfermline Athletic, and he was seen frequently at East End Park, sitting quietly and unobtrusively in the stand, chatting away with the supporters of both teams, nodding appreciation of a good save by either goalkeeper and keeping a tactful silence when a goalkeeping error cost a goal. It was often hard to imagine that this slightly-build, well mannered and dapper gentleman, who looked like someone's favourite uncle, was one of the best goalkeepers who had ever graced the game in Scotland and England.

He also played loads of golf, vying with

Ronnie, now officially retired is given the honour of leading out Celtic for the last appearance of the Lisbon Lions in May 1971. The Main Stand is in the throes of reconstruction.

155

that other great gentleman Steve Chalmers for the honour of Celtic's best golfer, and with his sports shop in Edinburgh and the work involved with being a local Councillor in Edinburgh, he was never short of anything to do. But he was, above all else, a family man remaining devoted to his beloved Rosemary and their two children, Stuart and Carol.

He died in April 2004 of a heart attack at the age of 73. His funeral in Corstorphine at St Ninian's Church was a serious obstruction to traffic; such was the attendance of everyone who was anyone in football. Pride of place went to the Lisbon Lions (Bobby Murdoch had predeceased him and Willie Wallace was in Australia, but the rest were there, resplendent in their green blazers) but there were people from Rangers, Newcastle and Hibs there as well as a few Englishmen like his friend the great Gordon Banks. The turnout was worthy of the man.

CAREER:

Appearances: 188
Scottish League medals: 4
Scottish Cup medals: 1
Scottish League Cup medals: 3
Glasgow Cup medals: 2
FA Cup medals: 2
European Cup medal: 1
Scotland Caps: 5
Shut Outs: 91

PAT BONNER (1978–98)

by Marie Rowan

In May 1978, a young lad aged just seventeen left the endless sound of the Atlantic breakers crashing against the shores of the West of Ireland as they made landfall, for a life amongst the flowing tide of humanity that was Glasgow. Pat Bonner was a raw talent signed by the great Jock Stein, his last signing, and also the last in a long line of goalkeepers the iconic figure had persuaded to put pen to paper for Celtic. Stein probably had his fingers crossed that this one would work out for so many of the others had sunk without trace. Willie Maley could spot a great goalkeeper a mile off, Jock could not. But Pat Bonner, a tall, lanky lad who had a habit of being late for training, fulfilled the promise Stein had seen in him. Bonner had in fact a long and successful career with Celtic on the domestic front and a glittering one with the Republic of Ireland on the international one earning eighty caps for his country. His haul of medals is impressive in a period where Celtic's play could vary dramatically from the very creative to the bordering on dire. The club was rapidly plunging into oblivion as, near the end of Pat's Celtic career, Rangers' star was in the ascendancy. Without Pat Bonner in goal, one wonders exactly where Celtic might have been as the days grew darker and all hope finally disappeared. Was Bonner's presence a blessing or did he inadvertently help paper over the cracks?

March 17 1979, was a day of huge significance in the life of Pat Bonner. He had signed for Celtic from Keadue Rovers and had found himself playing third fiddle to Peter Latchford and Roy Baines at Celtic Park. Billy McNeill had seen quality lurking somewhere in the youngster's performances and he had earmarked him as the eventual successor to Latchford when that time would come. So it was that on St Patrick's Day, 1979, having dropped Latchford who had virtually gifted Aberdeen two goals that had put Celtic out of the Scottish Cup, McNeill said he was simply doing it to help Latchford and the Celtic fans get the result into perspective. Latchford and Baines had been battling it out for a supremacy all season that would give one or the other the regular berth but neither one had made it his own. McNeill had ended the contest in his own decisive style and Roy Baines found himself transferred to Morton. McNeill was now placing his faith in Bonner as understudy with high hopes that one day he would fulfil the potential Billy McNeill had also seen in him. McNeill informed Bonner he was in the team on the Friday before Celtic were due to play Motherwell and the big Irish lad must have hoped that a good show would lead to his occupying the number one spot on a permanent basis. The newspapers made a great play of the boot-shining youngster himself shining on the pitch. The Celtic team were an eclectic mix with a seventeen-year-old from Donegal lining up alongside Lisbon Lion, Bobby Lennox from Saltcoats. Who could have blamed Pat if he had thought of keeping and framing the team-sheet? Unfortunately, though, it had been printed before Latchford's cup howlers and it was his name that was still there among the chosen eleven. That team contained figures destined to be prominent in Celtic's history; Danny McGrain, Tommy Burns, Roy Aitken, Davie Provan and Murdo MacLeod. Some of them were in fact only a few years older than Bonner but they were already idolised by the Celtic fans.

Celtic were still suffering from the mid-week defeat but Motherwell failed to capitalise on it in the initial stages of the game although they became more confident as time went by. It was a good debut by the young Celtic 'keeper for he had to pick the ball out of his net only once to his opposite number's twice. Bobby Lennox was yet again the sharpest tool in the box scoring all of his team's goals and so Celtic took all points in the 2–1 victory. Bonner had acquitted himself well, handling safely and confidently and impressed all with a particularly fine save from Mike Larnach.

After the game, Billy McNeill praised his temperament and tantalisingly declined to rule out to the pressmen that day the possibility that Bonner could be selected ahead of Peter Latchford for the Rangers game the following week. That game set Pat Bonner on a lifetime's roller-coaster ride if he had but known it. The Rubicon had been crossed and there was now no going back.

October 1984 saw Celtic take on the road once more in their quest for European glory in the form of the European Cup Winners Cup. Their destination this time was the cultured and architecturally beautiful city of Vienna, home in days gone by of the Straus family and the Viennese waltz. Perhaps because of being brought up on the fancy footwork of the latter, Austrian football had a reputation for highly-skilled players and the scary 1984 scenario of George Orwell's book, although deeply disturbing, was obviously lost on the Celtic team as they eagerly looked forward to the game. Joe Kennaway, the Celtic 'keeper of the 1930s, had played for Scotland against the Austrian national team at Hampden Park and the 60,000 spectators who had turned up to see the fabled skills of the Austrians, were definitely not disappointed.

That evening, 24 October, in Vienna, Celtic and Rapid Vienna were vying for a place in the quarter-finals therefore a great deal was at stake for both clubs. It was

A Footballer's Wedding with Frank McGarvey and Roy Aitken doing the honours.

the first leg of the tie and Rapid had some truly great players in their side, such as Panenka and Krankl, players who had made their names both in top-class European games and also World-Cup ones. Celtic probably had great need of Bertie Auld in the tunnel as the teams lined up side by side. But Pat Bonner in the Celtic goal could look out at his own teammates and feel that there was enough collective talent out there to give the Austrian side a game. Any Celtic supporter would have been more than happy to put his or her money on Bonner, McGrain, Reid, Aitken, W. McStay, Grant, Provan, P. McStay, McClair, McGarvey and MacLeod. The Celtic fans had been led to believe that European nights could – and in this case as the opposition was skilful to the nth degree – and would be a feast of fiercely competitive football. 'Fierce' as in a battle of wits and skill. Unfortunately, it turned into 'fierce' as in 'brutal' where civilised behaviour and good sportsmanship went out the window. The home of Straus's gentility and charm witnessed its team disgrace itself by their extreme behaviour.

Gamesmanship, unfortunately so common in the game everywhere today, was considered a rarity here but part and parcel of football on the Continent. The Celtic players of that day were in no way prepared for what they were subjected to in the form of physical contact designed to hurt and to provoke retaliation. As Rapid found themselves the winners by 3–1 with McInally for Celtic being sent off, they were left congratulating themselves but quite probably had regrets at having lost an away goal as Parkhead was famous for being a venue where, in European competition, Celtic were very difficult to beat. If Celtic were to capitalise on the away goal advantage, Pat Bonner was going to have to play the game of his life in the return leg.

Although there had been nasty incidents aplenty in the first-leg, none of the Celtic players anticipated anything they could not handle of that nature in the return game on 7 November. Ignorance is bliss! Rapid were 3–1 up so with an advantage like that, desperation had not been thought a likely scenario and if they did come under pressure, they were not expected to buckle to the extent of demonstrating unbridled indiscipline on the pitch.

The atmosphere inside the stadium was electric, anticipation high, the fans very much aware of how quickly skill could degenerate into debacle where Rapid Vienna were concerned. Celtic came out of the blocks determined to take every opportunity that came their way either by design or good luck. Bonner more than most was up for it. He thought three goals lost to this particular team were three too many. And Pat was a proud Irishman, well aware of the Irish roots of his team and the legacy those players of old had left. Mr Johannson of Sweden, the referee, immediately showed he was not going to stand for any nonsense, especially rough play, early on as he booked a Rapid player for a mild foul on Murdo MacLeod. Celtic did not look like a team over-anxious to score with its concomitant mistakes as they made determined, well-organised raids into Rapid's half of the pitch. It was an entertaining first thirty minutes, both teams showing their skills. Celtic were, of course, two goals down so it was the bhoys in green and white who had to make all the running and hope they did not leave themselves wide open to the counter-attack. A quiet start, therefore, to the game but it suddenly burst into life when Brian McClair scored in the 32nd minute and set the Parkhead faithful's hopes well and truly alight. Paul McStay who was absolutely inspirational that evening, pushed the ball out to Davie Provan. Provan in turn produced a wonderful cross over to Rapid's far post where the lurking McClair beat Ehn, the Austrian reserve goalkeeper, and slid the ball into the net. One goal pulled back. Another and Celtic would be in the lead owing to that away goal scored in Vienna. After that, it would all be in Pat Bonner's hands, literally. But that night, Aitken and McAdam were superb and let nothing threaten the big Donegal man's peace of mind. With Celtic still pulling out all the stops, still going for that decisive one, the referee added some stoppage time and those Celts certainly made the most of it. Murdo MacLeod volleyed a ball Davie Provan had sent flying into Rapid's penalty area and MacLeod left everybody in no doubt as to where he intended it to go. Murdo was famous for his ferocious shot. As the referee blew his whistle for the end of a superlative period for Celtic, the bhoys went into the dressing-room with the score on the night standing at 2–0 in their favour and 3–3 over the two legs with Celtic still having that away goal in their favour.

Celtic appeared for the second half and their intention was obvious – business as usual. It seemed only a matter of time before the visitors would give vent to their frustrations. From beginning the game with a 3–1 lead, they were now wondering what had happened. If things stayed as they were, their European campaign would be guttered before it had really started. The final whistle would blow their dreams away if they did not do something positive to prevent that. But 'positive' in this case equated with 'negative', which seemed to come more easily to them regardless of the talent in that side. The catalyst for it came in the 68th minute when Tommy Burns scored goal number three. After a clash with Ehn, Burns had picked himself off the ground, got to the loose ball and hit it into the back of the net. Cue for minor mayhem to be followed shortly by a major version as the Austrians let desperation become aggression. No doubt Ehn would take the flak on the plane home. Well, someone has to be the fall guy and it would definitely not be the high-profile guys. Frank McGarvey's shot had been saved by the 'keeper, but he then fumbled and dropped the ball. Burns, on the ground beside the kneeling Ehn, arose fast and taking the opportunity afforded by the ball running loose, accepted this present and Celtic, now 3–0 up, were definitely in the driving seat. Rapid were now down on players as well as goals as Reinhard Kienast, a Rapid defender, had been sent off for hitting Burns after Tommy had scored the third goal. Shades of the infant playground! But a major incident was in the offing. Ehns had tackled Burns in a manner, which resulted in a penalty-kick being awarded to Celtic. Obviously not a single member of the Rapid team seemed to find Tommy's own brand of charm captivating. Seems they all wanted to have a go at him. The resultant fracas saw the Austrian players demonstrate to the referee their fury at his decision as Mr Johansson tried to consult his linesman. Both officials stood firm. Unfortunately, during this melee, a Celtic supporter threw a bottle onto the pitch and an Austrian player gave notice that he was putting himself up for an Oscar. With the usual histrionics, bad acting and a distance of several yards from the bottle, Rudi Weinhofer did his best and ultimately failed to have the game abandoned. But the people who had thrown that bottle and some coins could take some of the blame for Celtic's eventual exit from the competition. All the fuss was eventually for nothing as after fifteen minutes, when play resumed, Peter Grant stepped up to take the penalty – and missed. He succeeded in sending the 'keeper the wrong way and also the ball, for it missed its objective by several yards. The referee added the lost fifteen minutes back on to make up for the lamentable scenes by the Austrians but there was no more scoring.

Rapid Vienna had been beaten by a better team and Pat Bonner had had an enjoyable time watching it and feeling grateful he was not his opposite number, no doubt. The 3–0 win was no fluke. But the Austrian team were determined that they were not going out of the Cup Winners Cup at any cost and the very next day saw UEFA bombarded with protests from them in the hope of being granted a replay. The instances of precedence that they could cobble together and put before the UEFA disciplinary committee were very much flawed in themselves. Perhaps Rapid hoped no-one would look too closely at them. Their main complaint centred round Weinhofer being hit by that bottle. The committee considered all the evidence put before it by both its own officials present at the game and also the television footage of the incident available. They concluded that the bottle had not injured any Rapid player and both Weinhofer and Rapid Vienna were censured for making a false claim. Reinhard Keinast was suspended for four games and the club coach was banned from the touchline for three games for throwing a bottle onto the pitch. The clubs were both fined, Rapid £5,000 and Celtic £4,000. Another Rapid appeal and this time they decreed that their player was not hit by a bottle but by a coin. An easy mistake to make! The epitome of bad losers. This time the committee doubled their fine and then, to everyone's astonishment, declared the game void and to be replayed at least 100 kilometres from Celtic Park. Celtic chose Old Trafford but there they were beaten by the only goal of the game. Celtic did suffer for a long time because of the stupid actions of that bottle-throwing fan.

The Scottish Cup had always been seen as the Blue Riband of Scottish football and repercussions can be great within Celtic and its supporters involving the manager of the club if it is dismissed from the competition. Although the Cup, the oldest football trophy played for in the world today, has occasionally seen a less fancied team battle its way to the Final, this year of 2016 has been remarkable inasmuch as two teams from a lower division, Hibernian and Rangers, have provided the combatants in the Final of this year's prized trophy. Hibs, the victors, had last won it in 1902 beating Celtic 1–0 at Celtic Park in front of a crowd of 16,000. It had taken Hibs a while to complete an Old Firm double but no doubt their fans thought it was worth the wait.

The coveted medal, instant success and euphoria, was Pat Bonner's for the first time on Saturday 18 May 18, at a rain-soaked Hampden Park. Great teams had emerged in the 1980s from the east coast as Aberdeen and Dundee United brought both home and European success to their supporters. And it had been those two teams plus Celtic and Motherwell who contested the semi-finals. Both games went to replays with Dundee United edging out the potential league champions Aberdeen. Quality football was coming from the wise men from the east. Despite a 3–0 score in their replay, Celtic was no goal-scoring machine and the forwards seemed to need the benefit of a map to find the net at times.

Pat Bonner walked out with the Celtic team on the day of the Final into a cauldron of emotion, expectation and unbelievable noise from 60,346 people, 52,000 of whom were reckoned to be followers of the green and white. The massive self-confidence of recent signing Mo Johnson had filtered throughout the entire team and Roy Aitken, who has become the epitome of Celtic midfield influence, was determined to erase the memory of his ordering-off in the previous Final.

David Hay, who had taken over from the departing icon Billy McNeill, was more than aware that Celtic had been without a trophy since they had beaten Rangers 2–1 in December 1982 in the League Cup Final. The wall of noise metaphorically erected by the Celtic support was a double-edged sword, both encouraging and intimidating at the same time. To let the fans down with a poor performance was unthinkable, the responsibility for the players, nerve-wracking. They were all aware that winning the Cup was always important, but winning with style and flair was the real prize. It was the 100th Final of the Scottish Cup and if Celtic won, all the hints and rumours written by gleeful sports journalists of turmoil behind the scenes at Celtic Park and a manager about to walk, would be put on the back-burner. Hay would have his first trophy and Pat Bonner's Irish eyes would be smiling as he clutched his medal.

The first-half was a dour struggle. Every Celtic attack came to a dead halt as Paul Hegarty and David Nary did a magnificent job of closing down all Celtic forays into their space with astonishing regularity and efficiency. Although the midfield had consistently won the ball and fed the forwards, their hard work had all gone for nothing as the forward-line had a lethargic air about it. The forward-line, including, the bank-breaking signing Johnston, seemed to be going nowhere very slowly and. The half-time whistle was blown by the referee, Brian McGinlay, and the teams trooped off level and goal-less.

Play was restarted and the massive Celtic support must have entertained thoughts of déjà vu when Roy Aitken was bypassed by Davie Dodds and Beedie beat Bonner to put Dundee United one goal up after fifty-four minutes. Disappointment in the Celtic camp was soon overtaken by the sheer determination to please the massive crowd whose consistent level of ear-piercing noise must have had the wally dugs rattling on the mantlepieces of Mount Florida. Bonner and his defence had remained solid both before and after that surprise goal by Dundee United. With fifteen minutes to go, Celtic were one goal down and Hegarty and Nary still repelling all boarders. The Celtic players later admitted to thinking that right then, they were dead and buried. But not the faithful and ever-optimistic supporter who had been brought up by his or her da and granda to believe that a man lucky enough to be privileged to pull on the Celtic jersey would give his all until time had run out. Jock Stein's oft quoted 'inferior player' words encapsulate not only utilising any ability with the ball to the greatest degree but also a work ethic that should be second to none. Effort, 100% of it, ended when the final whistle went. That team that day fully embraced that ethos despite unwelcome thoughts lurking at the back of their minds that it was a hopeless cause. Who could let those fans down? Certainly not that group of players. Manager Hay then made one of his best and bravest decisions ever. He substituted Paul McStay, Celtic's world-class player. Roy Aitken then moved into the midfield and his influence in that position transformed both attitude and play. The two Celtic goals that came in the dying minutes were variously described as dramatic, spectacular and opportunistic. Celtic won a free-kick and Murdo MacLeod and Davie Provan had a discussion before Provan stepped up to take it. He later said he thought the Dundee United goalkeeper, Hamish McAlpine, reckoned Provan would jump over the ball and McLeod, with his famous ferocious shot, would be the one to hit the ball. Not so. Davie Provan took the most stylish free-kick of the season and Celtic were now on level terms and had the crowd and the unrelenting driving force of Roy Aitken behind them. The green machine was in full throttle and with more than four minutes left to play, a superb Roy Aitken cross saw Frank McGarvey's head, as he came tearing into the penalty area, direct the ball accurately into the back of the net. With that goal, Celtic had won the 100th Scottish Cup Final, the team that had always considered it to be their trophy by right.

Roy Aitken had erased the memory of being the villain of the previous year's piece against Aberdeen. He had left the pitch that day and Celtic had had to contest the Final against one of the best teams in the land with only ten men. An impossible task. This time Aitken left it as Man of the Match. He had that day in 1985 the opportunity to make amends and he had grabbed it with both hands. His name is always the first on Celtic supporters' lips when there is no-one to dominate the midfield and the game on sheer force of personality alone. 'If only we had another Roy Aitken.' That wish will no doubt resound down the generations. It was Aitken who had engineered the incredible comeback against a Dundee United side who

Two Irishmen at Celtic Park. Pat and Pierce O'Leary who played a vital part in the Scottish Cup Final.

thought that with only thirteen minutes remaining, the trophy was once more heading for the east coast. Fate and football can be cruel to the wary and unwary alike. Mr McGinlay, the referee, had an excellent game and had only two names in his book at the end of the ninety minutes, those of Danny McGrain and Willie McStay. Not bad for a match on which so many jobs and reputations hinged. So Pat Bonner was able to take home his first Scottish Cup medal knowing that he had held firm in a most demanding match against a very fine team.

Celtic embarked on their Cup Winners Cup campaign in September 1985 with an enormous first-round home leg disadvantage. The game was to be played behind closed doors. Celtic's supporters had always played an enormous part in the team's success but the consequences of the fracas relating to the Vienna Rapid games were very real indeed and to Celtic's disadvantage in this particular tournament. When the draw was made in the European Cup Winners Cup, Celtic found out their opponents in the first round would be one of the most dangerous sides in the tournament, Atletico Madrid. Two weeks before the first-leg was due to be played at the Vicente Calderon Stadium, Celtic's manager, Davie Hay, had watched Atletico defeat Barcelona 2–1 and he rated them the best side he had ever seen in his time as manager. Celtic's main purpose in Spain would have to be one of containing the side, which had some formidable players. The massive input which the very vocal Celtic support had traditionally made to the club's success would be missing due to the Vienna Rapid legacy. This knowledge would no doubt also relieve Atletico of the fear factor guaranteed by the superb backing and influence the crowd has on the team. This had Atletico's manager, Luis Aragones, expressing his relief and acknowledging the edge over the two legs it would give his team.

As one reporter commented after the game in Madrid, Celtic's 'keeper, Pat Bonner should have been given the freedom of Parkhead. Bonner's display was nothing short of inspired, his handling brilliant, his anticipation superb. Throw in a superlative save from a penalty-kick and the result was a Republic side that should have thanked their lucky stars that Bonner had been born in Donegal. A breathtaking, heroic performance by the Irishman. Mo Johnston was there at the opposite end of the pitch to contribute the goal that could very well prove to be the decisive one. In the match as a whole, Bonner not only saved the penalty from Rubio in the most instinctive manner, but he also had another three exceptional saves. All this from a team who were definitely on the pitch that evening as the underdogs despite having some superb, not to say, world-class players in their team.

The game set off at a cracking pace in the kind of heat that made simply breathing a hard task in itself. Little wonder the Spanish team and their officials who had expected their Scottish opposite numbers to provide them with that extra edge by wilting under it, could not believe the energy and pace shown by the Celts in the second half. Although a few names went into referee Volker Roth's book, it was a match with little or no trouble both on and off the pitch. Atletico, being joint leaders of the Spanish League, were expected to control and dominate the proceedings. They were an attacking side in the first half, full of purpose and determination and had Celtic on the railings on several occasions. This only succeeded in bringing out the best in Pat Bonner as he set about dealing defiantly with all Atletico could throw at him.

Within eight minutes of the kick-off, he had Da Silva bearing down on him and only an incredible save with his legs allowed him to keep the Bhoys from being 0–1 down. The Atletico centre-forward did not realise it at the time but that was to be only the beginning of a very frustrating evening for him as he duelled with the Celtic defence and their almost impregnable goalkeeper, Bonner. Another Da Silva shot, unleashed after the centre had succeeded in beating Danny McGrain, was duly dealt with in great style by Packie. Da Silva was beginning to wonder just what he had to do to get the ball past the big Irishman. But the Celtic 'keeper was not finished yet, not by any manner of means. This time it was Alreche who decided to have a go and Bonner with one hand punched his shot over the bar and the Celtic goal remained unbreached. What an incredible evening the big 'keeper was having and it did not end there. By this time, the great test the Celtic players had been led to believe they would be subjected to had materialised in a form they found they could contain and consequently concentration – no doubt allied to relief – slipped and suddenly they were 0–1 down. Setien, who had had his name taken for a bad tackle on Peter Grant, was the architect of Celtic's despair. Given a large degree of space, the consequence of poor marking and that lapse in concentration, Setien accepted the ball from a free-kick some twenty-five yards out on the thirty-five minute mark and beat Bonner with a fifteen yard angled shot as he ran in on goal from the left. That left-footed shot now put immense pressure on Celtic as a second goal would surely make winning the return game in an empty Parkhead stadium a very difficult task indeed.

Celtic came out for the second half determined to reimpose that control they had so negligently lost and all thoughts of the stifling heat were swept aside. Added to their firmness of purpose, the players found an amazing energy and pace which, allied to the sight of an Atletico team bent on protecting their lead and backing off, content to stay mostly in their own half, were all signs that it was game-on again. Every man in that Celtic team played his part without flinching and none more so than the in-form Davie Provan. That Celtic workhorse, Peter Grant, had been beavering away in midfield as the Spanish team backed-off. Grant's pass out to Provan was superbly picked up by him as he ran for the goalline and he in turn sent in the killer cross for Johnston in the 69th minute who timed his run brilliantly and equalised with a powerful, accurate header towards the far post which flew clear of Fillol, Argentina's World Cup 'keeper. How many heroes can one team have in one evening? Celtic were now definitely in charge. But Atletico were not finished yet. A reckless tackle by young McGugan on Setien resulted in that player hurling himself to the ground just inside the penalty area. Hard luck on McGugan as he had saved a near-certain goal in the first half. A penalty for Atletico Madrid. The mighty Bonner now carried the weight of all Celtic supporters' hopes and dreams on his shoulders as he prepared to face Rubio, an Atletico substitute. Rubio calmly placed the ball on the spot, took a ten pace run up and fired a ferocious shot close to Bonner's right-hand post. Instinct prevailed as Pat dived towards it and, with one hand, made one of the best saves of his life.

Celtic's performance was a credit to Scotland and Pat Bonner a hero in the best Celtic goalkeeping tradition.

September 1986 saw Celtic due to face Shamrock Rovers in the first round of the European Cup in Dublin. The Celtic manager saw this test as a stepping-stone and proving ground to test Celtic's readiness to take on the best in Europe once more. The Milltown ground would no doubt hold as many Celtic supporters as those there to cheer on the Irish champions. David Hay was taking no chances for Celtic had pulled out all the stops in their determination to get the man who was to become an iconic figure in the club's history, fit for the match. Having restored their world-class defender, Danny McGrain, to the team choosing experience over youth, the team was now formidable. With Pat Bonner gracing the ultimate line of defence, what a treat was in store for his Irish compatriots! It was the manager's opinion that there was no better 'keeper in Scotland than the ever popular Donegal man. Hay and his Celtic team were not only up against Shamrock Rovers but were also being held to ransom by the club's illustrious past in the greatest of club competitions. Jock Stein had laid down the benchmark. Reaching the Final or semi-final was acceptable, the latter grudgingly and on anything else, you could pull down the shutters and go home.

There had never been an Irish team that was not fiercely competitive and Shamrock Rovers were no exception. They had been watched closely and carefully by Parkhead envoys and their strengths and weaknesses noted. The European Cup was the wrecking ground for those dismissive of their opponents and respect for the opposition at all times had been a keynote of Celtic's success. Hay's habit of dealing with one game at a time, his refusal to write off what was or perceived to be weaker opposition, was a trait that served him well. His aim was to defeat the Rovers over both legs but Hay was realistic enough to know that the crowd might just make a draw a good result in Dublin.

If there were any Irish people in that neck of the woods that night who had never seen the Republic's first-choice goalkeeper in action, they were in for a treat. Pat Bonner rose to the occasion and his performance in Dublin was breathtaking and even the most ardent of Shamrock Rovers supporters must surely have had, in his heart of hearts, enormous pride in the man to whom the Republic's goal, and Celtic's, was entrusted. A defeat, if that it was destined to be, was truly a double-edged sword. In any European Cup game, a rub of the green was a most welcome gift if it came your team's way. That evening in Dublin, two Irish teams were competing for that elusive ingredient but fortune smiled upon the Scottish team of decided Irish origins in the form of the incomparable Pat Bonner. Celtic would have been put to the sword if it had not been for his formidable presence and the reluctance with which the Celtic management would have settled for a draw before the game became a much-desired result as the home team pounded the Celtic goal. A 1–0 result in Celtic's favour was enough to promise an easier task in the return leg at Parkhead. A scoreline that at times that evening looked incredibly difficult to hold on to, in the end flattered the winning side.

Shamrock Rovers got off to a cracking start within minutes of the kick-off as they raced through a half-awake Celtic defence and Pat Bonner's alertness and ability were the only two qualities that stood between the Bhoys being on equal terms and a goal down. Bonner got down sharply and his diving save from a Noel Larkin shot was the wake-up call the rest of the team needed. This was more or less to serve as a pattern for the rest of the match. Shamrock Rovers versus Pat Bonner. Or was it Donegal versus Dublin? Bonner showed no sympathy for his fellow Irishmen as he thwarted the home side time and time again. His immense presence in the penalty area broke the Rovers supporters' hearts mercilessly that night and David Hay and his assistants must have wondered where the Scottish champions' skill had gone to. What should have been little more than a stroll in the park was rapidly becoming a very difficult and fraught confrontation. Celtic wilted and seemed devoid of ideas but the towering form of Bonner, who saved them repeatedly, gave them the breathing space that was required and allowed them to settle down and salvage their creativity and credibility.

With their composure restored, Celtic set about the business of making certain they went home to Parkhead with at least a draw, Bonner having played his part in great style earlier on. Again in the second-half, he made another great save when he was faced with a blistering shot. Skill and determination marked Shamrock Rovers' efforts but they did not outdo Celtic in the near-miss department. Mo Johnston and Brian McClair showed what a dangerous and creative partnership they could be as the first half saw a McClair header hit the crossbar and a fierce shot from Johnston in the second half hit the upright. Celtic gradually exerted some control in the opposition penalty area and this attacking partnership was a constant threat there. With no score and the minutes ticking away, neither side had anything to show for all their efforts, either composed or, at times, frantic. The long-held Celtic mantra of play until the final whistle sounds eventually paid off in style. Shamrock Rovers, ever anxious to press and harass the Celtic defence, had eight men in the penalty area when Celtic counter-attacked. A brilliant pass by Peter Grant into the sprinting Murdo MacLeod's path set the scene. McLeod powered a low ball past Jodi Byrne in the Rovers goal and sighs of relief could be heard all round the ground.

Celtic with that stunning goal seemed almost assured of progress into the second round of the competition. But their performance had fallen woefully short of a convincing superiority over the part-timers and but for the superlative goalkeeping of the man from Donegal, Kerrydale Street could have been more like Heart Attack Alley in the second leg of this particular tie. Shamrock Rovers had proved to be no pushovers and the victory Celtic took back to Glasgow was due mostly to one man, Pat Bonner, as he had repeatedly denied the Irishmen the open arms of his goal that night.

Celtic had entered their centenary year with defiant high hopes and in moments when reality kicked in, sinking depression. Billy McNeill had come home to manage the team less than a year before and it was to 'Cesar' all Celtic supporters looked to bring back, if not the glory of his playing days, at least some semblance of emerging hope. It was now March 1988, and the team had rallied to such an extent under McNeill that the League Championship was within their grasp. Next up – Aberdeen at Pittodrie. Victory over what was the most successful Scottish club in the eighties would ensure Celtic would be seven points ahead of their nearest rivals, Rangers, and needing only six more from the remaining six games to win the League.

The day after that game, the Celtic team's performance was variously described as exhilarating, brilliant and even stunning. What an incredible change from the lacklustre team McNeill had inherited, a team going nowhere fast. That they had practically sealed the title in magnificent style was acknowledged by all. Aberdeen had been left totally traumatised and devastated by a Celtic second half performance that was truly breathtaking and the final score of one goal to nil in Celtic's favour bore no resemblance to their vast superiority in the second forty-five minutes. But one goal of a difference is an all too slender lead and if Pat Bonner had not pulled off a save of some magnificence from a Willie Miller shot in the closing minutes of the game, justice would not have been done.

Celtic had taken the field with only one thought in mind – to win and win handsomely. It was all eyes on the ball, the goal and the League Championship. The crowd were treated to a marvellous spectacle of attacking football and Aberdeen were worthy contributors to that. Celtic were first to take the lead in what was, especially in that first half, an end-to-end thriller. Awarded a corner, Celtic's Joe Miller struck the ball well and Anton Rogers headed it on to Andy Walker whose shot at goal was simply unstoppable. With that lead, Celtic could have been forgiven for adopting a defensive mode but that had never been Billy McNeill's style. Twice more they beat Jim Leighton in the Aberdeen goal but unfortunately they were flagged offside on both occasions. Paul McStay and Frank McAvennie could not in all honesty argue with the referee's decision. The score remained a perilous 1–0 in Celtic's favour. But now Pat Bonner, the Republic of Ireland's first choice goalkeeper, had to bear the brunt of Aberdeen's determination to take something from what was, after all, a home fixture and he found himself bearing the brunt of some genuinely great shots in the first half. Three times he came to Celtic's rescue as Aberdeen's forwards cashed in on Celtic's more adventurous play.

When Celtic took the field in the second half, they could have been forgiven if they had adopted a very defensive mode. But they used these forty-five minutes to demonstrate the skill and talent they possessed and how football can entertain in a truly wonderful and exhilarating manner. The game, especially the first half before Aberdeen were completely overrun, was a great spectacle and in the true style of Celtic, a team effort. Celtic left Pittodrie with all the points and having reassured the folk of the North East that football of the very highest order was alive and well and at home in the west.

In the end, it was a triumph of flair and pace, all imbued with Billy McNeill's own never-flagging ambition to bring success to Celtic. The team had been expected simply to try to defend their own position in the League and leave all thoughts of attacking to another day. Not so and those who had turned up to watch Celtic digging in dourly had had the shock of their lives. This had not been a display of football by a team willing to settle for a draw. Far from it. They played with passion and pride. They were adventurous when even the most stout hearted of their travelling support had probably wondered if playing Celtic's traditional attacking style of football might prove to be foolhardy. But it was never that. Their complete mastery and dominance in the second half against an Aberdeen side that fought long and hard against this unstoppable force was a magnificent advert for Scottish football and left no-one in doubt as to who would lift the League Championship trophy. That centenary 'double' was now well and truly a tantalising prospect.

Every single Celtic player who played in the friendly on 30 April 1989, against an emotionally reeling Liverpool side could count it a privilege to do so. It was always going to be a deeply emotional occasion as Celtic and Liverpool came together with fans of both clubs to pay tribute to those who had died that day at Hillsborough.

Pat Bonner lined up with his Celtic teammates in what was a sea of green and white, red and blue. As all in the stadium held up their scarves and sang 'You'll Never Walk Alone', all thoughts were on the innocent fans who would no longer be able to experience that simple pleasure through no fault of their own. The Liverpool fans also displayed a huge banner proclaiming 'Merseyside Thanks Glasgow'. It was a very moving tribute from people who had suffered so much and for whom memories of that dreadful day would never be erased. The close ties between the two clubs went back decades. Ninety-five, later to become ninety-six, fans had died that day and a scarf for each memory lay knotted in front of the main group of Liverpool supporters. The game was being played for two equally valid reasons; to raise money for the Hillsborough Disaster Fund and to allow the players to ease their way back into playing again. Players and fans could unite in helping each other and begin the process of recovery and this game was the first step on that long and difficult road. Before the game, Glasgow's Lord Provost Susan Baird presented a cheque for £25,000 from the city to the disaster fund and Strathclyde Region were providing a banquet for both teams and their officials after the game.

Liverpool's manager, Kenny Dalglish, himself a Celtic hero in his time with the club, had chosen Celtic as the opposition knowing well the generosity of spirit which moved its supporters. Close ties had been formed between the clubs since the early sixties and 'You'll never walk Alone' had become a joint anthem. Kenny Dalglish had expected an exceptional welcome but he said later that it had surpassed anything he could have imagined. It was truly magnificent and heart-felt. But that evening was all about raising spirits, allowing some sort of normality back into people's lives through football and the players of both teams were more than willing to help accomplish that. Football was now being used as an instrument of healing.

That Liverpool side had been on their way to winning the League and Cup double in England and it was no surprise to anyone that night that they had the players to achieve that. Billy McNeill had set up his players well but they had already played the previous day so it seemed it might just be up to Pat Bonner in the Celtic goal to repel all boarders if the Celtic legs gave out. He had a mountain to climb as the fitness level between the teams was going to be very unequal. For the crowd, it was not just an opportunity to show solidarity with fans who were coming under the fiercest of attacks from the authorities anxious to divert all responsibility for the disaster, but also to see the superb abilities of that team which had so raised hopes amongst the Liverpool fans of the 'double' that season.

Kenny Dalglish, 'King Kenny', received an outstanding ovation from the crowd. He was a Celtic legend, a talent that had been discovered and nourished over a long period of years at Parkhead. Both teams gathered together in the middle of the pitch for a minute's silence. The whistle blew for the kick-off and the healing process had begun – a small step down the long road to normality for those Liverpool players and their fans. It was now business as usual on the pitch when KD put Liverpool into the lead after 29 minutes. At 38 years of age, he demonstrated he had not lost his fabled skills until he was replaced by John Aldridge, the man whose initial reaction to the tragedy had been to doubt that he might ever be able to play again. The familiarity of the mechanics of the game soon eased the grief and anxiety that had been deeply etched in the faces of the Liverpool players and officials and Aldridge scored Liverpool's second in the 62nd minute. A shot from Houghton had been half saved by Bonner but the ball had gone out to Aldridge. This was a game where the Celtic supporters were treated to the supreme skills of the visitors and they were left in no doubt as to why the 'double' seemed a distinct possibility. The Celtic defence before him delayed and hesitated, not sure of what to do. In all fairness to the Celtic players, Liverpool's superiority was enhanced by a tired opposition as Celtic had played Aberdeen at Pittodrie only the previous day and also the great question for them was, how hard do you go in against a team suffering from such a traumatic event as Hillsborough? A definite dilemma. Houghton gathered the Barnes pass and shot for goal. Pat Bonner did well to save it but it went only as far as Aldridge who lobbed it over Pat's head for Liverpool's second. As the game wore on, Aldridge made it 3–0 for the visitors against a rapidly tiring Celtic team. A moment of aggro showed when Roy Aitken and Steve McMahon crossed swords but this was a reassuring moment that demonstrated that normality was indeed beginning to return. When Pat Bonner lifted the ball out of the net for the fourth time after Ian Rush had chipped it over his head, the scoring was finished. Liverpool had scored four to no reply from Celtic. The game had been a good run out for Liverpool as they had been told to resume their League programme the coming Wednesday.

The score was of no importance really despite the highly competitive Celtic manager, Billy McNeill, being decidedly under-whelmed by his team's performance. Cesar never gave or took excuses for a poor Celtic showing. But the strains of 60,000 voices of both clubs supporters joining together in singing 'You'll Never Walk Alone' must surely have mollified Billy a little.

That season 1988–89, Rangers were totally dominant and it looked like nothing could prevent them from securing the near-fabled treble. Certainly the team from Paradise, which had been so heavily defeated already by them that season in the League were not seen as stumbling blocks to glory for the south-side team. But Cup ties were, and always had been, food and drink to Celtic, their traditional attacking style geared in the early days to death or glory. Win or lose, nothing in-between. Shades of grey were not attractive or even recognised by Irish minds or hearts. The fierce heroes of Celtic myths and legends had never settled for a draw and in football, playing the points system simply did not suit. That had always been viewed as compromising the Celtic heritage. The Parkhead teams had a reputation as Cup ties and one-off specialists and all supporters expected the team to embrace their history and win. If Celtic, though, were to win their fans' desire, that season, something had to give. And manager Billy McNeill, in line with the sublime

173

pragmatism of the early committeemen whose willingness to mould rules into their own needs ensured and secured such as Dan Doyle's services, which helped greatly in making the club a viable force, decided that creativity had to be sacrificed on the altar of realism. Rangers, with the League Championship and the League Cup already in the bag had to have the chance of adding the Scottish Cup to that haul well and truly snuffed out in whatever way McNeill could devise. The Scottish Cup simply had to remain at Parkhead and McNeill knew now, after a season of humiliating defeats at the hands of Rangers, just what tactics his team would have to employ in the final to achieve that. The purists among the Celtic support were in for a major disappointment that day 20 May 1989. The heart and soul of Scotland's people were historically lodged within legends concerning that great trophy and to the people's team it rightly belonged – Celtic. Billy McNeill and his assistant manager, Tommy Craig, were realists and acknowledged the quality of the Rangers side. Their tactics, simple enough, were a dazzling success in front of 72,000 as the winning score reflected on that day of wonderful sunshine and a moment when Celtic FC salvaged something of its past glories. Man to man marking was anything but beautiful to watch but it resurrected a pride in the club, a joyous crushing of their rivals' treble dreams while obliterating momentarily Celtic's abysmal season. Compromise was the name of the game. In fact it was the only one likely to succeed and Joe Miller's wonderful strike in the 41st minute, ensured that the Bhoys had won the Cup for the twenty-ninth time.

McNeil's preparations for this momentous meeting were perfect. Seamill and occasionally Rothesay, favoured spots for team breaks in Willie Maley's day, had given way to foreign parts with guaranteed sunshine. Portugal and a bit of bonding had set the Bhoys up perfectly for the fray and McNeill's orders to close down Rangers for the entire match while still keeping an eye open for a window of opportunity for the more creative Celts paid off. Simple it sounds, but difficult it was for a team representing a club that had always prided itself on flair and entertainment. But Cup ties were do or die affairs and whilst killing off the opposition's chances, this had to be balanced to afford themselves the opportunity to win. Some players are big game specialists and Joe Miller was one of these. Rangers had everything to gain that dazzling day at Hampden Park and they already had the success of a great season behind them. What could the crowning glory be other than inflicting yet another defeat on the other half of the Old Firm and securing the treble that season. The Rangers fans rolled up confident that this Scottish Cup Final was a scenario where their team was Brutus to Celtic's Caesar. The Celtic supporters turned up defiantly confident, more in hope than conviction, that this was a Scottish Cup Final and who knew better how to play it than the Parkhead Bhoys. Paul McStay would keep the Ibrox men at bay from the midfield and the rest of the team could just get on with winning the Cup. Wha's like us!

The tension on the terracing spilled over onto the pitch and the players took some time to settle down. An early scare did nothing to calm Celtic's nerves as their goal came under threat within two minutes of the kick-off. Rangers were awarded a free-kick which was quickly struck goalwards. Mick McCarthy intercepted it before it reached Bonner and headed it out to what he hoped was safety only to discover it whizzing past him as Sterland, picking it up, cracked it towards the goal from twenty yards out. Pat Bonner who went on to have a first-class match, was able to watch it fly over the bar. Minutes later, a neat bit of play between McStay and Miller gave Peter Grant a wonderful opportunity to score but Grant's shot was well wide of the goal. Celtic were not only holding their own but were now playing with a belief in themselves. On the fourteen minute mark, Miller was again involved and the fans groaned as his dipping volley just cleared the bar. Rangers who, in this somewhat dour struggle were certainly underachieving, were becoming more desperate as what they had envisaged would be little more than putting the time in until they lifted the trophy, had become a game which Celtic were now controlling. What looked like the prelude to a roughhouse as the Rangers team indulged in a series of fouls was halted by Mr Valentine, the referee, by booking Scotland's Player of the Year, Richard Gough, in the thirtieth minute for a foul on Peter Grant. The yellow card score was evened-up eight minutes later when Mark McGhee had his name taken for a late challenge on Brown. A somewhat harsh decision was the view of one and all. The Rangers team's day was about to implode and Celtic would leave the field at half-time a nerve settling goal up. Joe Miller, who was having a superb game, watched in amazement as Rangers England international defender Gary Stevens demonstrated that not only was he having a very bad day, but that it was about to get worse – much worse. His shocking attempt to pass back to Woods, who was having enough problems of his own, was pounced on by the ever-alert Joe Miller and the powerful shot he lashed low and to the right from twelve yards out, bulged the back of the net to the ecstatic joy of the Celtic supporters. But as often happens, their opponents took advantage immediately of the Celts letting their guard slip for a moment and Stevens, racing clear on the left, beat the big Republican 'keeper only to see his shot cleared off the line by the ever watchful Whyte.

Celtic began the second half full of confidence and belief in themselves and, of course, one goal up. Bonner and Morris in front of him were having a great game against what was now becoming a team of dismal failures. The Bhoys attacked,

Fellow Irishman Sean Fallon, here pictured at Pat's wedding, was always a great source of strength to Pat.

stringing together a series of wonderful passes and within three minutes had been awarded a corner-kick. Tommy Burns took it and with his left foot placed it beautifully into the penalty area. Woods' outstretched arms grasped thin air and, as it flew past him, McCarthy's head connected with it but his effort was a yard wide. Celtic had another attack thwarted on the edge of Rangers' penalty area as a wonderful pass by Grant into the path of the oncoming Miller was halted by a well-timed tackle by Gough on Joe. Sterland was substituted in the fifty-seventh minute and Davie Cooper came on with Souness warming up. Rangers had now recognised that they were being outplayed. Celtic had yet another chance when a perfectly timed header from Burns was cleared off the line by Stevens with his 'keeper beaten all ends up. Rangers now powered forward and threw everything they could at Pat Bonner but he dealt superbly with it all. The Parkhead lads were now oozing confidence and the final whistle saw the Scottish Cup return home to Celtic Park and Rangers dream of the treble receive a most unwelcome shattering.

Celtic had drawn Rangers as their opposition in the fourth round of the coveted Scottish Cup and it was due to be played on 25 February 1990. Manager Billy McNeill was following the age-old Celtic tradition of taking his team to Seamill for some extra training and intensive tactical seminars. What happened to Portugal? Mike Galloway and Dariusz Wdowczyk had been having intensive treatment for injuries over the weekend and it remained to be seen if they would be fit for inclusion in the team. It was likely that ten out of the twenty-four who had taken part in the Scottish Cup Final between the teams on 20 May 1989 were unlikely to take part – a remarkable statistic – when Celtic had defeated Rangers by a Miller goal to nil. Celtic had by this time to play without the massive presence of Roy Aitken, Mick McCarthy, Tommy Burns and Mark McGhee. It was all to play for with Celtic desperate to salvage something from a season where Rangers were by now virtually certain of the League Championship and equally desperate to complete the 'double'. Celtic were geared up for a battle and Billy McNeill was certain his team had peaked at exactly the right moment. Pat Bonner was the one man in the team the management found impossible to replace and he seemed fighting fit again after his physical problems of the previous few seasons. With Rangers being so dominant and Celtic's season lapsing into the abysmal, Souness, the Ibrox manager, could have been forgiven for taking the result as a foregone conclusion. If he did harbour such thoughts, he kept them to himself. Souness knew and understood the nature of Cup ties and Celtic's enshrined attitude to them regardless of current form only too well. Celtic Park had never been a happy hunting ground for Rangers and Souness knew that too. In answer to the formidable striking partnership of Johnston and McCoist, only one name was required to be voiced by the Celtic supporters, Paul McStay, a world-class player with a sublime touch. The Celtic faithful expected that their own strike force of Jackie Dziekanowski and wee Joe Miller, whose unpredictability warmed the hearts of Celtic fans who had a natural aversion to the predictable, could safely match that of Rangers. No doubt the optimists had already made arrangement for the quarter-final.

It was a match full of the crunching tackles, fierce determination and exemplary grit that has so marked confrontations between the Old Firm down the decades. Tommy Coyne had been having a rough time convincing the Celtic support that the £500,000 paid for him had been well spent but this time out, when he left the pitch limping fourteen minutes from the end, the Celtic fans appreciation of his skills was deafening. A Joe Miller shot had been parried almost on half-time by Chris Woods in the Rangers goal. As the Rangers defence stumbled about, Coyne pounced on the loose ball and sliding along the slippery surface, he sent the ball skidding into the Rangers' net. The Celtic supporters were euphoric. The Press, somewhat predictably, for they had been wracking up the possibility of that Rangers' League and Cup double achievement, suddenly ignored their hopes evaporating and consigned the

177

defeat in such phrases as, 'little more than a hiccup' on Rangers way to membership of the European elite club. Aye right! Roy Aitken, now of Newcastle United, was there to congratulate his old teammates especially McStay, a player of infinite skill and football nous and in contrast to the previous Celtic captain, a quiet, reticent man. Celtic, having been going through the mill both on and off the pitch, now found itself, momentarily, at one with its support. McStay maintained that the team had been prepared perfectly for the game and although the universal underdogs, he had known within five minutes play that his team would win the game.

This League thriller, which took place on 24 March 1991, between the Old Firm at Parkhead had it all and more besides with Pat Bonner being dubbed, 'an inspiration to outfield men.' The post game phone-in calls could have tied up the lines all weekend. A superb double-whammy within seven days for the Celts over the Ibrox men definitely brought a much needed feel-good factor to the support. Both players and fans were emotionally wiped-out when the final whistle sounded. A 3–0 victory by their team sent the Celtic fans into rapture and Rangers ones complaining bitterly about every tackle, shot, facial expression of the Celtic players and generally any team having the cheek to beat Rangers. The more things change, the more they stay the same. This was simply a verbal continuation of the barrage of missiles thrown from the Rangers end onto the Parkhead track. The situation had not been helped by Celtic fans taunting them by holding up red cards, a reference to the dismissed Rangers players at the previous meeting of the two teams.

That meeting the previous weekend had turned into something of a donnybrook. But despite Mr Smith, the referee, booking five and sending off the Rangers left-half, Scott Nisbet, who was mediocre at best, it was the general consensus of opinion that the players had behaved themselves on this occasion. It was also noted that the referee had had a good game but could probably find an easier way to earn £70. Having had ample opportunity to study the previous meeting of the teams, Mr Smith must surely have had a niggling notion that it was not going to be any picnic and that accepting the brief could well in retrospect have looked like a suicidal decision on his part. Fortunately for him and Celtic, it all worked out well.

It was never going to be a game where the old adversaries settled for a draw. Rangers were top of the League but if they lost to Celtic, it would see them only three points ahead of Aberdeen and there were still seven games left. Celtic, still in the Scottish Cup where winning it would guarantee European football the following season, were taking no chances and were looking to secure another route into Europe by overtaking Dundee United in third place and that could give them a spot in the UEFA Cup. The game set off at a frantic pace, the high expectations of the 52,000 crowd and the tension on the terracing transmitting themselves to the players on the pitch. Rangers suffered a major blow within seven minutes. Celtic had gone on the attack immediately and were quickly awarded a free-kick and so the stage was set for a Rangers howler and a Celtic goal. Joe Miller had taken the free-kick and sent it flying into the Rangers penalty area. A fine array of defenders awaited it and the normally safe Richard Gough's attempt to head it clear only sent it further into danger. Chris Woods, renowned for having a safe pair of hands, jumped head and shoulders above everyone else, caught the ball and then promptly dropped it as Gerry Creaney challenged. Both men hit the grass in time to see Anton Roger slam the bouncing sphere into the net. One – nil to the home side. If the free-kick leading to the goal had incensed the Celts who reckoned advantage should have been allowed, their complaints had now vanished. Rangers rallied despite the blow and Pat Bonner was kept busy as the crosses came in thick and fast. Three minutes from half-time, saw an incident that seemed set to allow the underlying tension to boil over. Paul Elliott and Richard Gough were the original players involved in the incident but everyone seemed to want to play his part. As players congregated around these two, the referee simply stepped in and extricated them from the group. After a sound ticking off, he booked both of them and play went ahead. Rangers continued to press but Bonner's handling and anticipation were perfection itself and the score remained a tense 1–0 when Mr Smith blew for half-time.

Both teams came out for the second half mindful of what was at stake for both of them with Celtic determined to increase their lead, Rangers bent on showing the form that had made them League leaders. Lady Luck herself came on and lined up alongside the Celts. Billy McNeill later conceded that they had definitely had a rub of the green but pointed to their positive defending and constant threat of scoring. Pat Bonner now had more than his fair share of opportunities to show Chris Woods how it was done by a top-class, international 'keeper and it was the latter who had the next opportunity to pick the ball out of the net.

Goal number two for Celtic was begun by the man who had converted the first, Anton Rogan. He played a brilliant forward pass to Tommy Coyne who, having beaten Davie Dodds, the Rangers centre-half, was dismayed to see the ball running away from him and heading for the bye-line. But he chased it, caught it before it went out of play and sent it across to the lurking Miller. Joe made no mistake and Celtic, the underdogs –how Celtic love being that! – were now two goals up. Throughout the match, Miller upset the Rangers defence with his astute passing of the ball, his clever runs and impeccable crosses. Celtic felt they were now well on their way to victory, but Rangers had no intentions of letting that happen. They battled on but the Celtic defence, with Bonner and Rogan excellent, held on firmly and five minutes from full-time, a fantastic header by Coyne, set up by McStay and Miller, ripped past Woods and into the net.

Rangers had been having their fair share of problems and their situation was not helped by Nisbet getting himself sent off for a foul on Paul McStay, which the referee had deemed deliberate and dangerous. The final whistle went and Celtic's chances of European football had been well and truly enhanced. When asked about that first nerve-settling goal, Anton Rogan simply replied that the ball had fallen perfectly for him and he had simply put it away. Apart from the Rangers squad and their fans, the only other group suffering from profound disappointment were the journalists from outwith Scotland who had been anticipating a 'warzone' after the scenes of the previous week's meeting between the two clubs. Rangers' defence had let them down badly. That plus the formidable performance on the day by Pat Bonner saw them concede vital points to their opponents. Celtic's forwards had taken full advantage of the service supplied them by their mid-field captain McStay who had had one of his best ever games. As a spectacle, it had been a tense, action-packed thriller and Celtic, the less fancied team that day, emerged worthy winners by a score of 3–0. British Telecom did not do too badly either from the phone-ins.

Long before he was awarded a testimonial game, Pat Bonner had already taken part in matches of that kind for some very special Celtic players. In these days when being dubbed 'world-class' when a very good player has played a very good game watched by pundits with university degrees in hyperbole, it is difficult to realise that there is sometimes a truly world-class player in amongst it all. Danny McGrain was correctly labelled that and Pat Bonner had the great honour of playing alongside him. Danny's testimonial was played on 4 August 1980, and a crowd of 45,00 turned up to pay homage. Bonner was still the reserve goalkeeper but Peter Latchford was injured so Pat got to play against Manchester United that evening. The game as a spectacle was nothing of note but the big Celtic 'keeper managed to keep the United forwards at bay with a very good performance and the game went to penalties. The future penalty-saver of note only managed to save one whilst his teammates only managed to score the same.

Another legend, another testimonial. In the opinion of most Celtic supporters today, all the club's ills would be swept away if we only had another Roy Aitken in the team. If ever a man could influence a game by personality alone, it was Roy. Another player who will live in the memory of Celtic fans forever was Tommy Burns and Bonner was in good form for his special game versus Manchester United on 25 March 1987 during which Bonner managed to keep a clean sheet in a 1–0 victory for Celtic.

Pat Bonner's own big day came on 12 May 1991, and it was fitting that the opposition was the team whose colours Pat wore on international duty, the Republic of Ireland. This was a great excuse for the older Celtic fans to stroll down Memory Lane and to dig out the old scratched Bridie Gallacher records. Pat's credentials and popularity as a member of the Republic's side was sky high after his performance in June of the previous year against Romania in the World Cup. The season just finished had been one of the poorest with Celtic trailing a long way behind both the League Championship winners, Rangers, and second-placed Aberdeen. To have been the goalkeeper during those lean days was something best forgotten for, as in the case of Willie Miller, the 'keeper's performance has seldom been separated from that of a very unconvincing defence. Overall, Pat Bonner's stay with Celtic was very successful and his popularity with the fans was never in doubt. Most supporters had been thoroughly disillusioned by the team's ineptitude and even two successive victories over Rangers could hardly be expected to brush from their minds the looming conviction that if they reached the unlikely heights of ending the season third in the League, they could count themselves lucky. The team did in fact achieve the somewhat dubious distinction of being runners-up to the runners-up but only on goal difference from Dundee United. Therefore, it was, on the whole, a great crowd of 38,000 who left their disillusionment at the Board's running of the club in abeyance to honour a favourite son. As it turned out, Bonner's teammate, Gerry Creaney, stole the show scoring three for the Bhoys in a total of five converted that day. 3–2 to Celtic but probably Bridie Gallacher won hands down.

This game had entertainment written all over it even before Mr Syme, the referee for the game, had blown his whistle to 'let battle commence'. Flags were all over the place, an Irish band – The Artane Boys Band – had been brought over from Dublin. Bonner's famed devotion to charity was given the nod as the band had always been heavily into helping the underprivileged through passing on their musical skills. But the Celtic supporters, although in a happy, accommodating mood, were hoping in their heart of heart, they would not see their beloved Celtic dancing to the Republic's tune.

The match had barely begun when Celtic went one goal up from a terrific Gerry Creaney effort. Eight minutes on the clock, a lovely piece of interplay with Charlie Nicholas and Gerry did what Gerry always did best. Enter the skills of the testimonial bhoy and a great save by Bonner from a Sheedy shot kept Celtic ahead. Unfortunately the ball only went as far as Bernie Sleven and he put it into the back of the net. The whistle blew for half-time and the teams left the pitch a goal a-piece.

There was no doubt about how serious Celtic were taking this game and their determination to win this encounter. Perhaps it was a last hurrah – if only until

Pat's iconic penalty save against Romania in the 1990 World Cup.

the new season began – and an attempt to curry favour with the fans who had been so badly and frequently let down that season. A massive crowd had turned up whereas only 10,000 had appeared at the last League game of the season. No doubt they had come to honour Packie, but was this also a desire to see the Celtic players playing for the jersey as of old despite the nature of the game and opposition? A throw back to the expectations of pre-war generations? They soon got their answer. The Republic scored within eight minutes of the restart through David Kelly and a minute later it was all square once again. Creaney to the rescue, helped along by a wonderful cross from Stevie Fulton. The winning goal gave Gerry Creaney his hat-trick and the whistle finally blew on a Celtic victory over the Republic. Mr Syme and his officials very kindly donated their fees to charity. A wonderful occasion for a wonderful servant of Celtic FC.

It is unfortunate in a way that Pat Bonner's great career has been reduced, in some people's eyes, to that one penalty save for his country against Romania in the World Cup, important as it was to him and his fellow Irish men and women. Great saves are often forgotten, saved penalties are never consigned to the margins of football history. But Bonner rightly takes his place in a long line of great Celtic goalkeepers and, perhaps knowing Celtic's history well, it was a daunting task for him in the beginning even to pull on the jersey. If personal charm and humility alone would make a great 'keeper a popular one with the fans, Pat would have walked off with all the honours. But this, coupled with his great ability, noted so early on by Jock Stein and 'Cesar' himself, makes Bonner one of the most memorable ones.

CAREER:

Appearances: 642
Scottish League Championship Medals: 5
Scottish Cup Medals: 3
Scottish League Cup Medals: 1
Republic of Ireland Caps: 80
Shut Outs: 172

MISCELLANY

IAN ANDREWS (1988–90) In the wake of Paddy Bonner's injury in 1988, Celtic signed Ian Andrews from Leicester City. He impressed in the pre-season friendlies and in the early games but had the misfortune to be in the goal for the trip to Ibrox in late August. The 5–1 defeat was a cataclysm from which Celtic would not recover for years, and Andrews was blamed for most of the goals. A defeat to Dundee United in the League Cup followed, and Andrews was roundly booed by his own fans as the team went down 3–1 to Aberdeen at Parkhead in the middle of September. He was dropped immediately afterwards and disappeared.

ROY BAINES (1976–79) was an Englishman from Derby who covered admirably for the injured Peter Latchford towards the end of the triumphant 1976–77 season. He was the goalkeeper on the night at Motherwell when Andy Lynch scored two late own goals and is credited with the remark that he was frightened that Andy was going for his hat-trick! He played most of his excellent career with Morton, and Celtic could have done with seeing more of him.

GRAHAM BARCLAY (1973–77) was brought in for one game in February 1975. It was generally agreed that Celtic were in decline in the early months of 1975 and finding it difficult to recover from the double whammy of losing to Rangers and then Motherwell in successive weeks. A couple of feeble draws against Arbroath and Dumbarton in February led to a not unusual knee-jerk reaction from Jock Stein who dropped goalkeeper Ally Hunter. Denis Connaghan was still injured, and Peter Latchford had still not arrived, so Graham Barclay it was for the Scottish Cup game against Clydebank at Parkhead on February. He played well in the 4–1 win, and Stein might have done well to persist with him.

DICK BEATTIE (1954–59) was sentenced to nine months imprisonment at Nottingham Assizes in January 1965 for having taken bribes while playing for Portsmouth and Peterborough. He was by no means the only one involved, nor did it happen on only one occasion. This made folk wonder about his time with Celtic, but it must be stressed that he was never accused or even suspected, in any official sense, of doing anything dishonest in the years from 1954 and 1959 when he was with Celtic for five tolerably successful (for Beattie) years, during which time he won two Scottish League Cup medals. The second of these was the 7–1 win over Rangers in 1957 when he was seen, wearing his trademark orange (!) cap and holding up seven fingers to the triumphant fans.

He was agile and athletic, but prone to howlers, and possibly for this reason never got International recognition beyond the Under 23 level. Following his conviction in 1965, a few people began retrospectively to wonder whether these were simply howlers. Most of his mistakes tended to be made in otherwise insignificant League games (insignificant because Celtic never really challenged for the League in these days) and often involved misunderstandings with other defenders, but there were two high-profile games over which questions have been raised.

One was the 1956 Scottish Cup Final where Beattie's vain dive to stop Hearts' second goal does not look any better the oftener that one looks at it on YouTube, and the other was the 1957 Scottish Cup semi-final replay against Kilmarnock where *The Glasgow Herald* is mystified by the amount of mistakes made by the Celtic defence, and Beattie in particular whose errors were described as 'amazing', for he was responsible for the loss of all three Kilmarnock goals and is described as being 'panic stricken', throwing his cap in the air in frustration at the final whistle. But was this all an act?

One hopes that these were honest errors – even the best of goalkeepers do have the occasional shockers, after all – and it must be repeated that no allegations were ever official brought against him. Indeed he retained his popularity even after he left Celtic. In March 1963 he was playing for St Mirren at Celtic Park and in the unusual role of goalkeeper/captain, was given a great reception as he ran up to toss the coin and then ran back again to his goal.

His mistakes must also be seen in the context of other Cup Final goalkeeping catastrophes. In 1955 against Clyde, Johnnie Bonnar's amazing gaffe at a corner-kick definitely cost Celtic the Scottish Cup, and in 1961 against Dunfermline, Frank Haffey seemed to misjudge completely the Pars' second goal in the replay – yet no-one has ever pointed the finger of suspicion at these goals, even though Crerand and McNeill tore into Haffey on the field in that awful Dunfermline Scottish Cup final.

Goalkeepers do have bad games – and the matter must be left like that.

JOHN BONNAR (1948–58) is famous for one great game and one awful game, but this does less than justice to his career at Parkhead, particularly in the Double winning season of 1953–54 when he was consistently superb. He joined the club in 1948 from Arbroath and was in and out of the team until 1953 when he had his greatest hour in the final of the Coronation Cup as he defied the Famous Five forward line of Hibs again and again. He continued his fine form for the next two seasons.

But it was the Scottish Cup Final of 1955 that was his nemesis. Celtic were leading 1–0 until late in the game when Clyde forced a corner-kick on the right. Archie Robertson took an in swinger and Bonnar made an absolute hash of it to give Clyde a draw. He was distraught, and even more so when Clyde won the replay. It is a shame that this one goal disfigures his memory. The following season he lost his place to Dick Beattie.

ARTUR BORUC (2005–10) was a personality goalkeeper. He played for five seasons for Celtic, winning the Scottish League three times, the Scottish Cup once and the Scottish League Cup twice, and playing under Gordon Strachan, Tony Mowbray and for a short spell, Neil Lennon. He joined the club, originally on loan, from Legia Warsaw and left for Fiorentina. He has since played for Southampton and Bournemouth, and has been capped for Poland more than 60 times.

He was called 'the Holy Goalie' because of his devout Catholicism especially at the Copland Road end goal at Ibrox where the reactions to Artur's religious observances among some Rangers supporters showed that Scotland has not advanced as far along the road to religious tolerance and diversity as some people would have thought.

He was particularly good at saving penalty-kicks, his most famous being in the Champions League Qualifying tie against Spartak Moscow at Celtic Park in August 2007 when he saved the last penalty in the shoot-out. He also saved a penalty from Louis Saha of Manchester United, and on one occasion took and scored a penalty-kick himself in the shoot out of the League Cup semi-final against Dundee United in 2009.

He owed most of his achievements to his immense self-belief. He was a fine shot stopper and reader of the game, knowing exactly where to be at the right time. His bad days were few, but there was one occasion at Parkhead where he was badly at fault for a couple of Rangers goals in a 2–4 defeat in August 2008, he once was beaten by a fluke goal at Easter Road scored by John Rankine, and he generally was not at its best during the rather chaotic 2009–10 season when the team was under Tony Mowbray.

He remained controversial during his time at Celtic Park, and one suspects that he was not as strictly devout when Rangers supporters weren't around. But he was well loved at Celtic Park, and his departure was an occasion of some sorrow.

DENIS CONNAGHAN (1971–76) vied with Ally Hunter for the goalkeeper's job in the early 1970s, but neither really enjoyed the total confidence of Jock Stein. Connaghan had been at Celtic Park in the early 1960s but then went to St Mirren before rejoining Celtic in 1971 in the wake of the 4–1 defeat from Partick Thistle in the Scottish League Cup Final. He won a Scottish Cup medal when Celtic defeated Dundee United in 1974, and one always felt that he would have benefitted from a longer run in the team under a Manager who was prepared to trust him.

FRANK CONNOR (1960–62) was a remarkable character who played eight games in goal for Celtic at the start of the 1960s. He was a man of many clubs, and became a Coach and a Manager, his best years being at Raith Rovers in the late 1980s where at one point the queue for the pie stall had to be re-routed by the Kirkcaldy Police lest the punters might hear the foul oaths delivered at full volume from the dressing room at half-time! He was Assistant Manager at Celtic from season 1983 until February 1986 when he was suddenly sacked by David Hay for no apparent reason. He then was the Acting Manager of Celtic in the chaotic days of autumn 1993 during which time Celtic did not lose a game. Many, including some of the players, thought he deserved the job on a permanent basis.

JOE CULLEN (1892–97) played for Celtic in interesting times. He joined the club in 1892 and played in Celtic's first ever Scottish Cup win in 1892. He was also the first goalkeeper to play at new Celtic Park, and won two Scottish League medals in 1893 and 1894, Celtic's first triumphs in those competitions. He was competent, but prone to injuries and lost out to Dan McArthur. He was one of the many players of that era, well known for being an entertainer and a singer with a wide repertoire of songs, but he appeared in Court, along with Jimmy Blessington for a 'disturbance' at New Year 1897. He went to Tottenham Hotspur in May of that year, and died very suddenly of pneumonia in 1905.

MICKY DOLAN (1888–94) deserves his inclusion for he was the first ever Celtic goalkeeper, playing in the game against Rangers Swifts at Old Celtic Park on 28 May 1888. He also may have won a Glasgow Cup medal for the club in December 1891 against Clyde on a snowy day at Cathkin. This was the first recorded game of goalnets being used in Scottish football, and although Celtic won 7–1, the loss of the one goal may well mean that Micky was the first Celtic goalkeeper to pick the ball out of the back of the net!

WILLIE DONNELLY (1900–01) was an Irishman who played five games for Celtic, but it was his game on 16 February 1901 at Dens Park that was his 'cometh the hour, cometh the man' moment. Celtic were outplayed by Dundee in front of what was a huge crowd of 16,000 at Dens Park in a Scottish Cup tie. Celtic were 1–0 up, but then an enormous crack was heard behind the Provost Road end of the ground as a temporary stand collapsed. Fortunately no-one was killed and only a very few were slightly injured, but the crowd encroached onto the pitch and had to be shooed back by the Dundee Constabulary. Willie ignored all these distractions to keep a clean sheet and earn Celtic passage to the next round. He then went back to Ireland to play for Belfast Celtic.

RAB DOUGLAS (2000–05) joined Celtic from Dundee and was part of the 2000–01 treble winning side with his form the following year being particularly outstanding. He was a fine shot stopper with good positional sense but had the unfortunate tendency to make mistakes in high profile games, notably against Rangers, and also against Porto in the UEFA Cup Final in Seville in 2003. He won three Scottish League medals and two Scottish Cup medals with Celtic, and played 19 times for Scotland before departing to play for Leicester City and a variety of other English clubs before returning to Dundee. He then joined Forfar Athletic and took the unusual step of resigning from the club in protest at the sacking of manager Dick Campbell.

TOMMY DUFF (1891–92) Tommy Duff was an interesting character. He played in the first ever game at Old Celtic Park on May 1888 for Cowlairs against Hibs, and it was generally reckoned that, when he joined Celtic in 1891, Celtic had acquired a good goalkeeper. There was something remarkable about him, though, but no-one made much of an issue about it at the time. He was a member of an Orange Lodge. Protestants had played for Celtic before, but this was the first one (that we know about) who actually attended the Lodge.

It says something about the early Committee that no-one raised any objections, and one often wonders whether we should be surprised at all. No-one seems to have cared or even noticed that Andrew Watson was black, yet he played for Queen's Park and Scotland a decade previously with no eyebrows being raised, so an Orangeman playing for Celtic was perhaps no big deal. The 1890s were possibly more tolerant than the 1920s.

Tommy may have played in the Glasgow Cup Final of December 1891. *The Glasgow Herald* clearly states that he did so, talking about, 'exciting moments near Duff's goal', but other sources claim that it was Micky Dolan or Joe Cullen in goal. The recognition of players by reporters was no exact science in 1891, but if Tommy did play that day, there cannot really have been too many 'exciting moments' near his goal, for Celtic won 7–1 against Clyde in conditions where, 'the snow fell like pancakes' – something that gives us a clue about why it was so difficult to distinguish the Celtic goalkeeper. But whoever he was, Celtic had now won the Glasgow Cup twice in the calendar year of 1891.

There was no competitive game on New Year's Day 1892, but Celtic had arranged a friendly with last season's joint League champions Dumbarton. It was the first day that Celtic Park had used goal nets, and they were still sufficient of a novelty to attract a large crowd of about 10,000 to see them. Not only that but Colonel Burke of the Buffalo Bill Wild West Show being held on Glasgow Green was the honoured guest who was allowed to kick the game off.

Admittedly, it was only a friendly, but friendly games were very important to Celtic in their early days. Ill-advisedly some Celtic players had celebrated the arrival of the New Year with some gusto the night before. If one thinks that Christmas and the New Year are a little over-cooked today, New Year was certainly even more of a celebration then. Tommy and some others had welcomed the New Year 'not wisely, but well'.

He looked well enough when he turned up, but did not play well. In fact it was a 0–8 defeat, and according to some accounts, it should have been 11, for the compassionate referee chalked three off. 'The Celts never played a more wretched game', and only Maley, Doyle and McMahon were anything like respectable, as the Sons of the Rock played a 'dashing, go ahead game'. The 10,000 crowd gazed in incredulity, before turning to anger, and *The Glasgow Herald* is adamant that; 'some changes will have to be made'. *Scottish Sport* in a masterpiece of meiosis says that Duff's performance was 'very indifferent'.

Indeed changes did come. Duff seems to have been summarily sacked, something that makes one think that there was more to it than simply a bad performance. Duff may have made an intemperate remark about King Billy or the Pope, but the more likely explanation is simply drink. A half-hearted attempt was made to claim that as he suffered from rheumatism, he took medication that made him unwell, but few were convinced by this. Jokes ran round Glasgow to the effect that Tommy (and the rest of the Celtic team) drank plenty but 'ate nothing' (8–0!), but the Celtic career of Tommy Duff, now commonly referred to as Tommy Duffer was at an end.

JOHN FALLON (1958–72) John had a fascinating if frustrating career at Celtic Park, in which he never really seemed to win the total confidence of Jock Stein, but yet was present on many great occasions and played his part for the club. His debut was as early as September 1959 and he lasted at Celtic Park until 1972. On only two occasions could he be called the first choice (from 1963–65 and most of 1969) but he managed to win two Scottish Cup medals and two Scottish League Cup medals as well as being part of the squad which won the Scottish League from 1966 until 1971. Technically he played in Lisbon in the 1967 European Cup Final, for substitute goalkeepers were allowed in the case of injury.

His best time was definitely 1969 when he was part of the team which won all three Scottish domestic trophies in the calendar month of April, then in October of that year, he won the Scottish League Cup again. He was called upon at short notice to play in the two games in South America in 1967 after Ronnie Simpson was felled by a missile before the game started, and performed creditably.

His darkest hour was the 2–2 draw at Celtic Park on 2 January 1968 when he was to blame for both goals scored by Rangers that day, but he deserves credit for the way that he fought back from adversity. He remains a Celtic supporter and is seen at more or less every Celtic game.

FRASER FORSTER (2010–14) Fraser Forster is only denied a full chapter on his own in this book because of his odd decision to leave Celtic for Southampton in 2014, a decision that can only be explained by the attractions of the mega rich English Premier Division. In terms of winning trophies and honours and the love that he was held by the fans, it is inexplicable. Many times did the chant 'Fra-ser For-ster' echo round Celtic Park

Fraser was born in 1988 in Hexham, and it was from Newcastle United that he joined Celtic, having been on loan to Stockport County, Bristol Rovers and Norwich City. He seemed to be permanent loanee, for it was on that basis that he joined Celtic in 2010. The loan was renewed the following season and then he joined the club officially for seasons 2013–14 and 2014–15. He was a marvellous goalkeeper, a great shot stopper and with a fine positional sense and ability to understand the other defenders. His greatest spell was in early 2014, when he went 1,256 minutes without losing a goal, beating the record of the Scottish League set by Bobby Clark of Aberdeen and an even older one set by Charlie Shaw in 1914. A fine performance against Barcelona gave him the Spanish nickname of La Gran Muralla – the Big Wall – and he was particularly good at saving penalty kicks, with one late in the game against Hearts at Celtic Park in December 2011 remaining firmly in the memory of those who saw it.

189

In his four seasons, he won three SPL medals, two Scottish Cup medals but failed to complete the set by winning a League Cup medal. He is, arguably, Celtic's best goalkeeper in recent times, and was well loved by the fans who were naturally disappointed when he opted to leave Celtic for Southampton. He is now an England Internationalist.

WILLIE GOLDIE (1960) was born in Newmains in 1937. He was the Celtic reserve goalkeeper in 1960. Celtic had started the season very badly. They were already out of the League Cup, and had lost in the Glasgow Cup as well. But Chairman Bob Kelly retained faith in his youth policy and in his own judgement.

On 1 October 1960, the reserves had no game. Willie, a supporter, set out to Airdrie where the first XI were playing and was waiting, green and white scarf round his neck, for his bus outside Monklands Hospital. A bus picked him up but it wasn't the one he expected. It was the team bus, ordered to stop by Chairman Bob Kelly who was impressed by the enthusiasm of the youngster.

Sometime after that, as the team bus made the short trip to Airdrie, Bob Kelly became even more impressed by the youngster and decided he was playing! John Fallon who had thought he was playing was flabbergasted, but it was Willie Goldie who ran out with the team!

Not surprisingly the youngster had a shocker, and the team lost 0–2 with young Goldie giving away goals 'like soap coupons', and he never played for Celtic again. He was transferred to Albion Rovers a few months later, and the following year lost a leg in a work accident.

CRAIG GORDON (2014–) raised a few eyebrows when he was signed by Celtic in summer 2014 to take the place of Fraser Forster. He had already had a great career with Hearts, Sunderland and Scotland, and had just recovered from a serious knee injury problem. He played virtually impeccably in the 2014–15 season winning the Scottish League and the Scottish League Cup, and in season 2015–16 winning the Scottish League again.

JONATHAN GOULD (1997–2003) was a goalkeeper who built up a tremendous rapport with the supporters, always being willing to turn up at supporters' functions and becoming, very quickly, very knowledgeable about the history of the club. On one occasion at Dunfermline when the sun was getting in his eyes, he turned to a supporter behind the goal and asked for a loan of a cap, a fine gesture of solidarity. The son of Bobby Gould, one time manager of Wales, Jonathan was the goalkeeper of the team that eventually won the League Championship in 1998. He also won three Scottish League Cup medals, but when Martin O'Neill bought Rab Douglas, his opportunities became limited. In spite of being an Englishman, he was able to earn two caps for Scotland because his grandparents came from Blantyre.

FRANK HAFFEY (1957–63)
In the early 1960s, he had many fine games for Celtic as well as his shockers. His best game was probably the first game of the 1963 Scottish Cup Final against Rangers. It was a 1–1 draw but it was generally agreed that Haffey saved Celtic particularly in the second half with headlines like 'Fantastic Frank' in the next

day's papers. He also had a fine game for Scotland against England in the 1960 International at Hampden Park, saving a penalty kick from Bobby Charlton.

But sadly his name will always be associated with Scotland's 9–3 defeat at Wembley in 1961. The loss of nine goals says a little about the rest of the team as well, but it was Frank on whom most of the opprobrium and vitriol was hurled, particularly by Rangers fans who could not accept that full backs Shearer and Caldow were at least partly to blame. Eleven days later Celtic fans turned on him as well after a colossal howler to give Dunfermline their second goal in that tragic Cup Final.

Yet he remained a character, playing over 200 games for the club, all the time identifying with the support who loved him in spite of his sometimes appalling blunders. Shortly before the injury which shortened his career in November 1963, he took a penalty-kick. Celtic were already winning 9–0 against Airdrie and Frank was invited to make it ten. He took the kick but his shot was saved by Airdrie's Roddy McKenzie. Frank stood and applauded!

He was also a singer, singing songs like *The Dear Little Shamrock* and *Slattery's Mounted Fut* before emigrating to Australia in 1964 via Swindon Town. His departure compelled the club to sign Ronnie Simpson as cover for John Fallon.

ALLY HUNTER (1973–76) was a fine goalkeeper for both Celtic and Scotland, and the fact that he lasted such a short time can only really be blamed on Jock Stein's infamous distrust of goalkeepers. Already a Scotland internationalist, he joined Celtic from Kilmarnock in January 1973 and played until 1976. He made a bad mistake on the night that Scotland qualified for the World Cup of 1974 when they beat Czechoslovakia 2–1 at Hampden, but he never really let

191

Celtic down with several fine performances. He played in the Scottish League Cup Final of October 1974 when Celtic beat Hibs 6–3, and he also won Scottish League medals in 1973 and 1974.

GEORGE HUNTER (1949–54) nicknamed 'Sonny' because of his youthful appearance, George's moment of glory came in 1951 when he played a large part in Celtic's capture of the Scottish Cup. He had several outstanding performances that year. One was at Tynecastle in the Scottish Cup when in front of a more than capacity crowd which overspilled onto the pitch on several occasions, the 20-year-old Hunter defied Willie Bauld and others while the crowd were actually sitting on the back of his goal net! He then performed creditably as Celtic beat Aberdeen 3–0, then Raith Rovers 3–2 in the semi-final before taking part in the rear guard action against the talented Motherwell team in the Final. He had several great saves, but one from Wilson Humphries in the second half at the Celtic End of the ground earned an ecstatic reception from the 134,000 crowd.

It was Celtic's first major trophy since before the war, and it was also the high point of Sonny's career, for the following season he developed tuberculosis. This being the 1950s rather than the 1930s, he recovered and regained his place but he was never the same goalkeeper again. He left Celtic Park in 1954 and played subsequently for a variety of English clubs.

PETER LATCHFORD (1975–87) served the club admirably from 1975 until losing his place to Pat Bonner in 1980 and even then he stayed around as a reserve until 1987. He arrived from West Bromwich Albion and was the brother of a famous English goalscorer called Bob Latchford. He was one of the very few Englishmen to play football in Scotland in the 1970s. He won three Scottish Cup medals, the first one a matter of months after his debut, and two Scottish League medals, famously having the ball in his hands when the full-time whistle went in what became known as the 'riot' Cup Final of 1980.

Although he played through the dreadful seasons of 1975–76 and 1977–78, he was usually comparatively exempt from criticism. Indeed he was one of the few figures in 1977–78 who inspired any sort of confidence as the club struggled with injuries and the self-inflicted blow of selling Kenny Dalglish. He had his bad days, of course, and possibly was not the greatest shot stopper in the world, but in the late 1970s he was a figure of reliability and stability in the Celtic goal. He stayed around with the club well into the 1980s, content to play for the reserves, and always a source of strength for youngsters.

RAB MacFARLANE (1901–02) a goalkeeper of many clubs, and his time at Celtic was not a distinguished one, for it was felt that he might have done better with Hibs goal in the 1902 Scottish Cup Final. He also played for Third Lanark, Middlesbrough, Everton, Motherwell and Aberdeen. When with Aberdeen (for whom he played from 1904 to 1908) it was felt that he could have done more to prevent the only goal in Scottish Cup semi-final at Pittodrie on 21 March 1908, an occasion marred by serious crowd trouble and Rab left Aberdeen under a cloud soon after. It was believed that he had been bribed and made little attempt to prevent McMenemy's late header from entering the net (some sources say it was Quinn), but no charge was ever brought against him.

ALLEN McKNIGHT (1986–88) played 17 times for Celtic in the 1987–88 season. He was a Northern Ireland internationalist (and thus, as Pat Bonner was the goalkeeper of Eire, Celtic employed the goalkeepers of both Irelands at that time!) It was difficult to replace Pat Bonner but Allen could argue that his contribution was vital in the League and Cup Double that Celtic won in their Centenary season. Pat suffered problems injuries that year, and McKnight was drafted in at the end of August 1987. His second game was the 1–0 win over Rangers at Parkhead and his final game in that spell was the infamous 2–2 game when some players ended up in court. Then he had another three games around the turn of the year and these included a last minute victory over Dundee United at Tannadice and a great 2–0 win over Rangers at Parkhead. Thus McKnight played Rangers three times and never lost!

But he had one more game to play, and it was quite a game. It was the Scottish Cup Final when Bonner reported injured yet again. The news was kept quiet in the run-up to the game, and thus everyone was surprised when McKnight took his place in the Celtic goal. McKnight was blamed by some, notably Roy Aitken, for not coming off his line to prevent Kevin Gallacher's goal for Dundee United, but had a good game otherwise as Celtic won 2–1. Thus in the course of 17 games, he won a Scottish League and a Scottish Cup medal. He then went off to West Ham United and a host of other English clubs where his career was a lot less successful.

EAMONN MCMAHON (1953–55) was an Irishman from Lurgan in Armagh who had played Gaelic football for a spell. He joined Celtic in December 1953 at a time when Celtic were on the crest of a wave. John Bonnar was the sitting tenant in the goalkeeper's spot, but you never know when the goalkeeper is going to be injured. This happened in October 1954 when Bonnar picked up a slight finger injury and Eamonn was chosen to play against Queen of the South at Parkhead on 16 October.

Celtic were top of the League, and were confidently expected to beat Queen of the South even though they were without Willie Fernie who was playing for Scotland that day in Wales. Indeed the game started before a crowd of about 36,000 with Celtic 'battering' Queen of the South's goal, and Eamonn not really having very much to do at all.

But then came what *The Evening Times* calls 'the day's sensation'. Bobby Black of Queen of the South ran down the right wing and fired across a low shot, which might have been a cross as well. 'McMahon had the ball covered and even touched it, but the spin beat him and it wriggled over the line.' It was what one might have called a goalkeeper's own goal. *The Evening Times* adds wryly; 'Queen of the South almost deserved this unexpected break, for they had stood up to the terrible hammering practically throughout.'

But poor Eamonn's confidence had gone. In the only other time that Queens got over the half way line, they got a corner out of another weak cross from Black which McMahon 'backhanded' out of play. But the Celtic team pressed and pressed and simply couldn't score, things not being helped for poor Eamonn by the fact that the Queens goalkeeper, Roy Henderson, was playing an absolute blinder. Eventually just at the death, Johnny Higgins equalized for Celtic, but it was a point lost.

It wasn't a great day for Celtic, for their main rivals for the Scottish League, Aberdeen, won 4–0 at St Mirren and thus joined them at the top of the table. Scotland beat Wales 1–0, but poor Eamonn more or less disappeared and was never heard of again. He was given a free transfer at the end of the season and later played for Glentoran.

DICK MADDEN (1962–64) was born in Blantyre in 1944 and joined Celtic from the junior team Blantyre Celtic in 1962. He was generally looked upon as the third team goalkeeper, but one night on 27 March 1963 he was given an outing for the first team.

It was just after the big freeze of 1963, and Celtic were faced with a mass of fixtures. They were out of the League race after a dreadful run before Christmas, but had a difficult Scottish Cup tie on Saturday 30 March against St Mirren. Frank Haffey was rested for the Kilmarnock game, and depute goalkeeper John Fallon might have expected a chance, but the nod was given to Madden instead on the slender grounds that his father had recently won the football pools and therefore the whole Madden family would feel relaxed and happy!

It turned out to be another one of Mr Kelly's big mistakes, for Celtic lost 0–6 to Kilmarnock at Rugby Park. Admittedly, it was a weak Celtic side and Rangers supporters were convinced that they lay down to Kilmarnock that night to strengthen Killie's chances of winning the Scottish League, but it was a humiliating night for Dick Madden who never played for Celtic's first team again, being given a free transfer in 1964. He did later join Albion Rovers, and he also a few years later followed his father's footsteps by winning the pools!

Celtic had another debutant that night – a small red-headed winger called Jimmy Johnstone. He also had a terrible game, but in the long run contributed a great deal more to Celtic than Dick Madden!

DAVID MARSHALL (2002–07) was a goalkeeper of whom it was felt that Gordon Strachan made a mistake in offloading, particularly when one considers his subsequent career with Norwich City, Cardiff City and Scotland, for whom he has excelled. He had one particularly brilliant performance against Barcelona in the Nou Camp in March 2004, and he also won a Scottish Cup medal that year.

JOHN MULROONEY (1911–13) was a gauche-looking character with ears which protruded and a funny walk. Nevertheless he played excellently in goal for Celtic particularly in the Scottish Cup final of 1912 (one of many that could be described as 'the hurricane final' when he defied Clyde and the wind for long periods in the second half of the game to help Celtic win their eighth Scottish Cup as they won 2–0). He was blamed disproportionately for the poor 1912–13 season and was transferred to St Johnstone. He died suddenly of rheumatism on the eve of the Great War in July 1914.

LEIGH ROOSE (1910) had a remarkable career and a remarkable life. He was born in Holt near Wrexham in 1877 and is one of only a handful of Welshmen who have played for Celtic. He was an amateur and had played for a wide variety of English clubs, notably Stoke, Everton and Sunderland. He was also a Welsh internationalist, and it was in this capacity that Maley saw him on 5 March 1910 when Scotland beat Wales 1–0 at Kilmarnock.

As chance would have it, Davy Adams was down with pneumonia, and Celtic had a Scottish Cup semi-final at Shawfield the following week against Clyde. Celtic didn't really have a reserve goalkeeper – Philip Quinn, the brother of Jimmy, was used in friendlies but wasn't considered to be good enough – so Maley engaged Roose for this one game, rather than risk young Quinn.

It was a disaster of a game. Sunny Jim Young was suspended, Jimmy McMenemy had been injured in the International against Wales, and in any case the great Celtic side was beginning to show signs of creaking. They would win the Scottish League that year, but today they were outplayed by the talented Clyde side. Although Willie

Kivlichan had scored first for Celtic, Roose was beaten; 'by a slow shot which came through a crowd of players', then lost another before half-time. It was the third goal that was much talked about, though, for Roose insisted on chasing after the Clyde forward to shake his hand!

This display of 'Corinthian good sport' from the Welsh amateur was not appreciated by the Celtic fans in the 37,000 crowd, for they sensed, in any case, that this was the beginning of the end of their really great side which had ruled Scotland since 1904. Roose was not offered another game for Celtic, but continued to play for Huddersfield Town, Aston Villa and Arsenal. He won a total of 24 caps for Wales before he met his death in October 1916 in one of the last phases of the Battle of the Somme. He was a Lance Corporal in the Royal Fusiliers and had already won the Military Medal.

ALAN ROUGH (1988) Not many people are aware that Alan Rough, more famous for his exploits with Partick Thistle and Scotland, played for Celtic, but he did manage five games for the club that he adored in 1988 as a cover for injuries. He was goalkeeper for Partick Thistle in October 1971 at the greatest moment of Firhill history as Thistle beat Celtic 4–1 in the League Cup Final. He also has the dubious honour of being Scotland's goalkeeper in the Argentina shambles of 1978.

PETER SHEVLIN (1924–27) Peter was unfortunate in the respect that he came between two superbly great Celtic goalkeepers in Charlie Shaw and John Thomson. Peter, who had arrived from the famous Celtic nursery of St Roch's, took over from Charlie in October 1924 in a team that was still developing and therefore inconsistent, an inconsistency that Peter shared. But 1925 was a  superb Scottish Cup year with Peter well involved in the 5–0 defeat of Rangers in the semi-final and the 2–1 defeat of Dundee in the Final with the back three of Shevlin, McStay and Hilley playing their part, even though the more spectacular stuff came from Jimmy McGrory and Patsy Gallacher at the other end.

His best season was 1925–26 when Celtic, with Tommy McInally back on board, won the Scottish League with a degree of comfort. But the sting in the tail came in the Scottish Cup Final when a sub-standard performance deprived Celtic of a double, and although Shevlin was by no means the only poor performance, he attracted a disproportionate share of the blame. His confidence was shattered to a certain extent, but he stayed on until early February 1927 when after a poor game at Glebe Park, Brechin in the Scottish Cup, he was dropped in favour of John Thomson.

He subsequently played in English and Irish football, and for Hamilton Accies and Albion Rovers before moving to England. He died in Manchester in 1948, possibly as a result of having suffered a few injuries in an air raid a few years earlier in 1941.

TOMMY SINCLAIR (1906) had a remarkable nind games with Celtic. He had eight shut outs and in the only game that he lost a goal (he lost two actually) he won a medal! After winning his medal he never played for Celtic again, and returned to the team who had loaned him to Celtic. The team concerned was Rangers! Later that same season he played a few crucial games near the end of the season for English League Champions Newcastle United. You couldn't really make this one up, could you? But then again, the unusual comes at no extra price from Celtic.

Possibly the only Celtic player ever to have been born in Dunkeld, Perthshire, Tommy Sinclair came to Glasgow to play for Rutherglen Glencairn alongside Alec Bennett and Jimmy McMenemy at the turn of the century before joining Rangers in 1904. He played for them in the notorious 1905 Scottish Cup semi-final, when Jimmy Quinn was sent off and the game had to be stopped early because of rioting. Rangers then lost to Third Lanark in the Scottish Cup Final and Sinclair was blamed for the loss of some of the goals.

He couldn't always command a first team place at Ibrox. Celtic's goalkeeper Davy Adams was playing in a pre-season benefit match at Ibrox in August 1906 when he cut his palm on a nail, which was sticking out of an Ibrox goalpost. He would be out for a couple of months. Celtic had no reserve goalkeeper, but Rangers very kindly and possibly suffering from a guilty conscience offered Tommy Sinclair, now their reserve goalkeeper, to Celtic. It is hard to imagine this happening today, but in the early days of the 20th century, things were different. Celtic and Rangers were proud of their good, symbiotic relationship in 1906! Their respective Managers Willie Maley and William Wilton were close personal friends. Not without cause were the teams called called 'the Old Firm'.

Settling in very quickly at Parkhead, Sinclair now proceeded to keep eight straight clean sheets in a row as the brilliant Celtic team of that era got off to a flying start in season 1906–07. As with other clean sheeters in Celtic's history, Tommy was helped by the fact that he had an excellent defence in front of him. Not many teams got past Young, Loney and Hay, but if they did, Tommy was there to mop things up, earning a great deal of praise from the support and from the taciturn Willie Loney and the raucous Sunny Jim. Motherwell, Kilmarnock, Morton, Hearts, Third Lanark and Airdrie all failed to find the net in the Scottish League, and Partick Thistle and Queen's Park were similarly unsuccessful in the Glasgow Cup, while at the other end Jimmy Quinn was scoring repeatedly and consistently.

Then in the Glasgow Cup Final of 6 October at Ibrox. Sinclair won a medal… but lost two goals! He was very upset when he lost one in the first minute and when he lost another just before half-time, he was inconsolable for Celtic went in at half time 1–2 down to the competent Third Lanark side. But he and Celtic rallied in the second half and 3–2 was the final score. Thus Sinclair won a Glasgow Cup medal, but on the Monday he had to return to Ibrox, for Davy Adams would be fit next week. Tommy thus returned to Ibrox but with a medal, something of which there had been very few in that part of the world for the past few years!

He also returned to reserve football at Rangers, a state of affairs which continued until he moved to Newcastle United in March 1907. He played a few games for them and as Newcastle won the English League that year and Celtic won the Scottish one, he is one of the few players ever to have played for the Champions of Scotland and England in the same season! He later played for Dunfermline Athletic and Kilmarnock, and was always given a hearty reception from Celtic fans.

DAVID SYME (1918) played twice in October 1918 when Charlie Shaw took ill with Spanish flu and was out for a couple of games. Syme had been to the war but had been invalided out in 1917 with a nervous complaint. He was playing junior football for St Anthony's when Celtic signed him as cover just in case Charlie would be called up in those desperate days of 1918 when every man, even those previously granted exemptions might be 'combed out', as the phrase went. David Syme, declared unfit for military service was considered safe. When Charlie took ill, Syme played in the goal at Kilmarnock in a disappointing 1–1 draw on 12 October (with hopes now being entertained that the war would soon be over) and then the following week played against Rangers at Celtic Park in what was Celtic's worst performance for many years – a 0–3 defeat which included the loss of a goal at the very start of the game. Charlie returned the flowing week, and Syme's services were never called upon again. Nothing else was remarkable about this guy except that his son was a Willie Syme who refereed the 1967 Scottish Cup Final, and his grandson was another David Syme who was also a referee, distinguishing himself (if that's an appropriate way of putting it) in the League Cup Final of 1986 which Celtic lost unluckily to Rangers and Syme sent off a Celtic player called Tony Shepherd then changed his mind!

ROLANDO UGOLINI (1944–48) was an Italian who was fine goalkeeper but could not replace Willie Miller and left to join Middlesbrough and later Dundee United. Being an Italian at the tail end of the Second World War was not easy and he found himself on the receiving end of a lot of ignorant abuse from opposition fans. At Celtic Park, he was always much in demand to entertain the other players at social functions.

EVAN WILLIAMS (1969–74) was virtually unheard of (although he had played for Third Lanark for a couple of years) when Jock Stein signed him in autumn 1969, yet by the end of that season he was playing in a European Cup Final, one of the few Celtic players to emerge with any credit from the fiasco of the Feyenoord Cup Final in Milan on 6 May 1970. He then went on to win the Scottish League and Cup double in both 1971 and 1972 as well as a League medal in 1970 and 1973. A League Cup medal always eluded him, however, and he was (unfairly) given the blame for the loss of the League Cup final to Partick Thistle in October 1971, when there were other factors at work as well.

And then there was **SUNNY JIM YOUNG (1903–17).** Sunny Jim was of course one of the great Celtic heroes of all time as right-half and captain between 1903 and 1917, a phenomenally successful time for the club. On one occasion on 2 January 1909 he played in the goal. The circumstances were bizarre but the episode tells us a great deal about the level of commitment of the great Sunny Jim.

He had been injured in a game against Clyde on Boxing Day 1908. He this missed, to his intense frustration, the New Year's Day game against Rangers at Ibrox. The team however played well and won 3–1 with Sunny sitting in the Ibrox stand, cheering on his mates and assuring everyone that his leg was getting better.

Celtic had another game against Kilmarnock at Rugby Park the following day. A crisis approached when Davy Adams, who had been injured at Ibrox, reported unfit and Celtic, like most clubs in 1909 did not employ a reserve keeper. Maley thought he would have little option but to ask for a goalkeeper from a junior team, but he was, to his surprise, approached by Sunny Jim who volunteered for the job on the grounds that his leg was getting better and if he played in the goal would not have had to run about quite so much. Maley, always a great admirer of Sunny, reluctantly agreed.

In 1909 goalkeepers did not wear jerseys of a different colour, so the crowd would have thought that Sunny was fit again. But he took up his position between the posts, with Joe Dodds, who would become a brilliant left-back, lining up in Sunny's place at right-half. The team lost 3–1, but in contemporary accounts,

Young was absolved from blame. 'He saved several shots in good style, his height and reach of arm standing him in good stead', according to *The Dundee Courier*. The first goal was a penalty kick, and the other two goals came late in the game after Celtic had equalized and then, in accordance with the traditions of the club, committed themselves for a winner. But it was Kilmarnock's day, and one of the best performances in the forty-year history of a club which had not yet yielded much in terms of trophies. Ironically Sunny Jim was a Kilmarnock man born and bred, but he never again played for Celtic in the goal.

ND - #0209 - 270225 - C0 - 234/156/9 - PB - 9781780915357 - Gloss Lamination